BUILD YOUR OWN

Overland
Camper

First published in October 2016

A catalogue record for this book is available from the British
Library.

ISBN 978 1 78521 076 1

Library of Congress control no. 2016930193

Published by Haynes Publishing,
Sparkford, Yeovil,
Somerset BA22 7JJ, UK.
Tel: 01963 440635
Int. tel: +44 1963 440635
Website: www.haynes.com

Haynes North America Inc.,
861 Lawrence Drive, Newbury Park,
California 91320, USA.

Printed in Malaysia.

BUILD YOUR OWN
Overland
Camper

STEVE WIGGLESWORTH

Designing, building and fitting out vans and trucks for overland travel

FOREWORD BY STEPHEN STEWART

Contents

Chapter 1

INTRODUCTION, DEFINITIONS AND SCOPE

- An introduction to the concept of overlanding vehicles — 9
- Overland campers defined — 9
- Overland travel in context — 12
- Common routes to ownership — 13
- The scope of the manual — 15

CASE STUDY – Nick Elton's cash-in-transit box on a Mercedes Atego — 16

Chapter 2

PROJECT CONSIDERATIONS

- An honest assessment of actual needs — 21
- Underpinning philosophies — 21
- Logistics — 23
- Base vehicle considerations — 24
- Project progression — 29

Chapter 3

THE MODIFIED MOTOR CARAVAN SOLUTION

- Not all conventional motor caravans are born equal — 31
- Physically traversing poor roads and trails — 31
- Ground clearance — 31
- Issues with weight — 34
- Traction — 34
- Improving structural integrity — 34
- External modifications — 35
- Improving autonomy — 38

CASE STUDY – Bruce Burrow's home-made 'woodie' on a Leyland DAF T244 — 40

Chapter 4

TAKING ON A BUILD-YOUR-OWN PROJECT

PART 1 – PRE-VEHICLE ACQUISITION
- Establishing final direction — 43
- Design strategies — 43
- Vans and trucks with proven credentials — 44
- Where to source suitable base vehicles — 45
- Commercial entities — 47

PART 2 – POST-VEHICLE ACQUISITION
- Preparing a base vehicle — 47
- Enhancing time spent driving — 47
- Racks, hoists and winches — 52
- Ladders — 54
- Fixing other large and heavy items — 55

Chapter 5

DEALING WITH TORSIONAL STRESS

- Understanding torsional stress — 57
- Three- and four-point torsion-free subframes — 58
- Simpler solutions — 63
- Vibration and impact — 67
- General subframe mounting principles — 68
- The single irrefutable fact — 71

CASE STUDY – Gary and Monika Wescott's structural-honeycomb module on a Ford F–550 — 72

Chapter 6

GETTING ROAD LEGAL (UK-SPECIFIC ADVICE)

- Caveat — 75
- What's in a name? — 75
- Becoming a motor caravan – used vans and trucks already registered in the UK — 76
- Becoming a motor caravan – used UK-obtained vans and trucks not previously registered with the authorities — 77
- A brief consideration of imported vehicles — 80
- A brief consideration of new vehicles — 80
- Tachographs — 81
- Driving licences — 81
- Downrating a mid-sized truck to 7.5 tonnes — 81

Chapter 7

PROCURING OR BUILDING A HABITATION BOX

- Ready-made boxes / box-and-vehicle combinations — 85
- Having a box professionally made — 90
- Building your own box — 90
- Thermal bridges — 102

CASE STUDY – Colin Woollard's kung shelter on a Gaz 66 — 104

Chapter 8

HATCHES, WINDOWS, DOORS, ROOF LIGHTS AND VENTILATION

- Connecting the cab to the box — 107
- Windows — 110
- Doors and lockers — 112
- Roof lights, hatches and vents — 115
- Ventilation — 119

Chapter 9

WATER AND GAS SYSTEMS

PART 1 – WATER SYSTEMS
- Fresh water — 121
- Waste water — 123
- Plumbing and fittings — 124

PART 2 – GAS SYSTEMS
- An introduction and overview — 125
- Design considerations for LPG systems — 127
- Building the system – general hints and tips — 129

CASE STUDY – John Nrooks' grp composite 'flat-pack' on a Mercedes 1124AF — 132

Chapter 10

ELECTRICAL SYSTEMS

- The basics — 135
- Charging systems — 136
- The question of capacity — 141
- Inverters — 143

Chapter 11

HEATING AND COOLING

- Space heating — 149
- Domestic water heating — 152
- Combination heaters — 156
- Integrating the base vehicle's cooling system — 156
- Heating snippets — 157
- Heating summary — 162
- Cooling (and a bit more about heating) — 163

CASE STUDY – Tom Hübner's dornier shelter on a Leyland DAF T244 — 164

Chapter 12

INTERIOR SPACE AND FURNITURE

- General layout considerations — 167
- A place for everything — 167
- Build techniques — 170
- Specialist structures — 175
- Hardware — 176
- Upholstery — 177

Chapter 13

KITCHENS AND WASHROOMS

PART 1 - KITCHENS
- Refrigeration — 179
- Cookers — 181
- Kitchen hardware — 183

PART 2 – WASHROOMS
- Showers — 183
- Toilets — 188

CASE STUDY – Patrick O'Neal's self-fitted ormocar on a Mercedes 1017A — 190

CONCLUSION — 192

USEFUL CONTACTS — 193

Foreword

In August 1999 I got my front-wheel-drive motorhome stuck on wet grass for the second time in a week. It was then I decided I needed something better, much better.

Thirty years earlier I had been a member of Comex 3 and had driven in convoy from the UK to India in one of 20 coaches. In 1971 I had driven an old Land Rover from South Africa to the UK via central Afghanistan. Later I had driven Bedford RL trucks across Asia and Africa for the adventure tour company Encounter Overland. On all these trips I had enjoyed the 'comforts' of sleeping under canvas.

In my front-wheel-drive motorhome I had the comfort, but not the adventure. What I needed was an 'overland campervan'.

So I sold my low-mileage, reliable, well-equipped motorhome and bought a 25-year-old ex-German army 7.5-tonne Unimog truck!

I wish this book had been available to me in 1999. It

would have saved me a lot of time and money. Reading it would certainly have helped me build a better vehicle.

But it wasn't available, so in 2000 I decided to create a website to document my two years of work converting my Unimog into an overland campervan. In 2002 when it was nearly (but not quite) finished I set off with several other campervans to drive to China and later to Mongolia, Siberia, Central and South America, Australia, Canada and Alaska. Over the years I added a record of these journeys to my website. As a result people began to ask me questions about designing and building overland campervans. Now I won't have to answer most of them, I will direct them to this book.

Building my own overland campervan quite literally changed the next 15 years of my life. Not only was building it totally absorbing for a couple of years and a very satisfying challenge but when it was finished I more or less *had* to drive it somewhere exciting!

However, building an overland campervan is not for everybody and not without its risks. It will take you longer than you expect, it will cost you more than you expect, and it will take over your life for a couple of years.

There is one significant omission from this book: there is no chapter on Relationship Counselling. If there are two of you involved make sure you both have the same objectives in mind, the same balance between comfort and utility, make sure you will both be happy to drive it as well as live in it. Make sure you both want to go, at least roughly, to the same sort of places for the same length of time. (I know one beautifully built overland campervan that never moves, he devoted years to building it, she calls it 'the cottage'.)

There is something really satisfying in waking up in the middle of nowhere in your own warm, dry, secure, and well-equipped home and knowing that all you have to do is get in the front and continue your adventure. It's a great feeling, even if you bought your vehicle already converted; it's an even better feeling if you built it yourself.

Stephen Stewart
www.xor.org.uk

AUTHOR'S ACKNOWLEDGEMENTS

This book has been made possible thanks to the generous supply of information and material by countless individuals and I'm sincerely grateful to all who have helped with contributions.

In particular, I extend special thanks to:

The team at Haynes Publishing for friendly support and for making this book project a reality.

Clive Barker, Les and Margaret Brook, Simon Coles, Tony Lee, Maureen Middleton and Nick Yu for providing images.

John Brooks, Bruce Burrow, Nick Elton, Tom Hübner, Patrick O'Neal and Colin Woollard for providing images and case-study material.

Brian Reynolds and Phil Seddon for providing images and in-depth information regarding their builds.

Stuart Savery for providing images and feedback on the book's stylistic content.

Ian Lang, the builder of 'Deep Red' (www. deepredmotorhome.com), for providing images and feedback on the frame-and-skinning furniture-construction method.

Doug Hackney for providing images and his work to bring together a pool of knowledge for self-builders faced with the dilemma of creating effective habitation-box-to-chassis mounting solutions.

Alan Crosby for providing guidance on the mystical art of the true cabinet maker. Alan can draw straight lines without a ruler.

Gary and Monika Wescott for providing images, case-study material and for untiring feedback on the book's thematic content. After 40 years of extensive overland travel, nothing much gets by them. Actually, *nothing* gets by them.

Jon Bull for providing images and technical guidance. Overland camper builds bring into sharp focus that a paper qualification and blustering waffle do not make for a real engineer: Jon is a *real* engineer.

Stephen Stewart. I owe an enormous debt of gratitude to Stephen. He was one of the very first to take the extra step beyond self-building an overland camper by actually documenting the process via a dedicated website. Though long since superseded by his current site (www.xor.org.uk), the original incarnation at URL www.unimog.org. uk was undoubtedly one of *the* most influential self-build entities of the early millennium. I, like countless hundreds of others, spent many hours staring open-mouthed at that site; truly amazed at the very concept of overland campers and utterly incredulous that it was actually possible to build one for yourself. Going full circle, this manual would almost certainly not exist in this form at this time had it not been for Stephen's early influence. It seems entirely fitting that I now find myself further indebted to him for contributing to the creation of the book by providing images, ongoing inspiration and the very generous foreword.

CHAPTER 1

Introduction, definitions and scope

- An introduction to the concept of overlanding vehicles

- Overland campers defined

- Overland travel in context

- Common routes to ownership

- The scope of this manual

Overlanding vehicles get you to where you want to be.

Overland campers are self-contained, go-virtually-anywhere vehicles that enable comfortable, adventurous and highly independent overland travel. But what exactly is 'overland travel', what constitutes an 'overland camper' and why would anyone want to build one?

▲ **Overlanding vehicles are unfazed by terrain and conditions that are simply unachievable in a conventional RV or motor caravan.**

An introduction to the concept of overlanding vehicles

If you're an independent traveller, you'll know that getting to the places you want to be to do the things you want to do can prove less than straightforward; particularly if your passion is for off-the-beaten-track adventure and visiting places less trammelled by organised tourism. If you're stirred by the notion of being immersed in spectacular landscapes, witnessing exotic wildlife and visiting diverse cultures – all at a pace set by you – an overlanding vehicle can open up a whole new world of highly independent adventure.

Overlanding vehicles are highly purposeful machines as they have to be able to support life on the road whilst withstanding the punishing rigours of travelling over rough roads and unsealed trails, often in arduous climatic conditions. They are a completely different entity to conventional RVs and motor caravans, which are essentially designed for use on well-surfaced highways and intended to offer limited independence whilst en route to formal campsites.

Of course, there's no obligation to travel to the far corners of the earth in order to enjoy the unique benefits that an overlanding vehicle can offer; their intrinsic robustness and go-anywhere capability confer advantages that may not be immediately obvious. For example, those who have already travelled by conventional motor caravan will know that tiny country lanes, especially those with encroaching vegetation, can quickly ruin acrylic windows, damage thin aluminium-sheeted wall sections and wreak expensive

havoc on protruding items like TV aerials and roof vents. In a well-made overlanding vehicle, such lanes can be tackled with impunity. Another, perhaps unforeseen, advantage of ownership is particularly relevant for those who enjoy remote outdoor pursuits or simply seek solitude. Overlanding vehicles can offer a newfound access to out-of-the-way places that, because of intervening terrain, are simply unachievable for the vast majority of road-based vehicles.

Overland campers defined

Whereas overlanding vehicles come in all shapes and sizes, this book is concerned only with those that boast a defined habitation area capable of providing self-contained live-aboard functionality, i.e. *campers*. Accordingly, some initial explanations and a qualification of terms may prove useful.

For a vehicle to be able to support truly comfortable, highly independent and long-term travel through inhospitable terrain and extremes of climate, it needs to boast good ground clearance and, importantly, also needs to be able to support *all* aspects of domestic life within its external dimensions. Accordingly, simply put, there's no escaping the simple fact that it needs to be quite large. Though smaller vehicles *can* be converted to accommodate limited living and leisure activities within their external dimensions – especially if occupants are very well organised and travel alone – it's common to find that with such vehicles activities associated with the *camping* component of the journey routinely spill into the great outdoors. With smaller vehicles, when the day's drive is done, it's popular practice to utilise roof-mounted tents and, unless conditions are prohibitive, to set up a seating/cooking area adjacent to rather than within the vehicle. Even in cases where truly comfortable domestic life can just about be contained within a smaller vehicle's dimensions, there will almost certainly be a knock-on effect in terms of a lack of remaining space or available payload to be able to carry a month's worth of water or sufficient fuel for a thousand-kilometre-plus range. Arguably then, when prepared for the rigours of extended independent travel, smaller overlanding vehicles are primarily people and equipment transporters and though they may very capably facilitate *setting up* a camp they cannot accurately be described as overland *campers*.

For the purposes of this book then, overland campers are to be understood as vehicles that boast at least a reasonable degree of all-terrain capability that *comfortably* permit occupants to move freely around within a defined habitation area and carry out such activities as cooking, eating, sleeping, relaxing and recreating, all whilst self-contained *wholly within* the vehicle's external dimensions. Additionally, vehicles qualifying for the definition should also be capable of extremely high levels of autonomy, i.e. they should be able to support *extended* periods away from civilisation and supplies. They should, therefore, have the ability to

▼ **Unquestionably an overlanding vehicle, but as most post-driving activities are intended to be done outside, not an overland camper.**

▲ **A good, unobtrusive set-up but again not an overland camper for the purposes of this text due to a lack of all-terrain capability and reliance upon outside space.**

carry at least one full-size spare wheel and tyre, tools and spares, ample personal effects plus large reserves of water and all required fuel types.

With distinctions drawn, here's what's specifically included in this manual, what's not and why.

Out – overlanders based on cars, small vans, MPVs and small utility 4x4s

Unquestionably, some spectacular overland journeys are made in lightly modified cars, smaller vans and family-orientated MPVs. Vehicles in these genres are frequently used to support travel to the far reaches of the earth – albeit mainly on reasonably well-surfaced roads – and there are undoubtedly many advantages to using vehicles of this type: their nimble and compact nature, for example, means that such potential journey-spoilers as rickety bridges, narrow mountain passes and weight-restricted city centres are rarely an issue. Additionally, countless genuinely *off*-road expeditions are successfully tackled in 4x4 utility-based vehicles such as Land Rovers, Land Cruisers and so on, and whereas it's freely acknowledged that *all* of the aforementioned vehicle types will sometimes be the best tool for the job – because they are variously limited in terms of their size, multi-terrain capability, or their potential for true autonomy – they are not the subject of this book.

In – overlanders based on larger vans and trucks

These are primarily the types of vehicle with which this book is concerned. Because of their relatively large size, and because standard/optional configurations often include rear- or all-wheel drive and good ground clearance, larger vans and trucks are an excellent choice as a base from which to create a truly autonomous, all-terrain-tackling and completely self-contained overland camper.

▲ **For our purposes, this is an overland camper: go-virtually-anywhere, extremely independent and offering very comfortable and completely self-contained accommodation for months or even years on end in remote and inhospitable terrain.**

In – modified conventional motor caravans

In spite of their intrinsic limitations, in some cases it *is* possible to modify conventional motor caravans to create a vehicle that can offer something approaching overland camper capability. Indeed, modified motor caravans have been known to traverse some of the world's trickiest routes and even completely standard ones can, as long as conditions are not *too* punishing, cope reasonably well in terrain away from smooth metalled highways. Though modified conventional motor

▼ **Tricky roads and trails can be conquered in conventional motor caravans, but sometimes the going gets very tough.**

OVERLAND CAMPERS COMPARED WITH CONVENTIONAL MOTOR CARAVANS

Though the point at which a conventional motor caravan becomes an overland camper can be blurred, the following characteristics may help in drawing a distinction:

Conventional motor caravan characteristics:
- Little ground clearance
- Nearly always two-wheel drive (often front wheels only)
- Road-based tyres
- Comparatively flimsy body construction
- Comparatively flimsy fixtures and fittings
- Easily damaged by rough roads or brushes with overhanging vegetation
- Habitation boxes are usually firmly affixed to the base vehicle meaning the chassis and superstructure are potentially at risk from destructive twisting forces
- Relatively small capacities for water, fuel and minimal off-grid electrical supply
- Often unable to deal with extreme climate or weather events
- Limited autonomy – frequently reliant upon formal campsite facilities

Overland camper characteristics:
- Good ground clearance
- Often rear-wheel drive or, more usually, all-wheel drive
- Aggressive tyres with good puncture resistance
- Strong body construction able to deal with poor road-surface-induced shock and vibration
- Strong fixtures and fittings
- Able to shrug off brushes with overhanging vegetation
- Habitation boxes are often attached to the base vehicle in a way that allows the chassis to move independently and thereby resist destructive stresses
- Relatively large capacities for water, fuel and off-grid electrical supply
- Usually able to deal with extreme climate or weather events
- Highly autonomous – designed to be self-sufficient and not reliant upon formal campsites

caravans will arguably be something of a compromise, Chapter 3 looks at a range of modifications that will give the best chance of success for travellers who might be interested in trying out this option.

Overland travel in context

Given an overland camper's capability for all-terrain travel, it's tempting to imagine yourself heroically traversing previously undriven terrain. However, the reality is that as well as such activity almost certainly being illegal, very few vehicle-based overlanding trips utilise anything other than established roads and trails. What *is* true is that many of the world's roads and trails, particularly in countries with developing infrastructure, are in very poor condition. Supposedly sealed roads are very frequently broken leaving yawning potholes, whilst some roads are not sealed at all and readily get cut up to form huge ruts, washboard surfaces and wheel-swallowing mud holes. It is *these* kinds of roads that overland campers are designed to traverse. Overland campers are *not* dedicated off-road vehicles; they are *not* rock-crawlers or trials vehicles.

It is unwise to even *think* of overland campers as off-road vehicles; there is, after all, a great deal at stake. Overland campers are quite a financial investment; they can also be

▲ **A typical unmaintained, vehicle-breaking 'sealed' road where traffic has taken to driving on the comparatively smooth unsealed verge meaning it's now safer to walk in the carriageway.**

▼ **Fording on unsealed trails – typical overland camper habitat.**

▶ It just isn't worth pushing the off-tarmac capabilities of an overland camper. This is the very van originally converted by John Speed in one of its less-happy moments. Readers will be pleased to note that van and driver were OK and the van is still in use today.

a huge emotional investment. Additionally, when you're on the road, they are your absolute everything. They provide shelter, your means of transport, your place to cook, eat and sleep, and will very likely be carrying all that is precious to you at any given moment in time. It's just not worth risking everything by pushing the limits of the vehicle's off-road capability. If you find yourself in a situation where you are canted at 45 degrees and requiring massive reserves of ground clearance and suspension articulation, you should probably *not be there* in an overland camper.

Common routes to ownership

If an overland camper is something that's currently missing in your life, there are several routes to ownership.

Buy new

Though there are both large and small companies around the world that build overlanding vehicles on a commercial basis, buying new is not as straightforward as might first be imagined. This is because the individual requirements of potential customers vary dramatically and it's very rare to find a manufacturer that will hope to be able to find a profit in producing a showroom-style finished product that just requires the addition of fuel to drive away. The reality is that overland campers are almost always custom built to order: to customers' very unique and specific requirements. This process takes time and money – often a great deal of both! It is not uncommon to find that a new truck-based overlander built to a very high specification by one of the better-known companies has required the proud new owner to part with several hundred thousand euros.

Buy second-hand

Second-hand overland campers do come up for sale and can provide a good solution. It would be incredibly fortunate to find a second-hand vehicle that met with a prospective owner's particular requirements, but it could be that the combination of base vehicle, dimensions, condition, equipment and systems might just be close enough to make this route to ownership viable. Some second-hand vehicles will have been out in the great wide world already and proven themselves in the field. Others may well be just at, or nearing, the point of completion and may never have turned a wheel in anger. It's surprisingly common for projects to reach the point of being ready to use, only to be sold on. In a similar vein, part-built projects are also fairly commonly found. In these latter two cases, it would be prudent to try to establish the seller's reason for wanting to exit stage left: there may be perfectly valid reasons, or there may be fundamental issues that need resolution. The material in this manual will help to enable prospective second-hand purchasers to assess the viability of taking on, and completing, someone else's project.

Build your own

It sounds daunting, and make no mistake: this option is no small undertaking. It is, though, with good planning, attentive project management and a good dose of determination, entirely within the reach of a person with average DIY skills. The notion of a self-build is very appealing on many fronts: it enables owners to choose exactly which base vehicle they prefer, to precisely specify equipment and systems, to build bespoke layouts tailored to very personal needs and – importantly – to control budget.

▲ A part-build subsequently finished by the owner to an extraordinarily high standard. Here the vehicle is fresh from the ORMOCAR factory and comprises a high quality but empty habitation box on an ex-military Mercedes.

▶ A different style of part-build. This commercially available demountable camper is augmented by several self-built storage units and mounted by means of a self-built subframe to a very capable Mitsubishi-Fuso 4x4.

Though building entirely from scratch is a highly popular choice, it isn't the only one: there is also the option to complete a build based on professionally constructed starting points. One part-built starting point is to enlist the help of specialist companies to supply a vehicle and empty habitation box, and then to fit and finish it yourself. Another option is to purchase a ready-made and fully fitted demountable camper – or even a caravan – to use as your habitation area, and to then suitably modify and graft such structures to a capable base vehicle.

The scope of the manual

To convert, partially build, or fully self-build an overland camper is an involved task and the undertaking requires considerable dedication. On the plus side, it's also a hugely gratifying experience and the enormous feelings of well-being and satisfaction you'll encounter when you're miles from anywhere and looking out over an awe-inspiring vista from the comfort of a fully functioning vehicle of your own creation are impossible to overstate. You absolutely *will* well with an overwhelming sense of pride and achievement.

If you're sold on the concept of overland camper ownership then this manual is likely to prove an indispensable companion. It is *not*, however, intended to duplicate already readily available books or regurgitate hardware manufacturers' fitting instructions. For excellent introductions to the fundamentals of things like gas and electrical systems, and detailed pictorial guides on how to tackle some common-to-all-vehicle jobs like, for example, adding insulation and fitting windows, other Haynes publications such as *Build Your Own Motorcaravan (2nd Edition)* and *Motorcaravan Manual* are likely to prove useful reads. That said, there is – inevitably – *some* overlap with existing publications, but where this does occur the focus of this manual is intended to highlight how hardware, equipment and systems are most successfully selected, fabricated and employed specifically in the *overland camper* context.

Overland campers are very unique creations and it would be extraordinarily rare to find two that were identical. You'll find that within the important guiding principles introduced in the next chapter – and which form an ongoing theme for the book – there's a great deal of scope for flexibility. Different builders demonstrate a range of equally ingenious solutions to commonly encountered problems and this manual is just as much about inspiring research, creativity and resourcefulness as offering a build-by-numbers template. To this end, several case studies are featured within. These give a direct window to owners who have faced the inevitable dilemmas and settled on their own solutions, some of which are utterly conventional, some of which are highly unusual. Few approaches and techniques are definitively right or wrong but some *will* be more or less appropriate given your own individual circumstances. In summary, though the manual is unequivocally intended to offer guidance, you're positively encouraged to think critically and creatively.

▼ **When this happens and you feel smug... that's forgivable: the sense of achievement is well deserved.**

Nick Elton

1   Name
Nick Elton.

2   Base vehicle
2003 Mercedes Atego 1823 (now known as 'Jim').

3   Drive
4x2 – Rear-wheel drive only (with diff lock).

4   Fuel capacity
A 400-litre aluminium tank fuels the engine – this was fitted as an optional extra from the factory. Additionally, we have a 250-litre auxiliary tank, which was taken from a Mercedes Actros and cut down to fit the available chassis space. This tank supplies the heaters and a generator. Fuel from the auxiliary tank can also be siphoned/pumped into the main tank in an emergency.

5   Weight when loaded and ready to travel
Somewhere around 13.5 tonnes.

6   Reason for base vehicle choice
I was looking for a tough truck with a high GVW, but that wasn't excessively long: ideally anything over 10 tonnes, and around 6–8m. Jim is extremely small for an 18-tonne box truck and would have been pretty useless as a general cargo vehicle; this meant that he was for sale for an excellent price. On my relatively low budget I was extremely fortunate to be able to buy a truck that was less than four years old.

I was originally looking at ex-army trucks with low mileage for around the same money, but when a truck came along with air-conditioning, cruise-control, air-seats, an Eberspächer heater, a well-proportioned box already fitted to the back, a huge pass-through between the cab and the back, and all very sturdily built, my plans changed. Jim has good ground clearance, a strong chassis, a diff lock on the back axle, and full international parts availability. I was happy to sacrifice the excellent mobility of an army truck for the advantages that Jim possessed.

7   Subframe solution
The box was mounted to the chassis by the coachbuilder that originally converted the truck for the Brinks security company. The box is fixed to the chassis rigidly, using plates bolted to both the outside of the main chassis rails and the subframe rails above. The truck cab also bolts rigidly to the box, which makes the use of flexible chassis mounts (at least at the front of the box) impossible. The box body is *extremely* strong though, and the combination of a very rigid box and the intrinsically stiff chassis means that there is no significant twist in the chassis on rough ground. This limits articulation slightly and can lead to odd and uncomfortable movement of the truck under certain conditions.

8   Habitation-box construction
The purpose-made cash-in-transit box is constructed around a skeleton made from 50mm x 50mm, and 75mm x 50mm mild-steel box section. Outside, the walls are skinned with 18mm plywood sheathed in a thin layer of fibreglass. The roof is skinned with riveted aluminium sheets and the floor is made from 8mm steel tread-plate. A mixture of aluminium and stainless-steel pieces are used at the edges and corners to protect the truck and prevent water ingress.

Inside, the walls and ceiling are skinned using a selection of materials. The front section of the box body originally comprised the security-crew area, and the inside of this is lined using a high-carbon bullet-proof steel that proved almost impossible to drill. Elsewhere the walls and ceiling are lined in a mixture of mild steel and aluminium sheet. Additionally, bullet-proof plywood is used between the frame members in certain places, presumably to make it harder to cut a hole in the bodywork using an oxy-acetylene torch.

9   Habitation-box insulation material
50mm fibreglass insulation was packed between the steel frame members on the walls and ceiling by the original coachbuilder, but there are cold bridges everywhere and the original insulation is not great. The bedroom area has an extra layer of 50mm PIR/PUR type board all round, and with the curtain closed between the bedroom and the rest of the truck, it maintains its temperature well. We have never used the truck below approximately –5°C, but at this temperature we could maintain a comfortable temperature inside.

10   Habitation-box manufacturer
The box was built for Brinks by Trumac Group, who is no longer trading. The body was modified by me, with help from Essex Bodies.

11   Habitation-box windows
The original non-opening windows were fitted by the original coachbuilder and comprise bullet-proof glass bonded in place and sealed using a custom aluminium profile. I fitted additional double-glazed sliding aluminium windows from Kellett Windows. Four skylights are also fitted, two are Lewmar Ocean acrylic-glazed units which open fully, and two are glass coach-type units from Stedall. These only partially open, but they are useful for good through ventilation whilst driving.

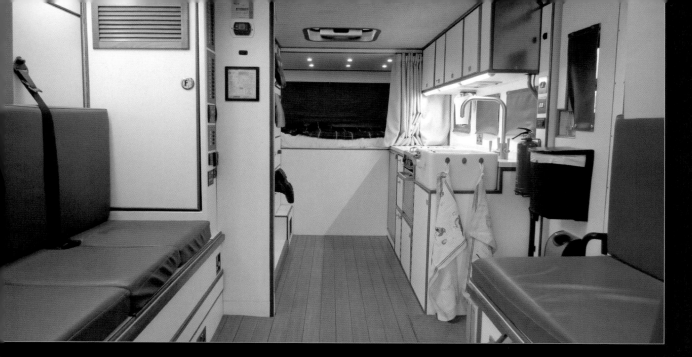

12 Habitation-box door(s) and locker(s)

The original entry doors were fabricated from steel and were absurdly heavy. They came fitted with electro-magnetic locks, 24V solenoid-operated sliding bolts, KABA locks, and manual shoot bolts. I removed them and replaced them with doors manufactured from 18mm GRP-faced plywood using commercial truck door hardware from Commercial Body Fittings Ltd (CBF). I also added locker doors – manufactured in aluminium by the Vehicle Window Centre – for access to the toilet cassette, the gas bottle, the electrical fittings and the generator.

13 Fit out done by

The complete fit out was done by me in my back garden. The only major items made elsewhere were the curtains and cushions. I learnt a lot of new skills during the course of the conversion and enjoyed the work so much that I've vowed to try and make a business of it sometime in the future.

14 Furniture construction

The furniture is all faced in white WISA Multiwall, which is essentially birch plywood laminated on both sides with a thin textured plastic film. Some of the furniture is built entirely from this structural board, but some areas, which I thought needed more strength, are built from a welded steel box-section frame and then skinned. Areas strengthened in this way include the bed frame, which supports the water tank (450kg), and the offside bench seat which supports 400kg of batteries. I wanted to be sure that in a serious accident these heavy items would not become detached and pose a hazard.

15 Fresh water

450-litre plastic tank, custom built to fit across the width of the truck. The only general filtration at present is a coarse filter fitted on to the input of the water pump; this is intended just to protect the pump's diaphragm. We do though additionally have a dedicated filtered-supply tap and this is fitted next to the kitchen sink. This tap delivers treated water via a General Ecology Seagull IV water purifier.

16 Refrigeration

Vitrifrigo C115i – 115-litre, 24V compressor fridge freezer.

17 Space heating

The primary space heating system is an Eberspächer D2 diesel-fired blown-air heater; this is fitted outside of the habitation box under the truck and the heat is ducted inside. The air heating is the most convenient system; it is quick to warm up, easily adjusted, and quiet when at low power. It is also fitted with an altitude compensator, which prevents the heater from coking up above 2,000 metres.

Additional heating is provided by a 'wet' central heating system using a Webasto Thermo Top C diesel-fired water heater plumbed into convection radiators. The radiators do not provide sufficient heat output to heat the whole truck in extremely cold weather, but the heater is practically silent. The wet central heating also heats a towel rail in the bathroom and a small radiator at the front of the truck. The addition of a blown-air water-to-air heater matrix would make the Webasto more user-friendly.

The truck can also be heated electrically, using the Dometic HB2500 air conditioner in its reverse-heat-pump mode.

18 Water heating

Water is heated in a 25-litre Quick BX25 calorifier. The water is normally heated using the Webasto Thermo Top C diesel furnace but can also be heated using a 240V immersion-heater element. The immersion heater can be run via an inverter if necessary, but it makes more sense to use it only when mains power is available.

19 Cooking facilities

Cooking is done with a GN Espace Levante gas cooker, which is equipped with three hob rings, a grill and a thermostatically controlled oven. The cooker can be run from propane or butane and a 13kg propane bottle lasts is around six months.

20 Habitation-box cooling

Cooling is primarily done passively; the back wall of the truck adjacent to the bedroom, opens completely, and provides a huge area of ventilation in hot climates. Sleeping so exposed took us a little getting used to, but the bed is around 2.5m above the ground, and I learnt to enjoy the feeling of being outdoors in bed. There are also four opening skylights, and numerous opening windows. There are three adjustable fans, one 24V Hella Turbo fan pointed at each of the two bench seats, and one 24V Caframo Bora fan in the bedroom area. In addition, the Eberspächer D2 air heater can be used in ventilation mode, blowing in fresh air from outside the truck. The Eberspächer duct outlet is at floor level, and our dog took comfort in the tropics by lying next to it.

21 Leisure-battery charging

The leisure batteries are charged from three sources: solar, engine and mains power. The solar system comprises eight 100W solar panels fitted to the roof rack and fed through a 45-amp Morningstar MPPT regulator. The batteries are also charged when the truck engine is running; some of the 100 amps available from the truck's alternator are diverted to the leisure batteries using a 30amp Sterling battery-to-battery charger. Finally the batteries can be charged using a 50amp universal input Victron Skylla charger; this accepts 90–265 volts and will accept both AC and DC incoming voltages. The Victron charger can be run from the generator, or can be plugged into the mains anywhere in the world.

22 Things to do differently next time

There are innumerable things that I would have done differently, but as a whole the truck works well and is extremely comfortable, even for extended periods of time in adverse conditions.

One of the biggest failings was the fixed diesel generator: a portable petrol unit would be better. Single-cylinder air-cooled 3,000rpm diesel generators are too loud to be useful in a motorhome and with 800W of solar panels we rarely need to use it anyway. We used the generator about three times in a year of driving around North and Central America, twice to run the air-conditioning unit and once when the Webasto heater coked up at high altitude in the Rockies, where after several days of a failed hydronic system and having to heat water with the immersion heater, we depleted the batteries.

CHAPTER 2

Project considerations

- An honest assessment of actual needs
- Underpinning philosophies
- Logistics
- Base vehicle considerations
- Project progression

If you know you will be encountering such conditions, tall and aggressively-treaded tyres will float and drive: non-specialist tyres won't!

Most successful overland camper builds are underpinned by considerable thought, research and planning. A good understanding of proven philosophies, concepts and vehicle attributes will prove indispensable in giving this, the all-important planning phase, a solid grounding.

▲ **Wherever possible, complexity is best avoided.**

An honest assessment of actual needs

If you've decided to undertake a self-build or a conversion project, then it would prove wise to temper enthusiasm for a little while and spend some quality time in *honestly* assessing your *actual* needs. This process will be a little easier if you've done a bit of travelling before, especially by motor caravan. It doesn't matter if you haven't though; you just need to turn your mind to the important issues of what you ultimately want from the vehicle, how you'll use it, where you are likely to go and when you are likely to go there.

Put quite simply, if you build a large truck-based overlander weighing in at 18 tonnes or so, then you may well run into trouble when crossing some of the world's very weak and rickety viaducts. Likewise, it may seem obvious, but tall vehicles will *not* fit under low bridges. Conversely, vehicles untroubled by low bridges may suffer from a lack of ground clearance and spend a great deal of time stuck in ruts. It's fair to say that there is no one-size-fits-all solution, and it would be useful, at an early stage, to grasp the reality of unavoidable compromise. The objectively perfect overland camper is impossible to create: all suffer from some shortcoming or other. What *is* possible is to balance the inevitable shortcomings in such a way that they do not affect overall performance *as it relates to you* too significantly. In other words, compromises are unavoidable, but the trick is to ensure that these are made in such a way that your overlander competently achieves everything that's most important to *you* for *most* of the time.

And so, the process of brutal assessment begins. It's very pleasant to court an image of yourself lounging on the roof of your camper lazily watching big game over a serene savannah, but if the harsh reality is that your vehicle will – in all probability – see most of its action north of the Arctic Circle, then the requirements for base vehicle, equipment, systems and layouts are likely to be very different indeed. It can't be stressed enough how important it is to try to establish exactly how you intend to use the vehicle, when, where, and what exactly you require it to do. Time spent at this stage can save a great deal of frustration and disappointment further down the line. Think it through, let ideas ferment, do some research, read this manual, think it through again…it *will* all pay off in the long term.

Underpinning philosophies

Thousands of people have trodden the overland camper path already and, over many decades and hundreds of thousands of miles – often traversed at the furthest reaches of the planet – some hard-won collective wisdom has been established. This wisdom has served to create some solid underpinning philosophies that any prospective builder would be wise to take on board.

Simplicity

At every stage, with every component, simplicity is your friend. Your personal skill set may tempt you, for example, to build a highly complicated and fully automated electronically managed multi-widget meaning that at the push of a single button your vehicle will self level, all the window blinds will open and the habitation box steps will deploy. However, such perceived time and effort saving devices, time and again, have proved utterly unreliable when exposed to the rigours of extended overland travel. All too often complex systems simply lead to massive frustration, constant attempted repairs and a vehicle full of dead or partially working components. Collective wisdom advocates that in the overlanding context, the choice to keep things simple is unlikely to be something you'll regret.

Reliability

Closely allied to the notion of simplicity is that of reliability. Modern vehicles are more and more dependent upon electronic control systems and these systems undoubtedly bring huge benefits both to the driving experience and to the reduction of environmental impact. However, they're not infallible and many an overlanding vehicle has been scuppered by malfunctioning electronics. Indeed, problems can even arise simply as a result of a control system's parameters being exceeded. With access to diagnostic equipment and a dealer network this may not be an issue: when you are at the far reaches of the undeveloped world, it most certainly can be. Electronic control of an all-wheel-drive system may be a far more sophisticated solution than engaging four-wheel drive with a manually operated lever, but it doesn't take much to work out which system is likely to prove the more reliable and, more importantly, the easier to fix when well off the beaten track. Reliability is an important watchword in an overland camper and should be borne in mind not only with base vehicles, but with *all* fixtures, fittings, equipment and systems added during the build process.

▼ Simple and massively durable ex-military vehicles tend to hold up well for overlanding use. There isn't much to break and many components are over-engineered by design.

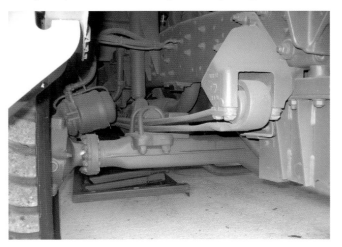

▲ Reserve systems – a combination of diesel- and gas-powered space heaters in this build give a sporting chance of avoiding uncomfortable or even dangerously cold conditions.

Durability

Basically, a tougher base vehicle, better quality components and attention to detail paid during the build process will, in combination, result in vastly increased durability of the finished product. Overland campers have a tough life. The constant punishment meted out to all components should not be underestimated; failures *will* occur. Again, at all points of vehicle selection and the build process, the importance of durability should be kept firmly in mind.

Reserve systems

When failures occur and in the event that the failure relates to something that is mission critical, then it's highly desirable to have a contingency. If, for example, a 'domestic' 12V battery were to fail, it *should* be possible to deploy a backup DC power-delivery system: especially with the ever-increasing need to charge handheld devices used for navigation and communication. Similarly, in very cold climates, if an LPG-powered heating system were to fail, it would, at the very least, prove uncomfortable were there no alternative heating system ready for deployment. Many overlanding vehicles have different-fuel-source heaters fitted for just such an eventuality.

Multifunctionality

Finding enough space and keeping weight down frequently feature as build issues. The more functions that a single component can fulfil then the more it earns its keep. If you fancy letting plenty of natural light in through the roof, why

▲ **Multifunctionality – at this stage of its evolution this camper was still incomplete and registered as a goods vehicle so, by law, it required a rear under-run protector. The requisite under-run was therefore designed to incorporate entrance steps up to the habitation box and also act as an outdoor seat.**

not choose a rooflight that can be opened so it can double its use to allow much-needed ventilation? Furthermore, why not select a hatch that opens fully to allow emergency exits? Could this additionally be positioned so that it also fulfils the function of a wildlife observation hatch? Similarly, can your space heater blow cool air as well as fulfil its heating function? A little extra ventilation on stifling days is always welcome. It's good to get into the habit of thinking laterally to maximise component functionality.

Logistics

A place to work

Overland campers tend to be comparatively large vehicles and will not fit in an average domestic garage. Access to a covered and heated working area is ideal but in reality is a luxury that many successful builders have to do without. Don't be too discouraged if you only have space out in the open. Ready access to tools, mains electricity, a water supply and a flat (ideally hardstanding) surface are desirable and you can take encouragement from the fact that many very high quality builds have been completed on random scraps of sloping tarmac no larger than the finished vehicle itself. There are even cases where builders have had to endure really tough conditions but prevailed nonetheless. Builds in fields

PINNING DOWN IDEAS

Whilst still very much at the brutal-assessment-of-needs stage, it may be useful to organise your thoughts in logical clusters:

Life in the vehicle
- How exactly do you want the vehicle to support your life on the road?
- Do you want a TV, stereo, or games console?
- Do you prefer lavish or austere fixtures and fittings?
- Where will you sleep, eat, recreate?
- Will you cook lavish meals or eat simply?
- What about ablutions, would a *very* simple toilet and wash facilities suffice?
- What equipment will you carry? Bikes, boats, a generator?
- What's the smallest vehicle you could comfortably use? How much space do you *really* need?

Climate
- Do you intend to visit very hot or cold destinations? Extremes may affect things like levels of insulation, number and size of windows etc.
- What about high levels of rainfall? Leaky roof lights are a nuisance; do you need a free-draining roof shape?
- Exposure to unrelenting sunshine may mean you need to prioritise effective internal cooling.

Terrain
- What level of poor-road capability do you anticipate requiring? Very steep terrain or off-camber traverses may require a particularly low centre of gravity.
- Will you be on soft sand, mud, snow or other tricky surfaces?
- Will you be tackling narrow mountain passes or frequently facing walls of thick vegetation?
- What about fording capability?

Autonomy
- How long do you anticipate being away from centres of population?
- Do you intend to use formal campsites?
- Will you be parked in the same spot for days on end or moving on each day?
- What about fuel range?
- Will you need to take on water from open sources like rivers, wells and lakes?
- Will you frequently be within reach of vehicle repair services?

with no mains utility supplies have been known, but be very aware that this *is* at the extreme of plausibility and will turn an already tough project into a real battle.

Tools and skills

In a similar vein to having a pristine place to work, having access to high-quality tools and being very skilled in their use is a boon; however, once again successful builds can be completed with surprisingly little equipment and a modicum of DIY capability. If you have access to: a compound mitre saw, a jigsaw, a router, a drill, a decent array of hand tools – and have the skills to use them – you absolutely will be able to build a high-quality vehicle. Even if you're a little unsure about using some of the tools listed, there are numerous online tutorials that will have you up and running in no time. Do not fear mistakes, they are part of the learning process. In cases where things are proving too difficult, or if something like specialist aluminium welding is required, it's no sign of weakness to buy in the skills required to help you on your way. The fundamental point to take from this is that you absolutely do not have to be supremely skilled or own a bespoke workshop to build an overland camper. Tenacity and patience go a very long way.

Budget and time

How much time and money is involved really is impossible to quantify; so much depends on the specification of base vehicle, the standard to which the overall project is completed and the skill of the builder. There are claims that some campers are converted over the course of a few weekends at the cost of a couple of thousand euros and, conversely,

it's certainly the case that some projects take many years to reach fruition with budgets in excess of €100,000. Such wide parameters are, naturally, of little practical help; so, a very brave guestimate *might* see a pre-used truck-based project complete with a brand-new habitation box and high equipment levels finished to a high standard with a total investment of 2,000–3,000 hours and €25,000–40,000. This is intended to be a *very* rough guide only – but may serve to either thoroughly enthuse, or utterly dissuade.

Base vehicle considerations

Having contemplated the points raised so far and started to pin down your *actual* needs (and more importantly dispelled fanciful daydreams) it's probably a good time to continue your deliberations and consider the type of base vehicle that will best suit your own individual purposes. It cannot be overstated how relevant the underpinning notions of simplicity, reliability and durability are when contemplating base vehicle choice and you're urged to bear these notions uppermost in mind as your planning quest continues.

Size and weight

In the context of overlanders, bigger is not always better: in fact, the opposite is more often true. Having scoured the internet and seen images of monolith trucks carrying all manner of off-road buggies and other playthings, it's easy

▼ **Arriving here in a 9m 6x6 weighing 18 tonnes could mean a several-hundred-kilometre diversion.**

to imagine that big equals good; however, there are many downsides to very large and heavy vehicles. These include:

■ Difficulty fitting under bridges, low-slung wires etc.
■ Overstressing weak viaducts.
■ Heavy fuel consumption.
■ A propensity to bog *very* readily on soft/loose surfaces.
■ Difficulty in recovery *when* (not if) bogged or broken down.
■ Potentially problematic on small ferry services.
■ Increased toll charges on some highways and bridge crossings.
■ Difficult to negotiate narrow streets, especially in built-up areas with overhanging eaves etc.
■ Terrifying and downright dangerous to drive on precipitous or narrow mountain passes.

Though there is no magic formula – it really is a case of horses for courses – a very rough guide to the *upper* limits of size and weight for a *go-almost-anywhere* overland camper might arguably read:

■ Height: 3.5 metres.
■ Width: 2.5 metres (excluding mirrors).
■ Length: 7.5 metres (including racks and spare wheels etc).
■ Weight: 10 tonnes.

These figures are not carved in stone and the best time-and-again-proven guiding principle when considering size and weight is to go for the smallest and lightest set-up you can that is *just* large enough to satisfy all your indispensable needs.

The 80% rule

Overlanding vehicles are subject to far more mechanical stress than an average road-based vehicle. As a result, it is generally accepted as good practice to ensure that when fully loaded and ready to tour, the *actual* weight of the vehicle does not exceed approximately 80% of the vehicle's maximum design weight, i.e. the maximum weight that the manufacturer designed the vehicle to be able to bear. *All* mechanical components, when subject to the daily pounding that is the inevitable consequence of harsh terrain, will perform much more reliably and last longer, if they are allowed to operate well within their design limits. In reality, the situation is slightly more complicated than simply ensuring overall weight is kept within limit and it's wise to ensure that the 80% rule is applied not only to the vehicle overall, but relative to each axle too.

New versus old technology

The debate surrounding new versus old technology is nowhere more focused than when considering electronics and it's a simple fact that most modern vehicles are now *heavily* reliant upon electronic systems. Such systems essentially comprise a multitude of sensors that monitor

MAXIMUM DESIGN WEIGHT VERSUS MAXIMUM AUTHORISED MASS

A vehicle's Maximum Design Weight is not necessarily the same as its officially designated Maximum Authorised Mass (MAM) / Maximum Technically Permissible Laden Mass (MTPLM) / Gross Vehicle Weight (GVW). More about this subject appears in Chapter 3.

virtually all aspects of the vehicle's operation that in turn are 'overseen' by an electronic control unit (ECU). The ECU then controls all manner of functions such as, for example, the metering of fuel flow and the level of braking force applied to individual wheels. In a nutshell, these systems are splendid when they are working but a nightmare when they are not. In some cases, it has been reported that overlanding vehicles have had to be shipped thousands of miles before computer-dependent diagnostic testing could even begin, let alone debilitating problems fixed.

Another issue that comes to the fore when considering old versus new is a modern diesel engine's ability to run on High Sulphur Diesel (HSD). Though most of the world now utilises low-, or ultra-low-sulphur diesel, there are regions, including countries in South America, Africa and Asia, where only HSD is available. Modern electronically controlled engines are equipped with different kinds of emission control hardware and this can be very sensitive to the quality and composition of diesel fuel. Though ECUs and emission control hardware technology is improving – and in some cases is now supposedly able to compensate for fluctuating fuel standards – it is undoubtedly the case that many late-model engines simply do not cope well with HSD. Problems can range from blocked particulate filters to a barely running engine depending on the vagaries of how manufacturers have programmed their ECUs to deal with the information they receive back from the relevant emission control sensors.

Though very modern vehicles are undoubtedly very civilised to drive and have much better environmental impact credentials, the technology that enables these attributes can cause problems for overlanders in far-flung places where the only mechanic for miles around has barely enough tools for simple jobs, let alone a laptop brimming with diagnostic software. On the other hand, it's worthy of note that many zones in the developed world are now subject to stringent low-emission restrictions and you're simply not allowed to use engines that don't meet requisite standards in these areas.

In summary, though not without disadvantages, older technology currently remains the most popular choice and the recurring point most strongly advocated amongst those with worldwide overlanding experience is, essentially, the fewer electronics the better. In very general terms, the 1990s represented the changeover decade regarding the proliferation of electronics and much tighter emission standards and whereas it *is* possible to replace entire exhaust systems and update software/firmware on some newer vehicles to allow them to tolerate poor quality fuel or HSD, vehicles from the 1990s are perhaps the most recent that are both still readily available and not reliant upon modern, potentially stranding, technology.

Ground clearance

Good ground clearance is a fundamental attribute for overlanding vehicles. The grounding of differentials, sumps, suspension components and chassis members accounts for a good proportion of immobilised vehicles. Even ordinarily easily passable tracks can become a nightmare for vehicles with little clearance if the surface becomes rutted to leave a high central section between wheel tracks. Allied very closely to the clearance beneath the vehicle is the way that the vehicle approaches and departs from abrupt changes in the height of terrain. This phenomenon is readily witnessed when long/low vehicles attempt to board or disembark from ferry ramps. When the ground/ramp transition is encountered, it's not unusual to see bodywork ahead of the front wheels or behind the rear wheels fouling either the ramp, the ground,

▲ **Even with well over 300mm of clearance, it's easily possible to ground out when the going gets tough.**

or both. In extreme cases this can even lift driving wheels off the floor, completely stranding the vehicle. Even if not a 'stranding' situation, it is clearly highly undesirable to be dragging body or chassis components on the floor: damage is inevitable and could even be structural.

There are no hard-and-fast rules regarding under-vehicle ground clearance and approach/departure angles, but most established overlanding vehicles have a *minimum* under-vehicle ground clearance of something in the region of 200mm and a *minimum* departure angle of approximately 15 degrees. In both cases, more is generally better.

Traction

All-wheel-drive systems are a very useful overland camper attribute, but they are not essential. Rear-wheel-drive-only vehicles can perform extremely competently in the overlanding context, especially if equipped with a limited-slip or locking differential (diff). On the other hand, front-wheel-drive-only vehicles – though sometimes able to confound critics – are not, in general, terribly well suited to the rigours of overland travel. The main issue with front-wheel drive is that when fully laden, it is likely that the rear axle will have more mass over it than the front, and in many cases this situation is exacerbated because heavy items are built/placed *behind* the line of the rear axle. This leads to a fulcrum effect, whereby mass behind the rear axle not only 'pushes' the rear (undriven) tyres into the ground, but also – in see-saw fashion – actually lifts the nose of the vehicle too, thereby 'unweighting' the driven wheels. This phenomenon is often felt by conventional motor caravan drivers when ascending very step gradients where a combination of the unweighting effect and torque steer can see vehicles scrabbling for traction and direction. Imagine this scenario in loose dirt and the consequences are all too clear: the rear wheels act as a firmly sunken anchor whilst the driving wheels simply spin hopelessly.

▼ **Wheels dig in to leave high points that will snag the underside at any opportunity.**

▲ Good ground clearance, all-wheel drive and locking diffs are the usual fare for overland campers: they come in handy.

TRACTION AIDS – A VERY QUICK GUIDE

▪ **Diff lock** – a system for locking a diff to ensure that a wheel that has lost traction does not receive all the driving force and spin freely. Instead, the lock ensures driving force is diverted to both wheels across the axle meaning that *if* at least one wheel can find traction, the vehicle will be able to transfer power to the ground.

▪ **Transfer box lock** – found on all-wheel-drive systems and operates similarly to a diff lock but instead of locking wheels across a single axle, locks together the front and rear propshafts ensuring drive to both front and rear axles.

▪ **Limited-slip diff** – a system that allows a wheel that has lost traction to spin only a little before diverting part of the driving force to the other wheel on the same axle.

▪ **Traction-control systems** – electronically controlled systems that 'sense' wheelspin and then, utilising a combination of electronically directed power distribution and/or the application of individual brakes, ensure that driving force is directed to the wheel(s) able to find most traction. These systems are the most effective of all for avoiding getting stuck – when they are working correctly…

▲ Replacing the locking collar on a three-part split rim. NOTE: There can be fatal consequences if the disassembly/reassembly of a split rim is carried out incorrectly. You MUST become fully conversant with the risks before undertaking this job.

Tyres and rims

Tyres perform many duties in the overlanding context and collective wisdom gives some useful pointers regarding what works well and what doesn't. Frequently overlooked, but of particular importance, is load rating. Overland campers are comparatively heavy vehicles and thumping through potholes means the forces the tyres' structural components need to endure are considerable. The load rating of an overlander's

▼ If you can source them, two-piece rims are easier and much safer to work with. With some physical effort, a full truck tyre can be replaced using no more than a jack and just one socket and breaker bar.

DUALLIES

Twin rear wheels are very popular on road-going trucks as they improve load-carrying capacity considerably. In the overlander context, they can also offer more 'float' on really soft ground and increased traction due to the larger surface area. However, they are not particularly popular for poor road or trail use. There are *several* downsides, but by far the biggest issue is their tendency to trap rocks between tyres, which can, and does, cause sidewall failure. A tyre with a torn sidewall is basically scrap. In summary, seasoned overlanders do not generally advocate the use of dual rear wheels.

tyre should always exceed – preferably by some margin – the static weight that it actually supports. It's worth a trip to a weighbridge when fully loaded and ready to go to determine how much mass is actually distributed to each tyre.

Tread pattern is always a compromise as most overland journeys will take in a variety of surfaces ranging from smooth tarmac to deeply rutted muddy trails. The best plan is to steer towards a fairly aggressive tread pattern, but not to the point where this limits top speed or drives you crazy with road noise on well-surfaced highways.

In terms of profile, the trend for current vehicles is to go for an ever increasingly low profile: this is good for increasing ultimate roadholding capability, but it's exactly the opposite to the preferred profile of an overlander where tyres with tall sidewalls are the tool of choice. Tall sidewalls mean that you benefit from increased ground clearance, a compliant suspension effect on very rough terrain (where the increased air pocket and sidewall structure acts as a

very sophisticated bump absorption system) and increased traction, particularly if pressures are reduced. Lowering pressure allows the tyre to flatten out at the point of contact thereby vastly increasing the 'footprint' available to transmit power to the ground. Low pressure in a tall tyre is one of the most successful strategies for defeating tricky conditions and is one of the reasons why agricultural tractors have such tall wheels.

In the case of wheel rims, though they may look pretty, aluminium and similar exotica – unless specially made – are not that robust; a rim of simple steel construction is comparatively easy to repair if damaged and is the preferred option. Steel rims on overlanders fall broadly into two types: one-piece and split rims. As the name suggests, split rims are made up of several different components *usually* comprising an inner rim section, an outer rim section and a locking collar. The attraction of this type of rim for overlanders is that – with skill, practice and a very thorough knowledge of the steps involved – it's possible for just one person, with no special equipment, to replace tyres and/or inner tubes at the side of the trail, even in the case of very large truck tyres weighing in at well over 100kg. There is not even the need to unbolt the large inner rim section from the vehicle's hub. This is *not* an option readily open to you with one-piece rims.

Parts availability

There are no universal truths here as much will depend on where you anticipate spending your time travelling. For example, if you are heading for Russia and the vast surrounding regions then something like a GAZ or ZIL will be very well known to local mechanics and spares will be abundant. Likewise, for marques such as TATA on the Indian subcontinent, Ford, GMC or Dodge in the Americas and for Japanese trucks such as Isuzu or Mitsubishi in Australia. Conversely, a ZIL may not be the best choice for a tour of Africa. In very broad terms, for a base vehicle that may stand the best chance of support no matter where you may roam, Mercedes-Benz products are reputed to take some beating. This is not to say the support network for this marque is infallible and it can still take a great deal of time, even if they can be obtained, to have parts delivered to dealerships around the world – clearing customs can be a time-consuming process.

Though there is no single best choice regarding support, it clearly makes sense – if heading for extended off-the-beaten-track adventures – to avoid very esoteric or obsolete base vehicles and, whichever marque you ultimately choose, to carry an assortment of consumable spares. The definitive list of spares deemed essential is rarely agreed upon, but it would be a brave overlander who carried none at all. At a minimum, consumables like drive belts, filters and hoses are an absolutely indispensable start.

MISCELLANEOUS PLANNING CONSIDERATIONS

- **Left- or right-hand drive?** After a little familiarisation, most people easily adapt to any permutation relating to the side of the steering wheel or the side of road driven upon. In reality, there is no obvious better or worse scenario. One thing to be aware of, though, is that in some countries dotted around the world, particularly in Central America, right-hand-drive vehicles will be refused entry at border crossings.
- **Fuel capacity.** This is a popular campfire topic and one of the favourites for Top Trumps fans. In practical terms, a range of *at least* 1,200km is desirable with anything over twice that arguably being unnecessary and possibly even punitive in terms of payload and storage space. On the other hand, one plus side of mammoth capacity is that it allows cheap fuel to be purchased in bulk before crossing a border into a country with grossly inflated prices.
- **Modifications.** It's a widely accepted tenet that base vehicle modifications, particularly those that involve drastically uprating engine power or embellishing standard wiring systems, are the most common cause of breakdown in overlanding vehicles. Established wisdom dictates that if you really must make 'improvements' then make them conservative. Avoid heavily modified base vehicles: you have been warned.

Project progression

In brutally identifying your *actual* needs, understanding the basic principles of successful overland camper design and assessing desirable base-vehicle attributes, you should now be in a much better position to determine which kind of overlanding vehicle will best suit your own very specific requirements.

It may well be the case that you already own a modern conventional motor caravan and decide that it can be modified to successfully take on moderately tough overland travel. Conversely, it may be the case that you have designs on an extensive all-continents trip over very hostile terrain and a rugged truck with all-wheel drive is the only thing that will do.

Providing that you've fully considered all of the points covered in this chapter and been painfully honest in your self-assessment, do not underestimate how much vital work you have already done: even though you are yet to raise a power tool in anger.

CHAPTER 3

The modified motor caravan solution

- Not all conventional motor caravans are born equal
- Physically traversing poor roads and trails
- Ground clearance
- Issues with weight
- Traction
- Improving structural integrity
- External modifications
- Improving autonomy

Fitting taller (and moderately aggressive) tyres to this conventional motor caravan improved ground clearance usefully, and traction enormously.

If you already own a conventional motor caravan and want to try some off-the-beaten-track adventures, or having read the preceding chapters have decided that a modified motor caravan may be sufficient to meet your personal overlanding needs, this chapter is intended to help with ideas to prepare your vehicle for the best chance of success. Even if you have no interest in modifying a motor caravan, the information in this chapter holds good for any overlanding vehicle and may still prove relevant to your plans.

Not all conventional motor caravans are born equal

As previously outlined, some vehicle characteristics are highly desirable; some less so. Desirable attributes in a conventional motor caravan include:

- Rear-wheel drive, ideally incorporating a diff lock.
- The manufacturer's heavy-duty chassis variant. This will be more durable and may include such things as stronger suspension components and larger-diameter wheels.
- Good ground clearance.
- A full-height chassis. Some motor caravans utilise aftermarket chassis that are specifically designed to sit lower than standard to aid entry/egress, to improve road holding and to reduce overall vehicle height. Such lower aftermarket chassis are *not* well suited for use on an overland camper.
- Short front and, importantly, rear overhangs. Some conventional motor caravans have a great deal of living accommodation bodywork *behind* the line of the rear axle and this nearly always leads to grounding problems due to the resultant shallow departure angle.

Physically traversing poor roads and trails

Perhaps the most fundamental issue facing a conventional motor caravan when pressed into service as an overland camper is the vehicle's ability to physically traverse terrain without getting stuck. Getting stuck can happen in several ways, including:

- Losing traction.
- Getting into a cross-axle situation. This can happen where, because of very uneven terrain, the suspension

limits of the vehicle are exceeded, leaving a driven wheel (or wheels) dangling in mid-air.
- Grounding. This happens when part of the vehicle's underside bottoms out and acts as an anchor.

There are numerous ways in which the risk of getting stuck can be minimised but they all essentially revolve around maximising ground clearance and ensuring reliable traction.

Ground clearance

In the world of overlanding, ground clearance is a great ally and it's never really possible to have too much. One of the easiest ways to help minimise the chances of grounding is to physically inspect the underside of the vehicle and make modifications to anything that hangs obtrusively below the general line of the vehicle's underside. An example of this kind of fix is with the U-bolts that commonly clamp exhaust sections together. These are often mounted in the easiest way for mechanics to access the nuts, which means the tails of the U-bolt will frequently point towards the ground. By simply slackening, rotating and re-tightening, the chances of this simple clamp being ripped off when grounding are hugely minimised. A quick inspection of the underside will usually reveal many similarly quick and simple improvement opportunities.

Whilst under the vehicle, one area that requires particular attention is the underside of the rear overhang, especially the section right at the very rear of the vehicle. This is the section of body/chassis that ultimately defines departure angle and the part that will most often be grounded. Compounding issues at this vulnerable point is the fact that the edge that is most exposed will often be no more than a flimsy decorative apron or light cluster moulding. One commercially marketed solution revolves

around the fitting of heavy duty caster wheels but, note well, these are intended primarily to offer protection when driving on hard surfaces such as ferry ramps or steep driveways. Indeed, this 'solution' is arguably counterproductive in an overland camper as the hardware will actually reduce ground clearance and could well simply dig in to, or be ripped off by, softer surfaces. A far better solution would be to fabricate some kind of flat skid plate that would offer protection to the underside whilst harmlessly dragging along the ground. The approach angle bodywork/hardware should be given similar attention, with particular efforts being made to protect the base of any radiators and oil coolers that will more often than not be found lurking in this area.

▲ The perils of a limited departure angle.

Increasing ride height with wheels and tyres

Taller wheel and tyre combinations will improve ground clearance usefully. *Sometimes*, it's possible to obtain and fit

TYRE CONSIDERATIONS

Tyres of well-known brands are manufactured to high standards and manufacturers supply precise details regarding such things as the number of plies used in construction, the week and year of manufacture and parameters of operation for the finished product in terms of speed and load rating. This information is moulded into the sidewall of each tyre and should be noted carefully. If you're unsure of how to interpret the information, or of how to interpret sizing conventions such as 235/85x16 or 9.5R16, then a little internet research will quickly pay dividends.

In essence, it's worth installing the highest-load-rating tyres you can obtain that also satisfy the vehicle's speed-rating requirements. If you can obtain tyres constructed of an increased number of plies that furthermore contain specific puncture resisting materials, then so much the better. Additionally, the week and year of manufacture is important to take into account, even on ostensibly 'new' tyres. This is because the structural integrity of tyres deteriorates over time and this is exacerbated if they're stored in circumstances where they're exposed to UV rays or contaminants. It's generally accepted that once tyres pass five years from their date of manufacture, they are exponentially more likely to fail in normal use as each year subsequently passes, utterly irrespective of miles covered or rate of wear.

Tyres have a tough time on overland campers and it's worth taking the time to get this important component right, *particularly* on conventional motor

caravans where it's likely that the original equipment tyre will be approaching the limit of its load rating and will have been selected to prioritise low road noise and good fuel economy rather than crashing through pot holes and scrabbling for grip on loose surfaces.

▽ Even good quality and correctly spec'd tyres can succumb to tough roads and trails. Tyre-wrecking punctures in overlanding vehicles are not that uncommon.

a manufacturer's own original-equipment wheel-set ordinarily designated for use with heavy-duty chassis versions of the base vehicle in question. Replacing wheels of a 15in diameter with those of a 16in variant will, for example, be a very worthwhile starting point. With or without an increase in wheel diameter, tyres of a taller sidewall profile are a very worthwhile upgrade and depending on the profile of the original tyres, a 10% sidewall profile upgrade is *generally* possible without running into any bodywork-fouling issues. If, then, you find 215/65x16 tyres fitted as standard to your motor caravan, you will – in all probability – be able to fit 215/75x16 tyres instead without issue. Of course, it will be necessary to check that full steering lock and full suspension articulation can be achieved without the new taller tyres physically fouling any part of the vehicle and bear in mind that if you intend to make use of snow chains or similar traction aids, these will most definitely impact upon overall dimensions.

Though increases in wheel and/or tyre diameter will have a beneficial effect in terms of ground clearance (and traction), it should be borne in mind that the increased size and mass will invariably add to stresses on transmission and drivetrain components. That understood, as long as increases are modest – and *if* the vehicle is driven over rough terrain with due mechanical sympathy – it's likely that the drivetrain will cope without much protest. One other point to bear in mind is that increases in rolling tyre circumference will raise overall gearing slightly and perhaps necessitate a recalibration of the vehicle's speedometer, though in some cases the change of rolling circumference has been known to actually *improve* accuracy.

Increasing ride height with suspension modifications

Uprating suspension components is another way to improve ground clearance, with the added bonus that upgrades will reduce the probability of bottoming out on the bump stops in rough terrain: a sure-fire way to transmit unwanted shock to the vehicle structure and unwitting occupants. A good starting point for uprating suspension is to see if the vehicle manufacturer itself has any off-the-shelf parts available. It's often the case that tougher springs and shocks – originally intended for heavier-duty variants of the base vehicle – may be available and, if so, can provide a relatively simple bolt-on solution. In some cases, there may even be a factory four-wheel-drive version of the base vehicle in question and a parts-bin raid on the suspension components of such a variant could provide a really neat upgrade. If the original vehicle dealers are unable to assist, check for specialist companies who may be able to help in having existing springs modified, or make up completely new ones.

Air-assisted suspension kits are another consideration. These are available from stock for many light commercial vehicles and were originally designed to prevent the rear wallowing when vehicles are run at or near their maximum design weight. Ordinarily, the kits basically comprise two air-filled bellows that fit between the rear axle and the vehicle chassis and they can improve rear ride height usefully. It's possible to adjust the air pressure in the bellows, either manually or using a small onboard electric compressor, so fine-tuning of the ride height and suspension compliance is an option. The kits don't generally replace, but instead augment standard leaf or torsion bar springs.

Because light commercial vehicles generally utilise coil springs as part of their front suspension installation, the matter of air assistance for the front is less straightforward and, at the time of writing, is perhaps not a viable proposition. There *are* fairly crude solutions available known generically as coil spring assisters. These comprise either auxiliary 'helper' springs, or hard rubber inserts that simply hold coils further apart and these could perhaps be used to raise the ground clearance at the front of a vehicle: again, there are specialist companies that can offer advice and products depending on the specific vehicle involved.

Full air suspension is an entirely different proposition to air-*assisted* suspension. With full air suspension the vehicle's original steel springs are completely removed and replaced with air bags. These are compressor controlled with varying degrees of sophistication and complexity and though they are capable of raising ride height and providing a really smooth ride, they're ordinarily designed for carrying fragile cargo on roads that are in reasonable condition. The suitability of such systems for very poor road or mild off-road use should be discussed with expert suppliers because, in cross axle situations, it's possible that full air suspension – in attempting to automatically perform what it, by default, perceives to be an anti-roll requirement – could significantly increase torsional stress and thereby compromise the habitation box structure. In other words, in standard road-kit form, full air suspension can do exactly the opposite of what is actually required when exposed to more extreme poor-road conditions.

As with virtually every modification, there's no such thing as a free lunch and 'improvement' in one regard will often mean compromise in another. With improved ground clearance, the overall centre of gravity of the vehicle will be raised to the point that this may be noticeable when cornering. Raising height through suspension modifications will also increase the angle at which universal joints in driveshafts are forced to operate and could, if modifications are carried too far, lead to premature failure of these components.

Moderate improvement is the key and if, *with a combination of techniques*, you're able to gain something in the region of 50–75mm more ride height, you'll more than likely have made useful improvements with minimal risk of any significant compromise.

Issues with weight

Not only does excessive weight reduce precious ground clearance but when negotiating rough and bumpy roads, the stresses created by moving mass are significant and will do their utmost to break a conventional motor caravan apart. Remaining well within the reserves of the vehicle's maximum design weight is highly recommended. Note that the actual design weight is the weight the manufacturer constructs the vehicle to be able to cope with and is not necessarily the same as the maximum authorised mass (MAM) that is declared to satisfy the arbitrary legal requirements of licensing, revenue, and registration authorities. In the UK, and further afield, it's common to restrict the MAM of a typical motor caravan to 3,500kg but this does not necessarily mean the vehicle is only capable of coping with that specific weight. In some cases, that somewhat arbitrary 3,500kg *may* coincide with the actual maximum design weight but in many cases, especially with 'heavy duty' chassis variants, the vehicle may well still be *well* within its actual physical design limits at the administratively limited 3,500kg weight point.

It's worthwhile establishing the manufacturer's actual design limits when contemplating the vehicle's capabilities, and then taking heed of the 80% rule as outlined in the previous chapter. If you start to make some quick mental calculations, you'll quickly discover that a vehicle with a design limit of 4,000kg should weigh a maximum of 3,200kg when trip-ready *if* the 80% rule is to be followed. For anyone who has knowledge of the approximate weights involved when touring with a conventional motor caravan, you'll instantly realise that sticking to the 80% rule will be a serious challenge; especially in view of the fact that in preparing a conventional motor caravan for more autonomous travel, you're very likely to want to increase reserves of fresh water, fuel and battery capacity, all of which mean adding a good deal of extra weight. There's no simple solution to this dilemma and, practically, it's difficult to do much more than aim for the heaviest-duty chassis possible, travel as lightly as possible, and to *take it easy*. The simple solution of demonstrating mechanical sympathy when on really rough trails will pay dividends in the long run.

Traction

Mass also affects traction. The issue of ensuring that weight does not unload the driving wheels in a front-wheel-drive vehicle was considered in Chapter 2, but in summary: if you do have a front-wheel-drive vehicle, try to ensure that heavier items are placed at least on, but preferably ahead of the rear axle. Also, remember that simple physics dictates that heavy vehicles sink far more readily on soft surfaces.

Given, then, that you're travelling as lightly as possible and have your weight well distributed, the greatest influence that you can bring to bear on a conventional motor caravan's ability to lug through soft terrain is tyre choice. The merits of taller tyres are well established, but that is not the whole story: going slightly wider, as well as slightly taller, will help when the going gets tricky. If you do go to a slightly wider tyre, say from a 215 to a 225, the same earlier mentioned caveats regarding steering lock, bodywork fouling and snow chains apply.

When it comes to tread pattern, for some journeys, purpose-made, very aggressively treaded off-road tyres *may* be the correct choice, but these will almost certainly deliver compromised performance on well-sealed surfaces. If you know your journey will feature large tracts of decent surfaces (most do), then such tyres may ultimately raise more issues than they solve. In a nutshell, tyres marketed by reputable companies for 'all-terrain' and 'all-season' use – *and* which sport a distinctly open-tread pattern that extends over the shoulder of the tyre and on to the sidewall (to scrabble against the sides of ruts) – are arguably the best all-round choice. These *should* perform well over a mixture of both sealed and non-metalled road use across all climatic conditions.

Improving structural integrity

Conventional motor caravans are a mixed bag in terms of structural integrity. Some are very well built; others are not. On rough trails your vehicle will be stressed in two fundamental ways: through road shock in the form of vibration and impact, and through torsional stress where twisting forces are passed through to the habitation area as the chassis twists in response to uneven surfaces. The incessant repetition of these stresses will eventually find any weakness in fixtures and fittings.

Essentially, to give yourself the best chance of success, it's worth inspecting the interior with a very critical eye, working out how your furniture, fixtures and fittings are all fastened together and improving on any obvious weak points. This is especially true in the case of relatively heavy items like fresh water tanks, ovens, refrigerators, water heaters, LPG-bottle mounts and batteries.

One of the problems with the furniture board used in many contemporary motor caravans is that because it's specially manufactured to be as light as possible, it often lacks the structural integrity to allow it to securely hold a screw thread. Sometimes this is because material with a thickness of only around 3mm may be used, and sometimes, in spite of appearing quite thick, boards are essentially almost hollow: comprising a honeycomb construction with only a very thin laminated decorative face.

Techniques that can be used to augment the strength of construction include:

■ Bracing cabinetwork joints with brackets or battens
■ Using larger diameter and/or longer screws

- Securing screws in situ by applying suitable adhesive to threads.
- Replacing screws with a nut-and-bolt combination.
- Using specialist fixing inserts.
- Bonding cabinetwork using sealer adhesives.
- Fabricating stronger mountings for heavy items like batteries and LPG bottles in material such as aluminium angle.
- Bracing cabinetwork that supports heavy items like cookers and water tanks by adding extra wooden framework.

The specific structure-bolstering requirements for each motor caravan will be different and it may well be that yours is already well constructed. Even if it is, it will still be a productive exercise to check and augment where possible. Relying on magazine articles or forum posts that proclaim 'rock-solid build quality' will not stop your fridge shaking loose. Glossy articles that often just reproduce manufacturers' ambitious claims and uncritical casual comment from owners who subject their vehicle to a gentle potter to the local campsite twice a year are not good indicators of how a vehicle will cope with overlanding duty.

External modifications

Overhanging and encroaching vegetation can wreak havoc with external fittings, as can low-slung wires and things like impromptu washing lines. In developing countries in particular, it's common to find all manner of dubious cables drooping menacingly across urban streets. Items such as mirrors, roof vents, TV aerials and acrylic windows do not fare well when exposed to such challenges and though commercially available guards will help with some vulnerable

▲ **Upgrading flimsy standard fasteners with inserts such as these can make for a greatly strengthened interior.**

▼ **Good preparation will go a long way to preventing this unfortunate scenario.**

items like lights and mirrors, in order to protect other items, it may be necessary to be a little creative. As well as not wanting to be responsible for a power cut, or inadvertently stealing someone's washing, it will help to prevent losing roof-mounted hardware if you come up with some kind of effective deflector that will guide anything that would ordinarily snag vulnerable items uneventfully out of the way. In working out a solution, don't forget that you absolutely *will* also need to reverse through such hazards at some point…

The vulnerability of acrylic windows is well known to most motor caravan owners; even the slightest brush with light vegetation will scratch them mercilessly. Protecting them is something of a challenge, but not impossible. One solution is to make a box-section frame, mount this to the vehicle's external bodywork around the periphery of the acrylic window

frame, and then use this frame to mount a suitable shield. Those thinking ahead will quickly realise that with top-hinged acrylic windows this will (without a good deal of Heath Robinson engineering) mean a laborious process of opening/removing shields from outside of the vehicle. With sliding windows though, the entire opening/closing-of-shield scenario can easily be accomplished from within. Sheet aluminium is one good material from which to create appropriate shields, but other materials like a sacrificial transparent polycarbonate layer or perforated stainless steel would serve just as well and would also allow some vision out of the vehicle with the guards in situ. An added bonus of this kind of shield is one of enhanced security – vehicles certainly at least *appear* more secure, and with a little work can actually be *made* so simply by adding suitable locks of choice.

BUILDING ROOF BARS

Roof bars can prevent damage caused by overhanging vegetation and wires etc. They can be built in a number of ways, the simplest of which can be achieved with simple hand tools.

1 Bending 10-gauge aluminium bar should really be done on a proper jig or with pipe benders. However, there are always impromptu ways for the machine-shop-lacking self-builder. Here, a suitable brace is found and body weight judiciously added.

2 Neat stainless-steel fittings designed for railing around boat decks can be purchased to accommodate bars of various diameters.

3 Fittings can be screwed or – to avoid perforating the roof – bonded into position. In this case Sikaflex 512 is utilised. This should be strong enough to ward off relatively light brushes with foreign objects.

4 Rear of bars in place showing protection for vulnerable roof light – note bars are sloped at the rear too in order to lift foreign objects when reversing.

5 If you have the tools and skill, bespoke constructions in stainless steel are highly desirable.

6 Work in progress on an altogether more robust bash-bar system. This one should be able to shrug off pretty large branches.

BUILDING WINDOW GUARDS

This is just one way to approach the job of protecting vulnerable windows; other materials and methods can prove just as effective.

1 Sections of 16-gauge box section aluminium, suitably mitred, are bonded with Sikaflex 512 around the window's perimeter – it's wise to leave a

couple of channels during the adhesive sealer application for water to drain between the bodywork and the back of the frame, and to drill a couple of holes into the underside of the lower frame itself to allow any water that runs into the hollow structure to escape.

2 All is held in place until the adhesive sealer fully cures.

3 The full frame is detailed with runs of adhesive sealer to fill any gaps in order to prevent any frost-related issues and to make the job look neat.

4 Magnets are added to eventually hold the finished shields in place. This is a Neodymium magnet supplied with a convenient 6mm countersunk hole to allow attachment to the bodywork using a 12-gauge stainless steel screw and a dab of adhesive sealer (to weatherproof the body-perforating hole). Neodymium magnets were chosen for this relatively sheltered location because of their superior pulling power.

5 3mm-thick aluminium sheet pressed out to exact dimensions by a local supplier is attached to the frames using simple stainless-steel hinges. Hinges are riveted to the shields and screwed to the frame using stainless screws. A layer of strong double-sided tape can be added between the hinge and shield, and also the hinge and frame, to

both provide additional support and help to ward off any galvanic corrosion issues. Note the damage already visible on this shield from brushes with vegetation – the underlying window would, by now, be severely scratched if left unprotected.

6 Detail of the shield's magnet arrangement and rubber retainers. This magnet is a Samarium Cobalt item chosen for its strength and corrosion resistance.

It's attached using a slightly proud countersunk M6 stainless bolt. It's important to prevent magnets from physically crashing into one another as they 'connect' because they are very brittle and could shatter. The bolt head (and slightly proud countersunk screw on the respective body-mounted Neodymium magnet) are the only points of physical contact. The rubber retainer is a simple two-piece door stop of the type often used on horseboxes that can either be used as a simple rest, or, in windy conditions, fully plunged together (as in the image).

7 Retainer detail. For the shield fabrication, the diameter of the head of the male component of the retainer (which, incidentally, accommodates an M6 hex nut) was reduced by a few millimetres to make opening and closing the connection easier. As supplied these retainers are very strong and difficult to separate: they are designed to hold a full-weight door in quite windy conditions.

8 With shields down the view from windows is unmolested. When up the windows are not only protected but stay cleaner for longer, especially if

travelling in foul or dusty conditions. Furthermore, even when only closed with magnets, they also help with the appearance of security.

Improving autonomy

If choosing the trail less travelled, chances are you'll spend good lengths of time with no opportunities to replenish water and gas supplies. In very remote areas, fuel range too may be an issue. Subsequent chapters will introduce water, LPG and electrical systems in more detail and should be read in conjunction with the short generic sections that follow. It should be borne in mind that any enhancement of water, gas and other support systems on a conventional motor caravan will necessarily be fairly modest as space and payload are generally very limiting.

Enhancing water reserves

Specialist companies exist that are able to source or construct water tanks to bespoke specifications. It may well be possible to utilise space more efficiently and replace your original tank with one of larger capacity, or to add a second tank and connect the two. Another option is to simply mount an additional stand-alone tank, leave it as an 'unconnected' reserve and to access its contents by submersible pump or a simple manual tap. A further trick that has been used to good effect is to scrap the ubiquitous grey-water tank and substitute it with a secondary fresh-water tank. Grey water

▼ **The simple addition of portable water containers can make for great flexibility and convenience on the road.**

can then instead be collected in a portable container or simply drained direct to the ground – assuming it contains no harmful contaminants and is drained legally, respectfully and discreetly.

Some of the best solutions are the simplest and the versatility of portable containers should not be underestimated. The advantages of having at least *one* portable container are many, perhaps the most important of which is to be able to carry supplies from some distance away in the event that it's impossible to reach a water source by vehicle. Again, water held in portable containers can be siphoned, pumped, or in some cases simply poured into the vehicle's main water tank. Managing supplies from portable containers may involve a little more work than filling with a hose from a tap, but it's preferable to running dry.

Rate of consumption is something that can make a huge difference to reserves and, though it sounds obvious, the importance of good habits cannot be overstated. Pouring the cooled contents of a previously boiled kettle into a plastic bottle provides one source of drinking water and simple things like brushing teeth using a cup of water, rather than running a tap, can save significant quantities over time. Fairly clean grey water – perhaps collected after a shower – can be used to top up some types of toilet flush tank and it has even been known for enterprising overlanders to capture rain water for general domestic duty.

Enhancing gas reserves

Permanently mounted, self-refillable LPG tanks are readily obtainable and are a very good way to store gas supplies. They can be mounted in a number of positions (most frequently underneath a vehicle) and can free up the valuable locker space ordinarily occupied by portable cylinders. Frequently, conventional motor caravans are supplied with a gas locker that houses two portable cylinders and, for reasons fully discussed in Chapter 9, it's wise to create a gas supply system that will always enable the use of one local-to-where-you-are cylinder and regulator. The combination of a fixed tank and one locally obtainable cylinder is highly desirable as this will give useful self-refillable LPG capacity *plus* the option to use a portable cylinder if required – wherever in the world you happen to be. If a fixed tank is impracticable or undesirable, then a system that incorporates one self-refillable cylinder *plus* one local-to-where-you-are cylinder, as outlined above, is arguably the next-best option.

Enhancing electrical reserves

A detailed consideration of electrical systems follows in Chapter 10, but essentially, if you travel on a daily basis, you'll probably find the standard charging system

▶ **A refillable and local-cylinder combination takes some beating.**

and existing leisure battery (or leisure-battery bank) are sufficient. If, however, you're a heavy consumer, or spend several days in one place without access to battery-charging hardware (and do not wish to run your engine), then more battery capacity is the first port of call. It's usually a fairly straightforward matter to increase capacity, either by connecting an additional battery in parallel with the current battery(ies), or doing away with the original(s) and buying a single larger-capacity battery. A total capacity of 200–300Ah at 12 volts *should* ordinarily be good for a few days, but if this is still insufficient, it's probably wise to resign yourself to periodically running the engine, or maybe fitting a solar panel. Most other forms of off-grid battery-charging hardware are too bulky or heavy to form practicable solutions in a conventional motor caravan modified for use as an overland camper.

Enhancing fuel reserves

As covered in Chapter 2, a minimum range of 1,200km-plus is arguably optimal in a purpose-made overland camper, but, depending on frugality and terrain, this may simply be unattainable in a conventional motorhome without significant alterations to incorporate a long-range or auxiliary fuel tank. It is, of course, possible to fit either of these options and for the most adventurous it's probably worth serious consideration. In most cases though, portable containers in the form of jerrycans come to the rescue. Jerrycans have reliably served overlanders for decades and, as with water containers, it's always handy to have at least one portable fuel container to help with the transfer of diesel or petrol between vehicles – or when hitching a lift to the nearest fuel supply… A couple of jerrycans mounted in dedicated holders is a safe and convenient solution to increasing fuel capacity by 40 litres. Different types of can are available to suit all tastes and budgets and it's even possible to buy ancillaries like purpose-made pumps to aid fuel transfer.

Adapting a conventional motorhome into a vehicle capable of autonomous travel in difficult terrain is only ever going to be a compromised solution. There's an inherent tension in being able to increase equipment levels, reserves and capacities, whilst at the same time striving to keep that all-important weight down. Ground clearance, particularly in the context of departure angle, is always going to be an issue whilst traction, particularly with front-wheel-drive vehicles, will undoubtedly occasionally prove elusive. That said, it bears repeating that some conventional motor caravans have completed spectacular overland journeys and, with appropriate preparation, can be surprisingly capable.

GETTING STUCK

With good preparation and careful driving, a conventional motor caravan can be capable of surprisingly arduous journeys, but at some point you'll inevitably get stuck. It's beyond the remit of this manual to cover recovery techniques, but, when preparing your vehicle, you should consider carrying at least the following:

- At least one pair of sand mats or recovery tracks to stick under bogged wheels (home-brewed versions are possible and include, amongst other things, carpet and hessian sacks)
- A *high quality* recovery rope/strap
- At least two shackles to help secure ropes/straps
- A spade to dig loose surfaces away from bogged wheels and grounded bodywork
- A good-quality high-lift jack

Whole books have been written on the subject of recovery and for serious equipment and ideas off-road specialists have some brilliant solutions.

Bruce Burrow

7 Subframe solution

Self-designed three-point torsion-free arrangement made in box-section aluminium and mounted using two rubber-cushioned 'fixed' points at the front and one bearing-based fully pivoting point at the rear. The rear pivot was designed to sit at a height midway between the chassis rails. The cross member around the mounting point was also strengthened.

1 Name

Bruce Burrow.

2 Base vehicle

1990 Leyland DAF T244 GS – Winch variant.

3 Drive

4x4 / permanent all-wheel drive.

4 Fuel capacity

Standard (137 litres).

5 Weight when loaded and ready to travel

8.5 tonnes.

6 Reason for base vehicle choice

Simple, reliable, correct chassis dimensions for size of proposed habitation box.

8 Habitation-box construction

The box is made of wood. I used a 50mm x 50mm ash frame radiused at the top of the sidewalls and covered this with a 10mm plywood outer skin. Insulation material was then bonded in place and to line the interior I used 6mm ply.

9 Habitation-box insulation material

Celotex – 50mm foil-backed sheets.

10 Habitation-box manufacturer

Self.

11 Habitation-box windows

Seitz.

12 Habitation-box door(s) and locker(s)

I used an off-the-peg caravan door and an over-the-counter locker frame for the bike garage.

13 Fit out done by

Self.

14 Furniture construction

Made in plywood incorporating standard domestic kitchen units.

15 Fresh water

400 litres. One stand-alone tap is reserved for drinking water, which is provided via a dedicated water filter.

16 Refrigeration

3-way absorption fridge.

17 Space heating

We tapped into the hot water delivery circuit of the instant hot-water heating boiler and used a circulating pump controlled by a thermostat to feed a small 'wet' circuit containing a towel-rail radiator and a kick-space heater. I am not 100% happy with the way I have altered it as it means warm water is fed back into what should be a cold water inlet for the boiler. This is not a recommended modification and not something the manufacturer would approve, but it warms the truck quickly and has worked well for four years now.

18 Water heating

Morco LPG-powered instant water heater. This has a small built-in reservoir and supplies instantly heated water on

demand. The boiler's burner is activated when a hot-water tap is opened (or when the circulation pump operates as per the space-heating section above). The boiler needs a mains-voltage supply to run the control panel. An inverter takes care of this requirement.

19 Cooking facilities

LPG 3-burner hob, oven and grill.

20 Habitation-box cooling

We open windows and doors etc. I also have two domestic 240V extractor fans (one in the bathroom, one above the cooker) running from an inverter, which are very effective.

21 Leisure-battery charging

The alternator provides charge to the starter batteries, which then charge the leisure batteries via a DC–DC 24–12V battery-to-battery charger. We also have an AC to DC charger for use with mains electricity and 2 x 50W solar panels to provide a background/maintenance charge.

22 Things to do differently next time

I think I would use a fibreglass-faced ply in future to give better resistance to scratching on the exterior of the box but still try and keep the curved shape. Internally I think I would use a decorative-faced laminated ply similar to that used on a standard motorhome – purely for aesthetic reasons.

CHAPTER 4

Taking on a build-your-own project

PART 1 – PRE-VEHICLE ACQUISITION

- Establishing final direction
- Design strategies
- Vans and trucks with proven credentials
- Where to source suitable base vehicles
- Commercial entities

PART 2 – POST-VEHICLE ACQUISITION

- Preparing a base vehicle
- Enhancing time spent driving
- Racks, hoists and winches
- Ladders
- Fixing other large and heavy items

If you're reading this then the chances are you've decided that a converted conventional motor caravan is unlikely to meet your needs. If you've taken the plunge and are about to embark on a build-your-own project then it will definitely prove worthwhile, *before* handing over any cash, to formulate plans in finer detail. Then, when you're completely happy with a direction, it's time to source a vehicle and roll up your sleeves...

PART 1 – PRE-VEHICLE ACQUISITION

Establishing final direction

If you've addressed the points raised in Chapter 2, you should already have formed some fairly firm ideas on the kind of vehicle you ultimately aim to travel with and have some loose parameters in mind in terms of:

- Overall size.
- Weight.
- Driven-wheel configuration.
- Base vehicle age and level of technology employed.
- Whether you prefer a truck- or van-based conversion.
- The type of habitation box you'll use.

You should also have some fairly well established ideas regarding your preferences for layout, and equipment and systems, especially with fundamentals such as:

- Number of sleeping berths.
- Seating arrangements.
- Space-heating solutions.
- Water-heating solutions.
- Capacities for water/LPG supplies.
- Cooking preferences.
- Washroom preferences.
- Electrical reserves.
- Indispensable extras. Bicycles/motorcycles/kayaks etc.
- Entertainment. TV/media player solutions, sound system, ICT system etc.

If you're currently lacking clarity regarding any of your requirements or preferences, don't worry. At this stage you're still in a position to do more research and if you don't yet feel sufficiently informed about base vehicles, equipment or systems, it will be worthwhile selectively dipping into the later chapters of this manual, reading other written material, visiting shows or posing questions on forums. It's immeasurably better to take a little longer at this stage than to take a hasty plunge in entirely the wrong direction.

Design strategies

Around this stage in the process it will help to transfer ideas into some kind of tangible form. Simply *imagining* where you'll sleep, or how much space will be available to cook, eat and shower etc. can turn out very differently when actually drawing up scale plans; the space where you fancifully imagine you'll sleep may well turn out to be too cramped, or to be a hugely inefficient use of valuable space. When you actively engage in the process of working out the detail of your overall layout you'll inevitably be chasing millimetres so a useful exercise is to establish how much space is typically occupied by things like kitchen appliances, overhead lockers, washrooms etc., and to get to grips with the typical depth, height and width of items like worktops and seating. Visits to motor caravan shows armed with a tape measure will enable you to actually sit in vehicles with very different layouts and will be invaluable in allowing you to get an idea of which designs work best for you; remember to take copious measurements and make notes! Once you know what you really want, and what's dispensable, it's time to start modelling.

Making designs tangible

It doesn't really matter what technology you employ, as long as plans are to scale. Simple pencil and paper plans can

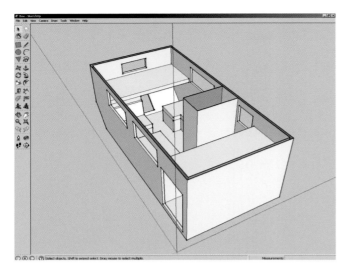

▲ With very little time spent learning the software, models such as this can be created. The ability to easily cut through cross-sectional views really helps with determining how things will actually work (or not) in an actual build.

prove very successful and if going this route graph paper will help with scaling.

For those who prefer an electronic interface, Computer Aided Design (CAD) software is now readily available and some design packages can be downloaded completely free of charge. Some are very easy to get to grips with and also benefit from good-quality online tutorials. One great advantage of CAD solutions is that visualisation of the finished product is so much easier when you're able to 'virtually' rotate and tilt models of the design that you have

created. The ability to create cross-sectional images of the model in all planes is also a tremendously useful feature. It really doesn't take that much learning effort to be able to create designs that are well up to the task of forming the basis of a successful build. Remember, this process is a means to an end; all you want to establish is whether your ideas work. Full architect-style blueprints and/or advanced CAD skill are not required.

Another really good technique, if you have access to a suitable space, is to use masking tape or chalk to mock up full-sized layouts. By marking out the floor plan in 1:1 scale you'll quickly see whether your plans will work in reality or whether there will be pinch-points that mean a rethink is required. This same technique can be used on vertical walls to determine suitable heights for seating and overhead lockers. Establishing three-dimensional measurements is critical at this stage as the positioning of items like seats and lockers will ultimately impact upon the subsequent dimensions and positioning of windows, hatches and doors – and, naturally, vice versa.

Vans and trucks with proven credentials

Successful overland campers have been built on all manner of vans and trucks and there is no simple right or wrong regarding the ideal base vehicle. Almost all well-known commercial vehicle manufacturers can offer, or have previously produced, vans or trucks with robust and simple mechanics, good ground clearance and all-wheel drive. Add to the mix that there are also companies that take brand

FREESTYLING

Collective wisdom advocates that the planning and design stages are crucial, and that substantial effort should be put into establishing clear vision, strategy and direction in order to produce an overland camper that will meet your own exacting needs. There are, though, several examples of owners who have successfully completed

▷ This is one example of a brilliantly executed 'organic' alteration following the realisation that the first placement of the habitation door caused too many compromises. It worked out well but involved considerable time, expense and frustration.

projects through a process of 'organic' development. On-the-fly builds sometimes turn out very well indeed but ultimately tend to involve quite a bit more work as alterations (and even alterations to alterations) are almost inevitable. These can be costly,

frustrating and can go on for some considerable time. If, though, you know yourself well and you work best when freestyling, it may be encouraging to know that some great vehicles have been produced this way.

new vehicles and perform all manner of (sometimes factory-approved) chassis and transmission modifications to make the vehicle more suitable for multi-terrain use and the range of suitable base vehicles can seem overwhelming. In reality though, it doesn't have to be: it's wise to take the line of least resistance and to take a steer from those who have trodden the path before you. An internet search for images of overlanding/expedition vans or trucks allows quick and easy access to the hard-won collective wisdom of people that have driven to all corners of the globe, and you'll quickly see recurring trends in base-vehicle choice.

When it comes to popularity and far-reaching global support, Mercedes-Benz rear- and all-wheel-drive products consistently feature and are undeniably well proven. Other very sound choices include brands that are arguably just as proficient and (almost) as well supported, if not yet quite so popular. These include, in no particular order, two-, four-, six- or even eight-wheel-drive products from MAN, Iveco, Tatra, DAF, Mitsubishi-Fuso, Isuzu and Renault.

Beneath this layer of often-utilised brands are other suitable if possibly slightly less well globally supported options from manufacturers such as Ford, Scania and Volvo, plus a whole array of Russian trucks. Thereafter, there are, without doubt, yet other very capable and desirable vehicles, but as brands become less well known reliance upon mechanical know-how and parts availability can become something of a geographical lottery.

When considering suitable base vehicles, it's worth bearing in mind that some major mechanical components, like engines and gearboxes, are very well known and widely used. For example, the engine found in ex-military Leyland DAF T244s from the 1990s is a Cummins six-cylinder diesel and this very same engine is still happily thrumming away in all manner of applications. It's currently commonly used in large pickup trucks in the USA as well as in boats, plant and generators the world over. During your deliberation process, particularly if straying from the usual brands, it pays to do a little research to check which major components form the basis of potential candidate vehicles. Ubiquitous components will hugely increase the probability of support in terms of mechanical assistance and spares availability.

Where to source suitable base vehicles

In thinking about sourcing a base vehicle – either with or without a basic box structure already attached – it helps to think about the attributes that make for a good overlander and then to imagine organisations and entities that would also find those attributes useful. It shouldn't take long to start to think along the lines of the military, utility companies, emergency services, local authorities, water companies, airfield operators, forest authorities, railway operations – and so the list goes on. Basically, any entity that has a requirement for vehicles to carry equipment and/or personnel over tough terrain will, at some point, seek to dispose of vehicles that are just about perfect as a starting point for an overlander.

▲ A 4x4 MAN former utility company crane truck. Vehicles like this are often utilised for transporting things like telegraph poles to difficult sites.

▼ A former local authority 6x6 snowplough/gritter. By their nature this kind of vehicle will usually be capable in inhospitable terrain.

▲ Airfield maintenance and rescue vehicles are often worth a second look.

▼ A runway de-icing vehicle awaiting its new overlander life.

Encouragingly, there are bargains to be had and though good deals can crop up anywhere, of particular note in this regard are ex-military reserve vehicles. These are almost-as-new vehicles simply mothballed awaiting deployment, and it's entirely possible to purchase such a van or truck in very good condition for well under €10,000. For the most patient of purchasers, occasional vehicles with odometer readings of well under 1,000km lurk in disposal agents' yards just begging to be discovered.

Sourcing online

These days, anyone wishing to sell anything almost invariably turns to the power of the internet. It is indisputably *the* place to start to look for a base vehicle and well-known auction sites frequently throw up all sorts of suitable candidates. Indeed, at some point, vehicles initially disposed of through methods detailed in the sections that follow will themselves very probably end up being offered online. Entering a term like 'expedition camper for sale' in search engines or popular auction sites will undoubtedly throw up some excellent leads.

OLD LOW-MILEAGE VEHICLES

If you are lucky enough to find a very-low-mileage example of a truck or van that's been stored for years, a little caution should be exercised. It's undoubtedly the case that older, unused vehicles can suffer from insidious internal corrosion to mechanical components, perished rubber components and deformed tyre sidewalls etc. Commercial vehicles are designed to cover huge mileages without major mechanical attention and so a well-maintained and regularly serviced vehicle with relatively high mileage is not necessarily an inferior starting point to an unused ex-army-reserve vehicle.

Centralised asset disposal in the UK

The UK Government has responsibility for an entity known as the Disposal Services Authority (DSA), which acts on behalf of the Ministry of Defence (MoD). This authority is primarily responsible for disposing of military vehicles but has a further role in helping other public bodies like the emergency services, HM Prison Service and local authorities to dispose of surplus stock. At the time of writing, Witham (Specialist Vehicles) Ltd holds the contract to dispose of all vehicles on behalf of the DSA. Most of the vehicles at Witham's are ex-military but non-military (sometimes fully-road-registered) vehicles do turn up too and, with luck, it's possible to find some remarkable bargains. In addition to Witham's, there are other UK-based companies that make a commercial enterprise out of surplus stock disposal such as L Jackson and Co and this company in particular is able to source some very interesting vehicles as it has access to stock from overseas armed forces. Both companies will more than happily deal with non-UK purchasers. If you are considering this

DISPOSAL AGENT BUYING TIPS

It's worth bearing in mind that in the case of the larger disposal organisations, they're generally geared towards dealing with large-scale sales on a corporate basis. Aid agencies and foreign governments buying dozens of vehicles (often unseen) is a model they know well. Individuals wishing to buy just one vehicle, and insisting that it's in showroom condition, are not necessarily the kind of customer deemed worthy of their top-drawer sales service. This is not to say that you'll not be treated well, just be aware of their usual client base and usual scale of operation. A little understanding and humility on your part will serve you well.

direction, something to be aware of is that ex-military vehicles sold through disposal agents will not *usually* be recognised by licensing and registration authorities and it will take some work to make them road legal – this issue is revisited in chapter six. Such vehicles may also require export licences if sold overseas.

Commercial entities

Commercial enterprises abound and take different forms:

- Smaller dealers will frequently purchase job lots of vehicles from disposal agents like the ones above and then sell them on, often having taken them through the process of making them road legal. There are innumerable small companies who operate in this way and, as is the case with most sellers, they will ordinarily rely on the internet to advertise vehicles for sale as and when they have stock.
- For anyone with a healthy budget, main dealerships would undoubtedly be happy to discuss new or nearly new options and for fans of real exotica there are even

specialist companies out there that will modify brand-new vehicles to bespoke requirements.

- Such is the growing popularity of self-build overlander projects that at least one highly specialised expedition-truck brokerage service is now operating out of the Netherlands and is able to source anything from suitable base vehicles right through to complete and thoroughly travel-proven overlanders.

Once again, internet searches will quickly throw up potential sources of commercial entities able to supply suitable vehicles.

Organisational disposal

Some large organisations such as local authorities, forestry commissions and utility companies may well sell off vehicles directly and it's worthwhile tracking down the people or departments within such organisations that deal with the disposal of assets. Such people/departments will advise on when and how suitable vehicles may be made available and taking the time to create good relationships can prove very worthwhile.

PART 2 – POST-VEHICLE ACQUISITION

Preparing a base vehicle

Once you've made your purchase it's time to dust off the toolbox. Tackling jobs in a logical sequence will ultimately make life much simpler so before starting work on a habitation area – and while you still have easy access to the chassis – this is a good stage to carry out modifications to enable the finished vehicle to accommodate items like racks, winches and larger fuel tanks. It's also as good a time as any to consider improvements that will make the substantial amount of time you'll be spending driving as comfortable and pleasant as possible.

Enhancing time spent driving

You may be fortunate and have acquired a well-appointed base vehicle, in which case this section may not be too relevant; comfort levels and driver aids have improved a great deal in recent years. In many cases though, given that many base vehicles suitable for overlanding use have a utilitarian background, it makes sense to look for ways to increase comfort.

Insulating and soundproofing the cab

The utilitarian nature of suitable base vehicles will often mean that manufacturers have paid little attention to making sure that heat and noise from engines and transmissions, plus extremes of heat and cold from outside, are effectively isolated. It will pay to look for any areas within the cab that have been left as exposed metal, or have only been given a cursory covering of decorative trim and to improve these areas with sound-deadening and/or heat-insulative material. Happily, there are many kinds of commercially available materials that are up to the job. Acoustic and insulative material is available for just about every application within a vehicle's cab and comes in a variety of thicknesses, has a variety of properties, and – as a bonus – is often self-adhesive. The materials are generally fairly easy to work, but it will always pay to make templates in paper or cardboard before committing to making cuts to expensive acquisitions such as lead blanket. It's also possible to make acoustic and insulative improvements using more traditional methods such as utilising custom-made plywood panels covered in headlining carpet.

1 Expanses of metal such as this lead to a noisy environment and also promote the rapid transfer of extremes of heat and cold.

4 Automotive lining carpet is fixed to the rear bulkhead using contact adhesive. The quarter panels in view were made also from lining-carpet-covered 4mm exterior ply. The cavity-facing side of the ply was also varnished to assist with resisting any moisture produced in the cavities.

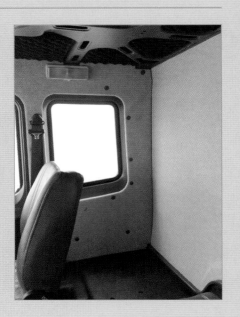

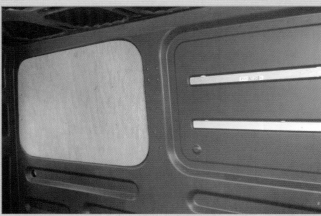

2 Battens are bonded to the rear bulkhead with Sikaflex 221 before suitably cut 4mm exterior ply is screwed to them.

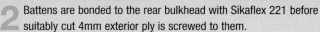

3 Smaller recesses in the metal pressing are covered with strips of self-adhesive closed-cell sponge.

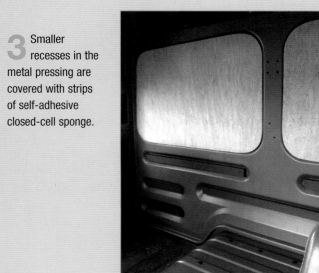

5 Sections of foil tape and self-adhesive lead blanket are cut to shape and used to cover holes and irregularities in this engine cover pressing.

6 A full and unbroken layer of lead blanket is then overlaid. A good tip for working this material is to gently tap it into position using a rubber mallet. With care, a ball peen hammer can also be useful for getting it to conform to tight concave sections.

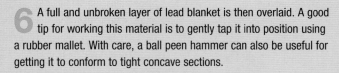

7 More lead blanket is added to fully insulate all parts of the exposed engine cover. This material is primarily a noise suppressant, but it also helps to a degree with heat insulation.

8 A final layer of professionally manufactured carpet makes for an even quieter and aesthetically pleasing result.

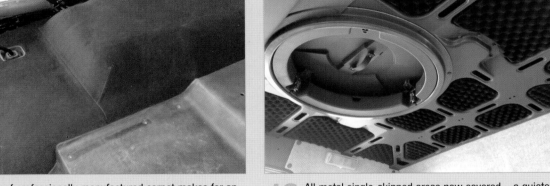

10 All metal single-skinned areas now covered – a quieter and better-insulated result.

9 Areas of the cab roof that are not double skinned in steel are covered in self-adhesive 'egg box' foam. Templates for each cut were first laboriously made in thick paper/thin card.

11 A different approach in an identical cab. In this work-in-progress, ply covered in a natural-fibre material is used to great effect and the use of structural ply means extra cubby holes and media solutions also become an option.

Adding finishing touches to the cab area is much like personalising a normal car: things like phone and cup holders are available anywhere and are straightforward to fit. There is one area, however, that may require a bit more thought. Many overland campers utilise 24V DC electrical systems, but most in-car entertainment and luxury items like stereos and device chargers need a nominal 12V supply. One answer is to fit a purpose-made DC-DC converter. These self-contained units are available with different current-carrying capacity ranging from a continuous 3A for things like small mobile phones, up to units capable of dealing with very high current requirements. Physical fitting is straightforward and the wiring requires just four connections: a positive and negative from the vehicle's 24V circuit (the input), and a positive and negative to the 12V device to be powered (the output). The units draw very little power when on standby so can theoretically be left permanently connected to the vehicle's 24V battery supply. That said, *any* unnecessary current draw from a vehicle's batteries when stationary is arguably a bad thing so it's highly recommended that you isolate the 24V supply to the converter with a simple switch.

Suspension seats

A combination of commercial vehicle suspension, very rough roads and (ideally) adherence to the 80% rule mean that most vans and trucks, particularly those that seat occupants directly above the front axle, deliver a ride most politely referred to as harsh. Suspension seats do much to improve comfort and, for longer/rougher trips, are arguably indispensable. The suspension action can be mechanical or pneumatic, but, considering ease of installation, reliability, cost and ease of repair, mechanical seats are generally favoured. Mounting will almost certainly require some minor fabrication of brackets in order to affix the seats in a position that will not foul hardware like the engine cover/transmission tunnel, seatbelt mounting points, handbrake and so on.

ISOLATED AND NON-ISOLATED DC-DC CONVERTERS

Two types of DC-DC converter are commonly marketed: 'isolated' and 'non-isolated'. The 'isolation' refers to the existence of an electrical barrier between the input and output of the converter. Simplistically, in non-isolated converters there is an internal electrical connection between input and output circuits, in isolated converters there isn't. Isolated converters are only critical if complying with a strict health and safety policy dictating their use: in overland camper applications, non-isolated converters are usually all that is required.

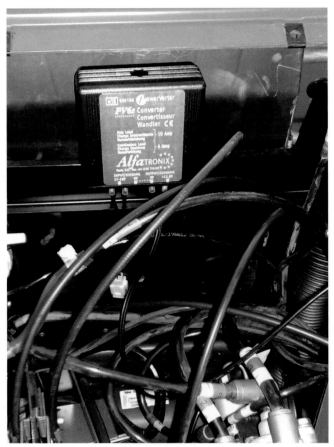

▲ A small DC-DC converter is added behind a dash panel to create a stable nominal 12V supply to allow mobile device chargers to run from the base vehicle's 24V supply.

▼ The angled bracket in view was supplied with these KAB mechanical suspension seats but has been cut down, shaped and painted to give the impression that it's an original part of the standard vehicle. It can be seen how the bracket allows the seat base to be offset from the original mounting holes.

Fortunately, manufacturers and suppliers recognise this and it's usually possible to purchase rudimentary brackets along with seats that at least give a starting point for successful integration. These are predrilled and offset at points that take into account the (often fairly standardised) bolt patterns found in commercial vehicles and with a bit of thought and tweaking will see the job done. In the worst-case scenario, custom brackets may need to be made and new mounting holes drilled. If this is the case, be sure to mount to sections of the floor that are at least *as* strong as the points used by manufacturers and brace as required. Always use high-tensile fasteners of at least 8.8 grade.

Keeping the cab cool

In very hot conditions cabs can get warm, even after a careful insulation/soundproofing job. Though cab air conditioning (air con) is quite common in modern commercial vehicles, it's rarely found in older vans and trucks. If you don't have factory-fitted air con and find the cab overbearing, there are a few ways in which you can avoid wilting. These include: fitting a self-contained electrically powered air-con unit, retro-fitting a full air-con system or adopting the relatively simple solution of relying on decent quality fans.

Self-contained air-conditioning units are readily available and are ordinarily roof or rear-of-the-cab mounted. Some are marketed towards leisure vehicles like caravans, others towards passenger carrying vehicles and trucks. Installation is relatively straightforward and usually entails the three major steps of cutting an aperture, physically fitting the unit, and arranging an electrical supply. Some units are designed to work on AC voltage only, in which case an inverter will usually be required, whilst some are specifically designed to work with 12/24V DC voltage, thereby allowing direct connection to the base vehicle's electrical circuits. This kind of air-con unit is relatively power-hungry and will rapidly discharge batteries if the engine isn't running so can, practically, only be used whilst driving or whilst taking very short breaks. Owner reports are varied; some claim good performance whilst others claim the units can barely cope. The volume of cab space, ambient temperature and the power rating of the unit itself all undoubtedly influence performance. If you decide to go this route, it's probably wise to err on the side of choosing a larger or more powerful unit than might initially seem adequate.

Retro-fitting a full air-conditioning system is not a job for the faint hearted, but it can be done. At its simplest, work involved would initially mean obtaining suitable parts including:

- A compressor to pump refrigerant around the system. These are belt-driven from a crankshaft pulley so a suitable pulley will also need to be sourced and fitted;

unless you're very lucky and have a spare groove in your existing setup just waiting to receive a belt.
- A suitable bracket to mount the compressor. This will also ordinarily need to be adjustable to allow tensioning of the belt.
- The drive belt itself.
- A condenser. This is effectively a radiator to cool the refrigerant. It has to sit in a position to receive good air flow and/or be served by a fan.
- A dryer/receiver. This removes moisture from the refrigerant, preventing ice crystals forming and causing blockages.
- An expansion valve to regulate pressure allowing the circulating liquid refrigerant to vaporise.
- An evaporator. This is effectively a heat exchanger that, with the assistance of a blower passing air across it, allows the much reduced temperature of the refrigerant to be transferred to the vehicle's interior (the cool blown air you feel).
- Suitable plumbing and fittings to connect all these components together.
- A control panel or switches to engage the compressor and activate blowers, usually at varying speeds.

Finding suitable space to physically fit, actually mounting, and then connecting all of this hardware is not a job to be taken lightly and – if you're not yet committed and simply weighing up options – it should also be borne in mind that air-conditioning systems are generally not renowned for their reliability. Crashing around on the bad roads of the world can, and does, hasten the failure of pipes and fittings and finding replacement parts on the road with such a bespoke system might prove a very frustrating affair. All this said, some owners have successfully been through this process and it's not unknown for bespoke cab air-con systems to be extended with a second evaporator and associated hardware to allow effective cooling to the habitation box whenever the vehicle engine is running. An added benefit of a full air-con system is that the dehumidifying properties are useful on cold wet days when condensation can lead to heavily misted cab windows.

If air-conditioning systems sound too involved, good quality fans are a comparatively cheap and reasonably effective solution. Better quality units are quiet in operation and are often specifically marketed for leisure vehicle, truck-cab and marine use. Many are available for both 12V and 24V electrical systems. A well-paced fan is likely to be a very cost-effective and reliable solution and only really loses out to other cab-cooling methods when temperatures really soar.

It's stressed that these solutions are all about addressing the issue of keeping the cab cool whilst actually driving or taking a short break. Keeping the habitation box cool is a very different matter and is considered in Chapter 11.

Racks, hoists and winches

If you're building a larger overlander and intend to carry heavy items like motorcycles, or plan to attach winches or hoists, then it will very likely save frustration in the long term if you address ways of mounting such items at this stage. As the build grows, then available space to mount hardware rapidly diminishes and because the optimum mounting points for items like racks and winches are very often precisely dictated by their function, it's all too easy to tie up the exact space that later turns out to be required to support a heavy fabrication.

Your intentions regarding carrying very heavy equipment may also have implications for your chosen habitation-box construction method. Motorcycles, spare wheels and so on perched on the rear of a truck subjected to rough-road use result in huge stresses so if you plan on utilising a lightweight composite-panel-based habitation box, you'll need to be mindful of this construction method's load-bearing limitations. In simple terms, a lightweight composite panel build will not – by itself – reliably support heavy racking so if this is going to be your build method of choice, be sure to plan for (or indeed get on with) fabricating mounts for an 'exoskeleton' or other bespoke load-bearing components at this stage. More about different habitation box construction methods and their suitability to support heavy racking appears in Chapter 7.

WINCHES

Winches pull along, hoists lift upwards: they are task-specific. Permanently mounted winches are a very popular addition to overland campers, but their effectiveness is rather less clear cut. Many owners have found themselves in tricky situations but for a variety of reasons have found their onboard winch useless. Some seasoned overlanders advocate a fully portable hand-cranked winch and cite their flexibility and lack of dependence on a power source as major advantages. Yet others consider all winches as little more than false friends that promote ill-advised risk-taking. Unquestionably, winches *can* save the day but equally unquestionably they don't always...

▶ Reducing tyre pressure and lots of digging is – more often than not – the only way out.

▼ Towing – an alternative to lowering tyre pressure – but not to digging.

▲ ▶ Work on this spare-wheel (and bicycle) carrier was wisely completed long before the lightweight composite panel habitation box build started.

▶ An example of an 'exoskeleton' type structure. This habitation box is also made from lightweight composite panels so the rack intended to carry spare wheels and a scooter relies completely on the purpose-fabricated braced skeletal structure to bear the substantial weight and stresses.

FABRICATING A WINCH MOUNT

Though this sequence looks at the key stages of mounting a winch, the principles are exactly the same for other heavy brackets such as racks and wheel carriers.

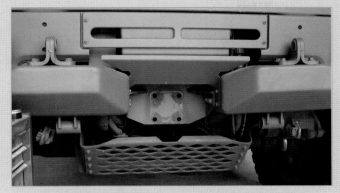

1 The manufacturer-designated towing point on this truck is identified as a suitably robust winch-mounting area.

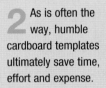

2 As is often the way, humble cardboard templates ultimately save time, effort and expense.

3 The winch is mocked into position to enable further detailed measurements. ▶

4 A drawing always helps to establish exact dimensions, even a quick pencil-and-paper plan will help to avoid wasting time and (expensive) materials. ▼

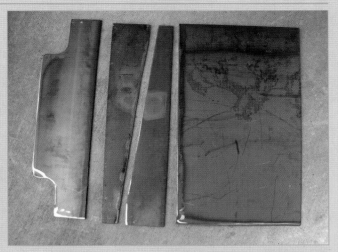

5 6–8mm steel plate is – thanks to the drawings – confidently cut to dimensions.

6 The structure is tack-welded into place and clearances checked.

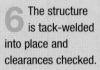

7 More steel is added and the fabrication tidied up. ▶

8 All is looking good, almost ready for cosmetic finishing with a final powder coating or paint. ▼

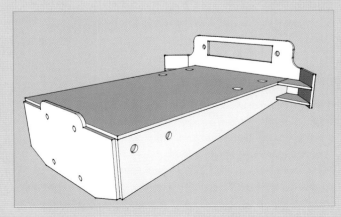

▲ This arrangement provides for a slide-out 'platform' area from which portable ladders can be deployed either to the front, side or rear. Ingeniously, the fabrication also includes two fixed rungs that allow vertical access in the event that deployment of the full system is impossible or undesirable.

Ladders

In the case of truck-based campers particularly, storing and deploying ladders that afford safe and convenient access to the habitation area is not as easy as might first appear. The conundrum only becomes apparent when you consider (at a minimum):

▪ You ideally need to be able to deploy ladders from both inside and out.

▪ For security, it's better not to leave them out whilst you are asleep inside – especially if a situation develops that requires you to move off quickly.

▪ Surprisingly often, you will find limited space in which to deploy them.

▪ They are bulky and, if over-engineered, they can be heavy.

▪ In the real world of overnighting away from formal sites, there will rarely be a fixed distance between the ground and your habitation door. This can dramatically affect the angle of the ladder and its treads if your ladder is one that works by resting on the ground.

▪ If it is of such a design it will readily sink in soft ground.

▪ Ladders get dirty and wet making them unpleasant to handle and store inside.

▪ If they are stolen on a trip, you have a problem.

◀ **A purpose-made commercially available (but expensive) solution. These are self-supporting ladders that do not, by design, rest on the ground so are guaranteed to present acceptably flat and stable treads under all circumstances. Additionally, they neatly collapse (almost) flat thanks to their parallelogram-style design and then slide smoothly out of the way into a purpose-made carrier housed in the subframe.**

► A completely different approach. By doing away with a conventional entrance door this simple, hinged solution doubles as both a ladder and a lockable security grille.

Access ladders sometimes prove the Achilles heel or a tell-tale 'afterthought' on otherwise brilliantly engineered overland campers and though countless solutions are possible, the accompanying images illustrate just three that might help in your thought processes.

Fixing other large and heavy items

If you're going to fit an auxiliary or longer-range fuel tank, or items like chassis-mounted storage boxes, this will probably involve mounting directly to the chassis' frame rails. If this is the case, it's wise to be mindful of introducing potentially damaging stress. Chassis are strong but not infallible.

Chassis are put under great stress in the overlanding context and placing extra strain on frame rail members is not something that should be done without critical thought. Mounting a 500-litre fuel tank on a chassis rail in the place of a standard 150-litre item will ultimately mean that over three times the original mass, much of it in sloshing liquid form, will be constantly attempting to twist the rail outwards. The extra stresses unwittingly introduced may well be in excess of the chassis' design limits. Chassis can, and do, break.

Modifications *can* be made, but it's wise to make additions conservative and to take cues from where manufacturers have already placed heavy items. For example, fuel tanks will frequently have their mounts situated

directly adjacent to chassis cross members, which will help spread load and support the mass across the entire chassis structure. In other cases, manufacturers may use thick steel brackets to bolster the chassis webs or flanges. Manufacturers do not want their products to fail so it's reasonably safe to presume they do things the way they do for good reason.

DRILLING AND WELDING CHASSIS FRAME RAILS

Chassis frame rails are often made in 'C-section' steel. The vertical section is sometimes referred to as the web and the horizontal sections the flanges. Manufacturers are very specific about any frame rail modifications that may be made and welding and drilling holes is generally discouraged. *Any* changes to standard specification should be done in accordance with manufacturers' instructions. Some manufacturers are willing and able to produce literature or advice to guide modifications; some are less approachable. If brand-specific advice is unavailable, you should at least familiarise yourself with the principles involved and, for example, utilise existing holes in the chassis members where possible. It's better to spend time to fabricate an awkward bracket and use existing holes rather than the temptingly quick solution of drilling new ones. Drilling, welding and introducing stress risers into chassis *can* lead to rail failure. If you absolutely must drill or weld, at least steer clear of the flanges. Do not drill or weld these at all and keep drilling or welding on the webs as far away from the flanges as practicable.

▼ Doubling up of brackets to help ease twisting stress on this chassis rail – the large angled bracket extending to the right carries a spare wheel and tyre combination of about 150kg, but stress is reduced by siting it near a cross member and cleverly using the clamping effect of a load-bed bracket.

CHAPTER 5

Dealing with torsional stress

- Understanding torsional stress
- Three- and four-point pivoting subframes
- Simpler solutions
- Vibration and impact
- General subframe-mounting principles
- The single irrefutable fact

A real-life play on the Unstoppable Force Meets Immovable Object paradox. This is how a twisting chassis and an un-twistable box would prefer to sit in relation to one another when exposed to difficult terrain.

If your base vehicle of choice is a panel van of unibody construction then this section will not be mission critical. If, however, your base vehicle is a typical truck and comprises a separate cab and conventional ladder chassis, on to which you intend to graft a habitation box, then it's vital that you get to grips with the concept of torsional stress.

▲ Chassis most definitely twist, it's not negotiable.

Understanding torsional stress

To begin to understand the issue, imagine a truck-type vehicle in its bare form comprising just a cab and a chassis. In the overlander context chassis are, more often than not, just two frame rails running side by side for the whole length of the vehicle. These frame rails are joined at intervals by cross members making the whole arrangement resemble a simple ladder. On to various parts of the 'ladder' are then mounted the engine, transmission, suspension, cab and fuel tanks etc. In this bare form, as the vehicle is driven down a relatively smooth road, any slight undulations in road surface will mainly be absorbed by a natural deformation of the tyres and the action of the suspension.

Now, imagine that the smooth road peters out into a dirt track with increasingly large and irregular humps and hollows. If you drive up a large hump with your left front wheel, initially the tyre deformation and suspension compression will absorb most of the forces at work but as the hump gets higher, the forces passing up through the front left corner will increasingly transmit load to the chassis frame. If you visualise the weight of the truck bearing down on the remaining three wheels and keeping them in the same plane (i.e. the flat ground), you should be able to envision how the chassis frame rails will begin to twist along their length in response to the 'up force' at the front left corner and the 'down force' at the remaining three.

Driving further along the deteriorating road, now imagine a situation where the front left and rear right wheels are driven on to large humps but – at the very same time – the front right and rear left wheels happen to be just where hollows appear. In the extreme, the result can be that the front right and rear left wheels end up suspended completely off the ground, whilst the full weight of the vehicle is supported entirely through the front left and rear right tyres. This is a 'cross axle' situation and at this point even very stiff chassis rails will visibly twist as they succumb to the opposing up and down forces.

If the effect is proving hard to visualise, imagine you and a friend are facing each other and holding opposing ends of a one-piece ladder. If you both simultaneously push down with your left arm and pull up with your right, you will be able to see roughly what the chassis is going through.

In itself the twist is no real issue, but a problem arises when we wish to attach a box structure to the chassis rails. For our purposes, the bottom line is that habitation boxes full of seat bases and bulkheads (i.e. boxes within boxes) *cannot* twist. If a box were to be fastened directly to a chassis along its entire length, then regularly driven over very uneven surfaces, one of two things could eventually happen: the box and furniture might twist apart or, if the box were very strong, too much stress would be localised in the chassis rails and the chassis itself might break – either outcome would spoil your day.

Though it might at first seem alarming, a chassis twisting and bending is entirely normal and in *some* cases manufacturers even exploit the phenomenon in order to enable wheels to stay grounded and therefore able to steer, brake and drive instead of being left suspended uselessly in mid-air. Several factors affect how much a chassis will flex: overall length, thickness and type of chassis-rail material, as well as cross-member configuration and bracing are just some of the factors at play. Some chassis flex spectacularly, others flex to a much lesser extent. However much or little a particular chassis deforms, though, we need to address the issue of how to successfully attach to it a non-deformable box.

Three- and four-point pivoting subframes

One chassis that is intentionally allowed to flex *very* freely is that of the Mercedes Unimog. Over decades, Mercedes engineers – in mounting rigid load beds to this chassis – have employed three- or four-point pivoting subframes to act as a chassis-to-load bed interface and indeed, the Unimog's chassis flex is so pronounced that such a highly articulating solution is indispensable. The Unimog pivoting-subframe design has been *very* influential amongst overland camper builders who have, for an equal number of decades, sometimes unquestioningly adopted the principle and fabricated home-made versions to the point where the design has been, and still is, extrapolated to trucks that

have comparatively *rigid* chassis and which, perhaps, do not therefore require such a complex engineering solution.

A 'Unimog style' pivoting subframe arrangement is generically known amongst overlanders as a 'torsion-free' subframe. With such subframes, the general (and for now greatly simplified) idea is that at just *one* point along the length of the chassis rails, the subframe will be mounted across both rails in such a way that it effectively forms a rigid cross member and – at this unique location – no matter how much the chassis twists, that cross member will be forced to stay faithfully perpendicular to both chassis rails. This 'fixed' cross member is usually situated in one of three places: towards the front of a habitation box, towards the rear of the chassis rails or approximately halfway between these two points. The base of the habitation box is then, simplistically, rigidly fastened (albeit often via compliant bushes) to the fixed cross member.

Placement of the fixed cross member will determine the positioning of the remaining subframe attachment points and will also influence whether the entire assembly is nominally designated a three- or four-point system. If the fixed cross member is placed towards the centre of the habitation box, then pivoting cross members will need to be added towards the front of the box *and* towards the rear of the chassis rails. Between them these members will effectively transfer the weight of the box to three longitudinal locations along

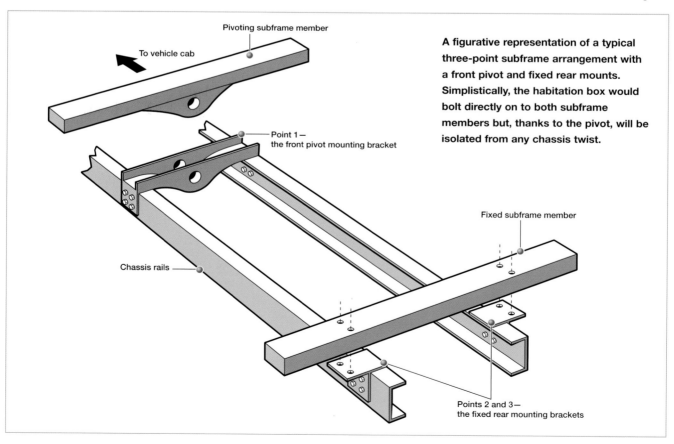

A figurative representation of a typical three-point subframe arrangement with a front pivot and fixed rear mounts. Simplistically, the habitation box would bolt directly on to both subframe members but, thanks to the pivot, will be isolated from any chassis twist.

Pivoting subframe member

To vehicle cab

Point 1 — the front pivot mounting bracket

Fixed subframe member

Chassis rails

Points 2 and 3 — the fixed rear mounting brackets

CROSS MEMBER PLACEMENT IN THREE-POINT SYSTEMS

In three-point systems, some people prefer to place the fixed member towards the front of the box, others towards the rear of the chassis rails. Forward-mounted fixed members are often chosen for the simple reason that they simplify the construction of a crawl-through from cab to habitation box. On the negative side, placing a fixed member just behind the vehicle cab *will add considerable extra stress* to a point on the chassis rails that is already a highly stressed hotspot. The section of chassis just behind the cab ideally needs to be allowed to flex quite freely and adding a rigid cross member bolstered by an un-twistable box clearly will not help in this regard.

the chassis length: this arrangement is (initially) somewhat confusingly known as a four-point system. If, however, the fixed member is placed towards the front of the box, or towards the rear of the rails, then a pivoting member will need to be added in the alternate fore or aft position and between them these members effectively support the weight of the box at two locations along its length. This arrangement is nominally known as a three-point system.

Regarding which multi-point system is ultimately the most suited for home-brewed overlanders is largely a matter of conjecture and here's a harsh truth: though most self-built designs are successful, there have also been those that have resulted in structural failure. Large manufacturers will devote well-resourced and highly skilled research-and-development teams to determining specific load-carrying solutions for specific applications. The world of the self builder is entirely different and though some fabrications are brilliant and inspired, it has to be accepted that intuition and a MIG welder have their limitations. If you intend to go the route of fabricating your own three- or four-point pivoting subframe, it would be wise to take the advice of a suitably qualified professional or, at the very least, to emulate designs that have proven successful in the field for your particular truck and habitation box combination. At the self-build level, pivoting subframe construction is *not* a precise science.

Chassis issues caused by poor weight distribution

As well as considering how a multi-point subframe is configured in order to isolate torsional forces (simplistically – up forces), it's equally important to consider how the chassis rails will cope with the weight of the habitation box bearing down upon them (simplistically – down forces). In three-point systems the full weight of the habitation box is supported *at only two longitudinal locations* along the chassis rails

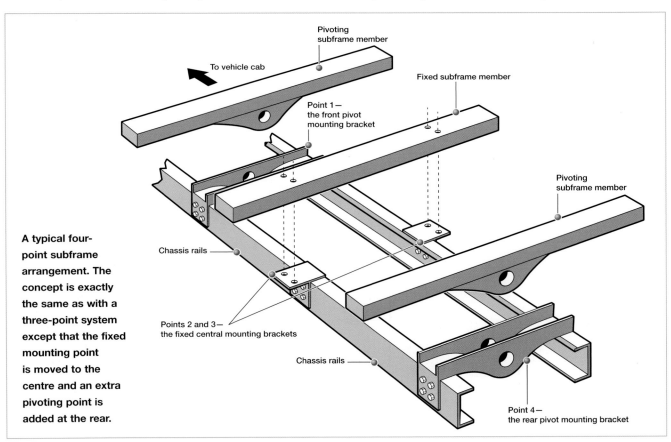

To vehicle cab

Pivoting subframe member

Fixed subframe member

Point 1 —
the front pivot mounting bracket

Pivoting subframe member

Chassis rails

A typical four-point subframe arrangement. The concept is exactly the same as with a three-point system except that the fixed mounting point is moved to the centre and an extra pivoting point is added at the rear.

Points 2 and 3 —
the fixed central mounting brackets

Chassis rails

Point 4 —
the rear pivot mounting bracket

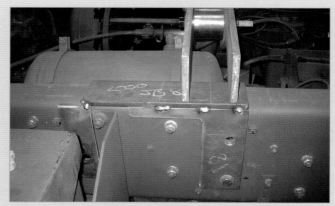

1 Work begins on creating the chassis-mounted component of this four-point system's fixed central cross member. When complete this member will stay faithfully perpendicular to the chassis rails no matter how much the chassis twists.

4 Fabrication begins for the chassis-mounted component of the front pivoting cross member. Note how existing chassis-rail web holes are utilised and how the chassis-rail flanges will be left free from drilling or welding.

2 At each end of the chassis-mounted component of the central cross member a metallistic bush is inserted and fixing plates are added to accommodate the actual framework component of the subframe. The bushes on this cross member are not intended to provide articulation but instead to absorb stress. The bushes take up any 'skew' effect caused by the subframe's pivoting axis being higher than the axis of the chassis rails and also help to absorb vibration and impact generated by irregular road/trail surfaces.

5 The chassis-mounted component of the front pivoting cross member following more steelwork. Note how the central pivot point is as low as possible in order to place the pivoting axis as close as practicable to the central axis of the chassis rails.

3 A mock-up of the fixed central cross member. The box-section steelwork clamped to the fixing plates is part of the framework component of the actual subframe, i.e. the surface to which the base of the habitation box will ultimately be attached.

6 Work begins on fabricating the chassis-mounted component of the rear pivoting cross member. All the visible holes in the chassis rail flanges were made by the manufacturer. Flange holes are acceptable in this instance as the chassis here is effectively solid thanks to the huge steel lifting eye insert which can be seen exiting to the left of shot.

7 Front cross member with metallistic bush added and the beginning of the steelwork for the actual framework component of the subframe.

10 The chassis-mounted component of the front cross member is about to be test-fitted to the subframe framework. Note the phosphor-bronze thrust bearing on the face of the cross member to stop any fore-aft stress on the rubber component of the metallistic bush.

8 Fixed central cross member and pivoting front and rear cross members. Remember the metallistic bushes at the extremities of the central member are only intended to absorb the effects of a little skew, plus vibration and impact stresses.

11 Mocked up and testing for full articulation.

9 The fully fabricated subframe framework itself with very obvious pivot-point brackets. Material is mainly 100mm x 50mm x 3mm rectangular hollow steel.

12 All three cross member mounting components finally bolted in place on the truck chassis and the subframe framework attached to the cross members via the metallistic bushes. One fully functioning pivoting torsion-free subframe – ready to mount the habitation box.

▲ Specifically made to utilise existing holes in the webs of the chassis' frame rails, this fixed four-point subframe member will eventually be bolted in situ on the site of the chassis' spring hangers/central cross member (visible beneath the fabrication). This fixed member is also particularly heavily engineered.

and, crucially, the forward mounting point will necessarily be somewhere between the front- and rear-suspension mounting points. On rough ground particularly, the up forces and down forces will be at their greatest and this could have dire consequences for your chassis. If you imagine a pencil suspended between two erasers, one at either end, and then push down in the middle of the pencil, it will initially bend and, given tall-enough erasers, ultimately break. Because it supports a large proportion of the mass of the entire

▼ If a subframe's pivot points are high above the chassis rails there will be a tendency for them to be displaced in relation to one another as the chassis twists. Keep pivot points as close as possible to the chassis rails' longitudinal axis.

habitation box, the forward mounting point of a three-point system *is* your analogous finger.

Four-point systems mean that the weight of the box is supported at *three* locations along the length of the chassis rails and, though arguably kinder to the chassis, it's still important to ensure the subframe is attached to the chassis in such a way that stress will be minimised. It's wise to take a steer from the chassis manufacturer and situate mounting points at the locations they themselves designate for attaching load beds or, if these cannot be ascertained, on the site of existing cross members.

Other considerations with torsion-free systems

If you've turned mental gymnastics and can visualise how a chassis twists under normal use you will probably have worked out that as it twists, it does so about its own longitudinal axis (situated at an approximate centre point between the frame rails). The reality of multi-point subframe construction means that in most circumstances it will be impossible to build subframe pivot points on this exact axis and they will almost invariably end up slightly higher. With such raised pivot points, when the chassis twists, a skew effect is introduced along with some fiendishly complicated geometry, but this can be summarised, in practical terms, as resulting in nominal extra stresses being passed into both the chassis and subframe. The bottom line is that the effect is not much to worry about, *but* it makes sense to keep the pivot points low and as close as possible to the axis of the twisting chassis.

A further complication, and one that might also have crossed your mind, is that as well as twisting, chassis also quite naturally bend from front to rear along their length. This effect is, for our purposes, negligible; but the forces introduced by this bending *will* tirelessly try to longitudinally

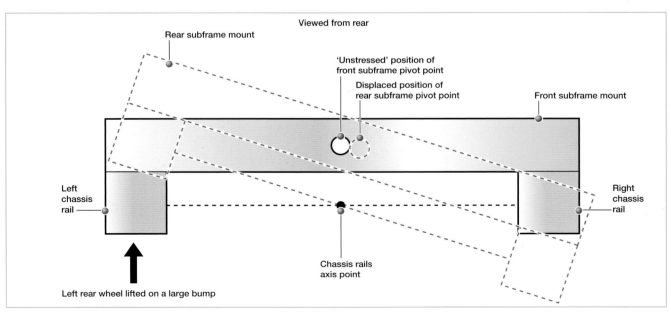

▲ **Four metallistic bushes. These were custom made but off-the-shelf versions can be obtained.**

compress or extend the floor of a solidly mounted box and introduce stress risers into the chassis.

Both of the above issues are far less of a concern than chassis twist but are briefly included for completeness and should ideally be countered. Some trucks even utilise a trunnion system on one cross member allowing fore-and-aft pivoting to help compensate for the undesirable skewing and bending forces at play. A good and relatively simple solution for off-axis pivots and front-to-rear bending is to build in some kind of compliance at all of the subframe mounting points and this is most easily achieved by the use of rubber/polyurethane mounts or metallistic bushes.

THREE- VERSUS FOUR-POINT SUBFRAMES

Though by no means definitive, here are some pointers to help decide whether a three- or four-point system will best suit an application.

Three-point subframes are often suited to:
- ▢ Vehicles with shorter chassis rails (rails under *circa* 5.5m *total* length)
- ▢ Lightweight payloads (i.e. ready-to-travel habitation boxes under *circa* 2 tonnes)
- ▢ Vehicles with thicker section chassis rails (over *circa* 6mm)

Four-point subframes are often suited to:
- ▢ Vehicles with longer chassis rails (over *circa* 6 metres *total* length)
- ▢ Heavier payloads (i.e. ready-to-travel habitation boxes over *circa* 2 tonnes)
- ▢ Vehicles with thinner section chassis rails (under *circa* 6mm)

Simpler solutions

Though pivoting subframes are sometimes exactly the right solution for vehicles designed for extreme off-road use, it is again stressed that overland campers are *not* extreme off-road machines. Transposing 'Unimog logic' to overland campers is common, but arguably sometimes misguided. Indeed, on trucks with fairly flimsy chassis there is even a possibility that, especially if poorly engineered, full multi-point subframes could actually create more problems than they solve, not least by failing to adequately distribute habitation-box weight.

It's worth remembering that you aren't trying to win any engineering awards and to focus on what needs to be achieved, i.e. avoiding torsional stress being passed to the box and avoiding damage to the chassis rails. There is no absolute right and wrong way to achieve this and pivoting subframes are only one solution. Self-builders have employed many ingenious methods to conquer the dilemma and air-suspension air bags, large floating rubber bushings and all manner of Heath Robinson contraptions have been utilised to greater or lesser effect. This is probably a good point for a timely reminder of one of the main tenets of overlanding: complexity often invites unreliability.

Rail-on-rail subframes

Fitting well with the principles of simplicity, reliability and durability, there's much to be said for a comparatively basic tried-and-tested method of managing torsion and load stresses that has proved reliable on countless all-terrain trucks, military vehicles and overland campers: rail-on-rail subframes. In very general terms, this method of mounting involves a steel frame, firmly affixed to the underside of the habitation box and comprising (in its most fundamental state) two longitudinal rails which simply rest on top of the vehicle's own chassis frame rails. These subframe rails are securely anchored to the vehicle's chassis rails *but generally at the very rear of the chassis only*. This is similar in principle to a fixed-rear-member three-point pivoting subframe in as much as the habitation box will stay perpendicular to the chassis rails at the very rear of the vehicle whilst allowing independent movement of the chassis and subframe at all points forward of the 'anchored' attachment.

As much as this solves the torsional-stress issue, in this simple state you may immediately perceive a problem. Clearly, if secured at the rear only, several tonnes of habitation box, especially when flopping around over rough terrain, will constantly attempt to slew from side to side at the (unattached) front and could, in the extreme, put enough stress on the rear mountings to tear itself clean off the chassis. Fortunately, there are two frequently utilised ways to guard against this issue. The first method is to affix locating pegs or vertical steel guide plates to the subframe rails to

BUILDING A RAIL-ON-RAIL SUBFRAME

1 The bare chassis frame rails on an ex-snowplough MAN. Note the flanged brackets down the length of the facing rail: the fixing points for the original load bed.

2 The rearmost chassis point: more than enough manufacturer-made holes to accommodate a very stable subframe anchor point.

4 Subframe laid on top of the original chassis rails and work under way to fabricate a pair of very sturdy anchor plates.

3 The very neatly welded and sculptured subframe taking shape. This particular subframe is owner-designed but professionally fabricated in S355 steel.

5 To observe the behaviour of the chassis rails and subframe, torsional stress is induced by hoisting the left rear wheel. At this moment the subframe is attached only at the very rear by means of the anchor plates which are, by now, augmented by the (just visible) spare-wheel-carrier fabrication.

6 This was the amount of separation of the subframe from the chassis observed at the front left of the structure. Note the flanged brackets welded to the subframe that will eventually mate up with their chassis-mounted counterparts by means of bolted opposing springs to both control the degree of separation and temper any side-to-side slewing effect.

9 Anchor plates detail.

7 Commercially available opposing springs plus suitable high-tensile fasteners and appropriately sized plain washers. Dished washers are also available to help centralise larger diameter springs – if required.

10 The opposing springs at the very front of the subframe. Note how these are longer and a larger diameter than the yellow version.

8 Chassis now painted, subframe galvanised and opposing springs being fitted. Note how the flanged brackets that hold the springs do not touch their counterpart when the subframe rails are resting on the chassis rails. This type of bracket is not designed to bear the weight of cargo and if they did touch they would pass potentially damaging stresses into surrounding members and/or themselves be damaged.

11 Subframe installed and about to receive the habitation-box floor. Note the subtleties of the opposing spring size and rate to allow for progressively more chassis/subframe separation towards the front.

▲ A locator plate bolted to the subframe keeps subframe and chassis in alignment and prevents the subframe from slewing from side to side.

keep the subframe rails located directly on top of the truck's chassis rails at all times. Though fairly crude, this 'free-floating' subframe mounting method works well and is even adopted by some quite high-profile professional converters.

A slightly more refined way to control slew is the 'sprung' mounting method, which involves adding flanged brackets to both the chassis rails and subframe and then utilising opposing springs or pliable bobbins to act as locators or separation controllers. By using different length springs and varying the position of brackets it's even possible to tune the system to permit varying amounts of separation at different points along the length of the chassis. If your chassis rails are intrinsically stiff, only a slight amount of total separation may be required; conversely, if your chassis is quite flexible, more separation may be desirable.

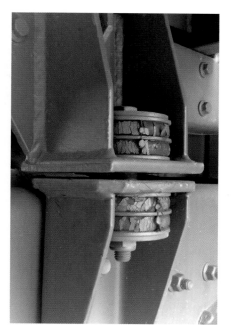

◄► Manufacturer's original outrigger brackets and opposing-rubber-bobbin-style compressible mounts on an ex-military Leyland DAF flat-back truck. The bobbins are under load and are allowing some relief from the torsional stress resulting from the mild articulation being induced in the image.

Building on the standard load bed of trucks designed for multi-terrain use

When vehicle manufacturers themselves produce trucks with flat-back type load-carrying beds on vehicles *designed from the outset* for poor-road use, they will often utilise some form of torsion *relief* system as a load-bed mounting solution. Load beds used, for example, on some military cargo-carrying trucks will, in all probability, utilise a combination of rigid and separable mountings. On such vehicles, the attachment points sometimes take the form of brackets commonly known as outriggers. Though there's a superficial resemblance between these and the flanged brackets used to mount opposing springs on a rail-on-rail subframe, they are different entities: outriggers are designed to bear the full weight of the load bed but in the event that they are separable, as opposed to rigidly bolted, the separation is usually similarly achieved with opposing springs or compressible rubber bobbins.

If you source a vehicle configured with at least *some* separable mounting points, it *might* be possible to press the standard load bed into service as a *ready-made* subframe on which to directly mount a habitation box. This method will, however, necessitate great caution and its feasibility is influenced by the rigidity of the vehicle's chassis plus the degree of in-built separation conferred by the mountings. If the truck's chassis is a particularly flexible one, and separation limited, the box would be subject to very high levels of torsional stress so in this instance you would need to build a very heavy duty structure that would *significantly* bolster the rigidity of the standard bed. Conversely, if the truck's chassis is inherently rigid, and separation generous, comparatively little torsional stress would be passed up to the load bed/box and *if* this is the case, the prospect of

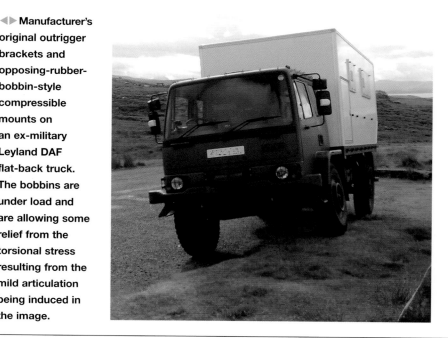

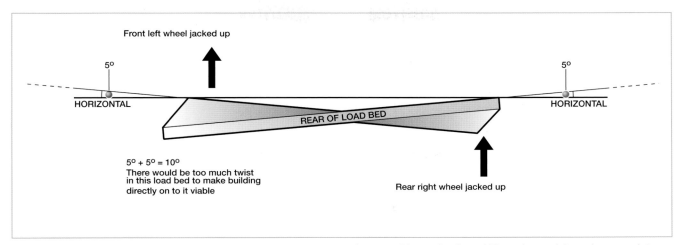

Front left wheel jacked up

5°

HORIZONTAL

5°

HORIZONTAL

REAR OF LOAD BED

5° + 5° = 10°
There would be too much twist
in this load bed to make building
directly on to it viable

Rear right wheel jacked up

▲ **Measuring the twist in a standard load bed.**

building a habitation box directly on to a standard load bed is potentially feasible and, for all but really tough terrain, is a comparatively quick and easy way to proceed.

To assess the viability of this build method, it's important to determine how much the standard load bed flexes when subject to high torsional stress. To do this, strip the load bed until you are left with just the structure you intend to retain and then, ensuring you are on level ground, jack up the truck's front left and rear right wheels until one other wheel is just about to be lifted off the ground. At this point, any built-in torsion relief system will be doing its work so using an inclinometer/angle meter, measure the angles from horizontal of both the very front and very rear of the load bed. If the *sum* of these two readings is nominal then providing the box is built with enough rigidity to significantly bolster the load bed you *may* get away with a habitation box directly mounted. If the sum of the angle is more than five

degrees this method *could* be a huge risk and a complete rethink may be required. The greater the sum of the angles of deflection, the stronger the box will need to be.

Vibration and impact

As well as the issue of torsion, the entire structure of an overland camper will be subjected to loads and stresses caused by vibration and impact. Nowhere is this more evident than on the infamous 'washboard' surfaces that are formed on unsealed roads the world over. Washboard comprises undulations in the surface that look like ripples on a lake with crests and hollows spaced at regular intervals. This surface sometimes goes on for great distances and is notorious for transmitting destructive vibration and impact forces into every last corner of every structure. These stresses are, perhaps, just as responsible for habitation box, fixture and fitting, and chassis failures as torsional stress. Whichever type of habitation-box mounting method you

◄ **Washboard – uncomfortable and destructive.**

▼ **This truck utilises a hardwood strip between subframe and chassis rails. Though not absolutely obligatory, there are many useful advantages to incorporating some cushioning.**

Though by far the most *common* solution to mounting a rigid box on a twisting ladder chassis is to build in some way of allowing the two to move independently of one another, it isn't the *only* solution. In very rare circumstances some cargo vehicles based on a cab and chassis are built in such a way that the end result means the chassis will be so well braced that under no 'normal' circumstances will it twist, bend or otherwise flex, certainly not to any significant degree anyway. Cash-in-transit or bullion trucks are often a case in point. Because such vehicles are built to be impregnable, in some cases the cab, box and chassis will, as a feature of design, be heavily reinforced and *all* bolted together – essentially forming one immensely strong and rigid 'cube-on-wheels'. If a vehicle is built this way, there is little chance that uneven surfaces will challenge structural integrity. Of course, there are downsides. On anything other than almost flat surfaces, as one wheel is lifted or dropped into a hollow, because of the 'super-rigidity', the rest of the vehicle will try to follow and this results in a lurching kind of driving experience. Furthermore, it's very probably the case that suspension mounting points will be under increased stress and almost certain that vibration and impacts will be transmitted throughout the entire vehicle *very* efficiently.

choose, a little cushioning from a compliant material will help to ward off the worst effects of vibration and impact. With pivoting subframes rubber mounts or metallistic bushes are commonly used and with rail-on-rail subframes it's good practice to use full-length strips of hardwood, rubber or other suitable material between the chassis frame rails and longitudinal subframe rails.

▼ **By profiling the leading edge of the subframe, the chassis frame rails will be relieved from potentially troublesome stress risers.**

General subframe mounting principles

If manufacturer guidance for the specification, placement and attachment method of load-bearing chassis-rail brackets and other hardware can possibly be obtained then this should be followed to the letter. If, however, it can't – and you don't have access to a heavy-vehicle-body-mount expert – here are some *very* generic guiding principles for subframe mounting.

Pivoting subframes

■ Take great care with the placement of mounting points, especially on intrinsically weaker chassis. Try to fabricate mounting points on the site of existing chassis cross members. If this is not possible, the mounting point should be constructed in such a way that it will itself form a substantial cross member.

■ *Directly* above rear leaf-spring hanger brackets is a good position for mounting points.

■ In three-point systems, if possible, mount the fixed member at the rear to avoid introducing inflexibility to the vehicle chassis at the already highly stressed point at the rear of the cab.

■ Build mounts to transmit the majority of the load directly to the web of the chassis – not the flanges.

■ Use high-tensile fasteners of at least 8.8 grade for all fixings and check the integrity of all mounts regularly.

Rail-on-rail subframes

■ With these systems, the longitudinal subframe member should run the entire length of the habitation box and so spread mass evenly over the chassis-frame rails.

■ Use full-length strips of hardwood, rubber or other suitable material between the chassis frame rails and longitudinal subframe rails to reduce noise, to act as a sacrificial wear surface and to add a little vibration and impact cushioning.

■ In systems where subframes are rigidly anchored at the rear only, locating pegs, suitably profiled brackets or steel plates are required to prevent the front of the subframe slewing from side to side.

■ The front of the subframe should not be finished in a

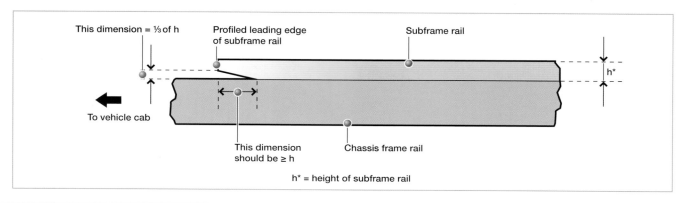

This dimension = ⅓ of h

Profiled leading edge of subframe rail

Subframe rail

To vehicle cab

This dimension should be ≥ h

Chassis frame rail

h* = height of subframe rail

simple square section as this could cause a stress riser in the chassis frame rails at this already highly stressed spot. Profile the forward edge to avoid concentrating stress.

- Use high-tensile fasteners of at least 8.8 grade for all fixings and check the integrity of all mounts regularly.

Standard load beds

- Outrigger brackets should extend at least halfway down the depth of the chassis frame rail and be bolted to webs only, never flanges.

- Experimentation with spring and bolt length or other compliant fixings in order to increase chassis flexibility and reduce torsional stress is possible but should be undertaken conservatively. The amount of separation allowed should be reduced progressively at each mounting point the further towards a fixed rigid mount you go. Do not go straight from huge separation to fixed mount: the fixed mount will become a huge stress riser or fasteners could fail.

- Keep at least two mounting points on each chassis frame rail (so four in total) solidly bolted to prevent the load bed slewing from side to side.

- Use high-tensile fasteners of at least 8.8 grade for all fixings and check the integrity of all mounts regularly.

▶ **A properly fitted load-bearing outrigger bracket.**

▼ **The standard opposing bobbins on this truck have been supplemented with a single spring to allow about 12mm more separation. Additional or differently rated springs could be utilised to further fine tune the separation allowed.**

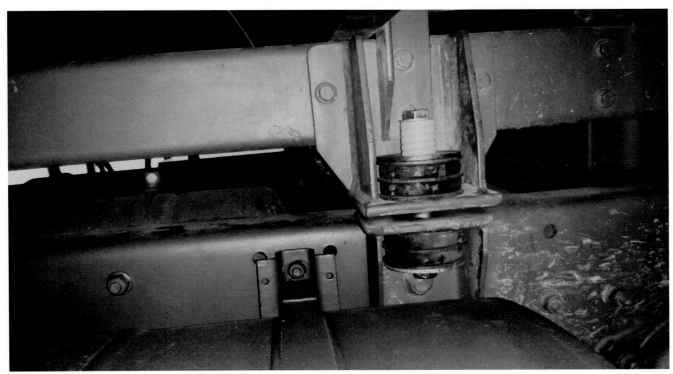

PROS, CONS AND SUITABILITY OF DIFFERENT MOUNTING METHODS

THREE- OR FOUR-POINT PIVOTING SUBFRAMES

Pros:
- Effectively isolate torsional forces.
- Permit maximum chassis flex which could, if inherently substantial, augment suspension and keep wheels on the ground.
- Minimise vibration and impact passed to the habitation box *if* mounting points utilise compliant bushes.

Cons:
- Complicated to construct.
- Habitation boxes can 'flop' from side to side and may, in extreme circumstances, cause instability in very testing off-road conditions.
- Mountings can cause load-point stress risers in vehicle chassis. that in extreme cases can lead to chassis failure.
- Because of the necessity to compensate for extra box movement, this mounting method often leads to a taller overall vehicle and a raised centre of gravity.
- Maintenance requirement associated with flexible bushings.

Suited to:
- Vehicles with very flexible chassis.
- Comparatively flimsy habitation boxes.
- True off-road terrain, i.e. places you probably shouldn't really be when carrying your worldly possessions in your temporary/ permanent home!

RAIL-ON-RAIL SUBFRAMES

Pros:
- Comparatively easy to construct.
- Effectively isolate torsional stress.
- Allow good levels of chassis flex to augment suspension and keep wheels on the ground.
- If properly constructed, do not cause point load stress on vehicle chassis.
- Reliable and serviceable.

Cons:
- Pass relatively high levels of road vibration and impact directly to the box.

Suited to:
- Vehicles with moderately flexible to stiff chassis.
- Moderately strong habitation boxes.
- The vast majority of terrain ever encountered in overland travel plus occasional difficult off-road conditions.

STANDARD LOAD BEDS

Pros:
- Ready-made subframe.
- Subject to manufacturer research and development so should not cause point load stress on vehicle chassis.
- Reliable and serviceable.

Cons:
- Pass high levels of road vibration and impact directly to the box.
- Generally not as effective at isolating torsional stress (NB this point is not particularly relevant for vehicles with an inherently rigid chassis)..
- Limit chassis flexibility reducing ability to keep all wheels on the ground stress (NB again this point is not particularly relevant for vehicles with an inherently rigid chassis).

Suited to:
- Vehicles with stiff chassis.
- Strong and rigid habitation boxes.
- The vast majority of terrain ever encountered in overland travel.

The single irrefutable fact

Deciding how to mount an un-twistable box on a flexing chassis that is also subject to insidious impact and vibration stresses is not a straightforward business. Failing to protect a box from the effects of stress may ultimately break the box whilst poorly conceived or engineered subframes can, and do, break chassis. Even professional manufactures suffer failures. There simply is no one-size-fits-all answer and the most suitable solution is influenced by factors such as the inherent flexibility of a chassis, the ultimate strength of the habitation box, the extremity of terrain to be tackled, the weights involved, materials used, quality of craftsmanship plus innumerable other variables.

Whichever mounting method you ultimately choose there is one overriding golden rule: when on anything other than smooth sealed surfaces, drive with a great deal of mechanical sympathy. Abuse will wreck even the strongest and most beautifully conceived systems. Avoid excess speed and heroics; do not traverse extreme terrain just because it's there. A slow and careful approach on bad roads will pay dividends and is the single most influential thing you can do to avoiding catastrophic structural failures.

▲ **Chassis can and do break. This one is thought to have failed due to too much point-load stress. Failures like this can take a long time to happen but the combination of bouncing around on rough terrain for months on end plus excessive concentrations of mass and/or stress will find weak spots.**

A STROKE OF GENIUS

The most frequently encountered methods of constructing and mounting subframes have been considered in some detail in this chapter, but, as previously mentioned, there are innumerable different ways to approach the task and it's not unusual to find variations on the common themes as well as some totally unique solutions. The exquisitely engineered subframe in the accompanying images is one example of a truly ingenious progression. This design takes the best characteristics of both pivoting and rail-on-rail subframes and fuses them together. It is the work of Riccardo Scalcon and encompasses a rail-on-rail system that effectively spreads the mass of the habitation box along the full length of the chassis frame rails whilst simultaneously providing the benefits conferred by a fully-pivoting system.

◤ **A full four-point pivoting system (complete with fixed-mount-point trunnions) is built – inspirationally – into a rail-on-rail system instead of directly to the base vehicle's chassis.**

▶ **The rail-on-rail system is then attached to the chassis fairly conventionally with fixed points and opposing springs. This hybrid design is arguably the current pinnacle of self-builder subframe evolution, at least in the case of base vehicles with conventional ladder chassis.**

Gary and Monika Wescott

1 Name
Gary and Monika Wescott / The Turtle Expedition, Unltd.

2 Base vehicle
Ford F-550 cab & chassis – 1999 (now known as
The Turtle V).

3 Drive
4WD with locking differentials.

4 Fuel capacity
Diesel 92.5 US gallons (350 litres): 47-gallon main tank,
35-gallon auxiliary tank, 2 x 20-litre fuel cans.

5 Weight when loaded and ready to travel
14,000lb (6.35 tonnes).

6 Reason for base vehicle choice
Ford has been the best-selling truck in the United
States, probably the world, for over 30 years and as the
bumper sticker up in Montana reads: 'Eat more lamb,
20 million coyotes couldn't be wrong.' The reputation
as a heavy-duty work truck is undisputed and because
there are millions of Ford, as well as GMC, Chevrolet and
Dodge RAM trucks on the road, there are thousands of
companies making aftermarket products to improve their
reliability, comfort and safety. The gross vehicle weight
capacity is variable from model to model, but in our case,
the rated GVWR of 17,500lb (7.94 tonnes) exceeds what
you would want to carry over the worst roads in the world.

7 Subframe solution
Custom-made 3-point pivot system – fixed points at
front resting on about 4 or 5 inches (100–125mm) of high
density polyurethane. Full pivot point at rear.

8 Habitation-box construction
An exo skeleton was made using heavy-gauge aluminium,
into which 4cm panels of NidaCore (a structural honeycomb
panel sandwiched between skins of fibreglass) were attached
using a marine-grade Sikaflex glue. The interior was covered
with 1cm closed-cell foam – which covered electrical wires
etc. – on to which Formica was laminated as a finishing trim.

9 Habitation-box insulation material
As above.

10 Habitation-box manufacturer
Self-built.

11 Habitation-box windows
Dometic Seitz dual pane.

12 Habitation-box door(s) and locker(s)
Custom – by Global Expedition Vehicles, USA.

13 Fit out done by
Ourselves.

14 Furniture construction
Cherry-wood laminated plywood. Corian countertops.

15 Fresh water
40 US gallons (151 litres) plus 2 x 20-litre portable water
cans. We use superchlorination to treat the water and a
dual Everpure water purification system fed by a Shurflo
3.5 gallons-per-minute 12V water pump.

16 Refrigeration
Dometic Coolmatic CR 110 compressor-type refrigerator.
Refrigerator capacity: 100 litres / freezer compartment
capacity: 10.2 litres.

17 Space heating
We run three heaters: 1) A Hunter thermostatically controlled
radiator taking hot coolant from the engine as we drive. 2) A
Hunter radiator taking water heated by a diesel-powered Espar
D5 Hydronic furnace. 3) An Espar Airtronic diesel-powered
blown-air heater. Note: both Espar Airtronic and Espar D5
Hydronic are equipped with high-altitude compensation kits:
tested by us at over 14,000ft (4,267m) in Tajikistan.

18 Water heating
Water heating is centred around a Kelvion / FlatPlate
double-walled, brazed-plate water-to-water heat
exchanger heated by the Espar D5 Hydronic and/or the

engine coolant depending on whether we are camped or driving. A WATTS series MMV thermostatic mixing valve restricts the domestic hot water supply to a comfortable 120°F (48.9°C) to avoid scalding.

19 Cooking facilities

1) Three-burner Magic Chef propane stove with one super burner. This features a Piezo ignition. 2) Weber Go Anywhere BBQ powered by propane. This also features Piezo ignition

Note: All propane tanks that are removable from the vehicle can be refilled anywhere in the world using the correct fittings normally available at the local hardware store and gravity from an exchange tank. Despite misconceptions circulating amongst travellers, the process of refilling a small/medium portable LP tank takes about three minutes. It is important to realise that you are not transferring gas; you are transferring liquid propane. The safety measure to prevent overfilling is either courtesy of an over-protection valve [NB such valves are not routinely fitted to all cylinders] or simply by monitoring gross weight using a fish scale. Obviously, extreme caution needs to be used because propane is flammable and a propane tank should never be overfilled to avoid danger of explosion. For the record, we have refilled our small portable propane tanks in Mexico, Peru, Chile, Brazil, Russia, Switzerland, France, Spain, Greece, Turkey and Mongolia without a problem.

20 Habitation-box cooling

2 x three-speed reversible Fantastic Vents with thermostatic control and a portable 12V fan. No air conditioner.

21 Leisure-battery charging

1) 2 x BP 85W solar panels. 2) Auxiliary 200-amp dedicated alternator controlled by an external marine Balmar regulator that measures battery bank and alternator temperatures to optimise charge and avoid overheating.

Note: We use a total of 6 x Odyssey Extreme AGM Group 34 batteries [Group 34 is simply a description of one of many standard sizes for a battery's physical dimensions]. These are 'combination' deep cycle and starting batteries. We use four in the camper and two in the engine compartment. The logic of this system is that if a starting battery should die, one of the auxiliary batteries in the camper can be taken out to replace it. Aside from that, a group-size 34 automotive battery can be found virtually anywhere in the world – and you don't need a forklift to take them out!

22 Things to do differently next time

1) The basic design of our truck and camper would not be changed… 2) …but we would never build it ourselves again. We are not electricians, fibreglass experts, welding experts, plumbing experts, cabinet makers nor engineers. The mistakes we made while building this camper – the fifth in our 40-year history of travel – could have been avoided by having people like Alu-Star, UNICAT, Langer & Bock or GXV (Global Expedition Vehicles) build the vehicle to our exact specifications in-house under one roof. They would eliminate 98% of the mistakes we made and the overall cost would probably be comparable. 3) The entire project should be designed on CAD, not with pencil and paper like we did. Unfortunately, most beginner camper builders do not realise what a can of worms they are opening. The complexity is easily underestimated. 4) In selecting the base vehicle, diesel is the obvious choice. The mistake many people make with diesel is using an under-powered engine. Our 7.3-litre intercooled V8 unit has performed flawlessly and we cannot stress how many times having the power and torque of the bigger engine pulling 14,000lb up a hill behind smoking under-powered freight trucks has given us the option of pulling out and passing. We average around 13mpg and the small gain by using a smaller engine would not be a good compromise.

Finally, many of the problems we have seen on the road from other expedition campers have involved electronics and, principally, automatic transmissions.

CHAPTER 6

Getting road legal (UK-specific advice)

■ Caveat

■ What's in a name?

■ Becoming a motor caravan – used vans and trucks already registered in the UK

■ Becoming a motor caravan – used UK-obtained vans and trucks not previously registered with the authorities

■ A brief consideration of imported vehicles

■ A brief consideration of new vehicles

■ Tachographs

■ Driving licences

■ Downrating a mid-sized truck to 7.5 tonnes

Many of the base vehicles forming a build-your-own project will already be registered with the Driver and Vehicle Licensing Agency (DVLA) as some or other variant of a 'goods vehicle'. In other cases, such as those of an ex-military or imported vehicle, it will often be that the vehicle is unknown to the UK authorities at all. Getting from either starting point to having your completed overland camper properly registered as a motor caravan can be quite involved.

Caveat

Legislation regarding all aspects of motoring is multi-layered and ever changing, as are the policies and procedures of the government agencies responsible for licensing, registration and vehicle standards. Though every effort has been made to ensure the information in this chapter is current and accurate, you are urged to check the legal and policy position with the relevant authority before committing to a course of action that could, in the best-case scenario lead to time-consuming frustration, and in the worst-case scenario see you on the wrong side of the law. Such are the complexities of some rules and regulations that it's even possible to find that different officials within the very same organisation will interpret legal requirements in different ways. Additionally, laws, policy and procedure may be subtly different outside of England and Wales and extra research is advised for inhabitants of Scotland, Northern Ireland and islands with their own legislature.

What's in a name?

The commercial transport of goods by road is heavily regulated as large vehicles driven for long hours over vast distances are considered a manageable risk to public safety. Accordingly, *goods vehicles* are subject to very stringent rules regarding their construction, use, maintenance and testing. The Driver and Vehicle Standards Agency (DVSA) is the authority responsible for, as the name suggests, maintaining standards.

Because of their commercial-vehicle origin, the vast majority of vans and trucks currently on the road will be registered with the (totally unconnected) licensing authority – the DVLA – as a goods vehicle of some description. There are numerous 'body types' within this generic 'goods vehicle' classification, for example: Panel Van, Drop-side Lorry and Insulated Van. The official body type classification of any van

or truck can be determined by reference to point D.5 on the vehicle's registration document (V5C). If you own a van or truck, you'll almost certainly be the owner of an officially designated sub-type of goods vehicle.

A legal distinction is made between goods vehicles and *passenger* vehicles and amongst the numerous passenger-carrying vehicle categories recognised by the authorities is the body type 'motor caravan'. Vehicles officially categorised as such, rightly or wrongly, are not perceived by the regulatory authorities as presenting anything like the risk to road safety as those presented by goods vehicles; accordingly, driver and vehicle regulation relating to this body type are rather more relaxed. Additionally, motor caravanning is generally viewed by insurance companies and entities such as border controls, police and military services, and even authorities that control things like parking allocation, as a benign and uncontroversial pastime that does not require the heavy hand of enforcement.

Paradoxically then, *the very same vehicle*, depending upon its official DVLA body-type classification, can be subject to greater or lesser regulatory control and more or fewer metaphorically raised eyebrows. Goods vehicles are heavily regulated; motor caravans are not. As a result, there are many advantages to having your overland camper registered with the body type of motor caravan, including:

- Access to comparatively cheap and bespoke insurance coverage (whilst in Europe at least).
- Potentially easier passage over some borders.
- Generally less punitive toll and ferry charges.
- Less onerous annual vehicle testing.
- No requirement for goods-vehicle-specific safety items. such as side guards and rear underrun protectors.
- No requirement for a tachograph to be fitted.
- Less regulatory control regarding access to parking and service facilities.

■ Less general suspicion from law enforcement or civil protection agencies when overseas.

Not only is it widely accepted as advantageous to have your overland camper registered as a motor caravan, it's technically the correct classification and, furthermore, if your vehicle meets the relevant criteria, there's actually an *obligation* to have it so registered. However, before we consider how to go about achieving this desirable designation, here's a word of caution. As a motor caravan you must never carry anything other than your personal effects, and these can only facilitate recreation. If you *ever* carry anything in your van or truck that could be deemed for use in any *commercial* context, then you run the risk of being interpreted as being back into goods vehicle territory. If, for example, you earn a bit of casual money as you travel by offering a mobile welding service, or if you race for prize money with dirt bikes or kayaks etc, you may well find your oxyacetylene bottles or racing kit are considered 'goods' by the official sporting the laminated badge. Be aware!

OVERVIEW – GOODS AND PASSENGER VEHICLES

In contemplating the implication of 'body type', keep uppermost in mind that though the vast majority of motor caravans will be *based* on goods vehicles, the conversion process, once ratified by the DVLA, leads to them being reclassified as *passenger* vehicles. As passenger vehicles, motor caravans are *no longer* subject to legislation which is specifically applicable to goods vehicles.

■ Simplistically, goods vehicles are defined as belonging to a class of vehicles with at least four wheels designed and constructed for the carriage of goods.
■ The term 'goods' is problematic and often left as a matter of fact for courts to decide but in general terms will not include personal effects like your clothes, books, jewellery, umbrella, but it *might* include your digital camera and tripod if you're a photographer chasing a cover shot…
■ Simplistically, motor caravans are defined as belonging to a class of vehicles used for the carriage of passengers and comprising no more than eight seats in addition to the driver's seat.
■ When the DVLA accept a change of body type to motor caravan there is a *presumption* of a change of use and that 'goods' will no longer be carried by the vehicle. If goods *are* then carried in a motor caravan, there may be legal repercussions.

Becoming a motor caravan – used vans and trucks already registered in the UK

The starting point in this scenario is that you're in possession of a used van or truck that's *already registered* with the DVLA and its body type is one of the officially recognised sub-types of *goods vehicle*.

The criteria that need to be satisfied in order for a vehicle to be designated a motor caravan can and do change, but at the time of writing the authorities will be looking for a vehicle that, at a minimum, incorporates as *permanent fixtures* to its structure:

■ A bed or beds. These can be fixed or made up by folding out seats etc.
■ Storage facilities. For things like clothes, food and recreational items.
■ 'Life support' systems. These must include cooking facilities.
■ Seating and dining arrangements including a table. The table may be foldable or removable to allow storage, but it must have a permanent fixture point like, for example, brackets on a wall.
■ An external door allowing access to the habitation area.
■ At least one habitation area window.

As and when you reach a point in your build where you can satisfy all of the current requirements, you need to apply directly to the DVLA to change the body-type classification. This is done by means of a formal request-for-change letter, which should describe how all of the above-listed criteria have been met and detail any further habitation-related equipment that's been fitted. In setting out a justification for your request you could usefully include that you need the correct body-type classification in order to: access appropriate insurance, ease the crossing of borders, ensure you're charged appropriate fares and tolls, and ensure you're in a position to present the correct vehicle classification to officials, especially on foreign soil. The letter should stress that the only items that will be carried will be personal effects to facilitate your recreation and that there's absolutely no commercial aspect to your intended use of the vehicle. Along with the letter you'll need to include:

■ Photographs showing details of the requisite fixtures and fittings and the external appearance of the vehicle, including one or more with registration plate(s) clearly visible.
■ Invoices or receipts for all of the fixtures, fittings and materials you've purchased and/or for professional work you've had done.
■ Your existing V5C document.

▲ In the process of conversion and still registered as a goods vehicle so side guards etc. are a legal requirement. Note how, for overlanding, the side guards compromise breakover angle and the underrun protector compromises departure angle.

If all goes well, the DVLA will (sometimes surprisingly quickly) return your receipts, photographs and a brand new V5C declaring that your truck or van is now a motor caravan. When you achieve official reclassification you're relieved of obligation regarding regulations that apply specifically to goods vehicles so if you choose, *following* your revised V5C issue, you're at liberty to remove any goods-vehicle-specific hardware still attached to the vehicle like, for example, the tachograph, side guards and underrun protectors.

Becoming a motor caravan – used UK-obtained vans and trucks not previously registered with the authorities

If you find yourself in possession of a used van or truck that you've purchased in the UK but which is unknown to the DVLA, the chances are you've bought something like a decommissioned military or specialist-off-road-only vehicle, in which case you basically have two options:

◼ To initially register the vehicle as a goods vehicle and, post camper conversion, apply to change body-type classification to motor caravan as outlined in the previous section.

◼ To fully complete the camper conversion first and then apply to have the vehicle recognised as a fully completed motor caravan at first registration by submitting it for inspection through the Individual Vehicle Approval (IVA) scheme.

Option 1 –
Initially becoming road legal as a goods vehicle

This is by far the less troublesome course to pursue. Providing your base vehicle is roadworthy and satisfies all of the legal requirements applicable to goods vehicles, it's generally a reasonably straightforward matter to get on the road. The current standards that the vehicle will need to meet can be accessed via the GOV.UK website, but if it *is* an ex-military or off-road vehicle we're dealing with (and is something other than a simple panel van), you'll almost certainly need to add, at the very least, side guards, a rear underrun protector and a tachograph in order to satisfy current legislation.

When you get to a point that you're confident the vehicle is ready for inspection, if your vehicle is no more than 3.5 tonnes MAM you'll need to book an appropriate MoT test, or, in cases where the vehicle *is* over 3.5 tonnes MAM, use form VTG1 to apply to the DVSA for a 'first test of a heavy goods vehicle'. In order to drive to the test station, you'll need insurance. This can be obtained by specialist providers who will, upon explanation of your intentions, issue cover (usually only for a limited period) based on the vehicle's chassis number only. Come test day it's a matter of turning up, submitting your vehicle, and hoping that no faults are found. All being well the inspector will issue you with an MoT Test Certificate (if your vehicle is up to 3.5t) or a Goods Vehicle Plating Certificate (if your vehicle is over 3.5t) and wave you on your way. In either case the certificate will be temporarily issued against a unique identifier in lieu of a registration number.

Once you've obtained your Test or Plating Certificate you'll need to apply to the DVLA to register your vehicle and this involves completing the very comprehensive and initially fearsome 'Application for First Tax and Registration of a Used Vehicle' form: the V55/5. The form comes with guidance notes and it's basically a case of filling in as much information as you possibly can. The process might involve supplying supporting documentation and the exact requirements will be different depending on the origin of your vehicle. If in any doubt, it's best to seek advice directly from the DVLA before submitting incomplete paperwork in the hope that someone will take pity on you; they won't.

As well as the completed form you'll need to furnish:

■ Your newly issued MoT Test Certificate or Goods Vehicle Plating Certificate.
■ A Certificate of Insurance (issued against chassis number).
■ Personal identity documents and proof of address, as directed on the V55/5 guidance notes.
■ Any required supporting documents. These might include, for example, MoD form 654 (Application for Disposal of a Cast Vehicle), again as directed on the V55/5 guidance notes.
■ The appropriate fee to cover both registration and vehicle excise duty.

Assuming there are no issues, the next thing that will happen is that you'll receive your Registration Document (V5C).

Congratulations, you may now have some registration plates made, attach them, and have a fully road-legal drive about, albeit being classified (for now) as a goods vehicle.

Once on the road, you can begin your overland camper conversion in earnest, but be sure to keep your insurance company updated with progress. If you're a speedy worker and complete the conversion within a year you can get on with the process of applying to change body-type classification to motor caravan before your first annual test is due. If you *do* succeed in having the body type officially changed by the test-due date, you'll be able to submit your vehicle for a Class IV MoT test; if you don't, you'll instead need to submit it for the appropriate alternative goods vehicle test.

Option 2 – Initially becoming road legal as a motor caravan: the IVA scheme

The Individual Vehicle Approval (IVA) scheme is essentially a formal testing regime that, amongst other things, is designed to assess the initial roadworthiness of one-off vehicles that are not mass produced and therefore not type approved. It covers all manner of circumstances and vehicles and is the test, for example, that most kit-car owners face on completion of their project. To see what's expected in relation to the preparation of a motor caravan, you'll need to access the very comprehensive IVA manual relating to vehicle class M1 (passenger cars) available via the GOV.UK website. If you

▼ **This old truck dash is an instant IVA test fail as it has far too many sharp-edged controls. One answer is to cover them. The covered version will now pass the test in spite of it being impossible to operate the windscreen demister and the engine-stop cable. This is just one of dozens of seemingly counter-intuitive modifications that may be required if submitting an older vehicle.**

MOT AND ANNUAL GOODS VEHICLE TESTS

■ Class IV tests apply to (amongst other things) *passenger vehicles* with a limited number of seats. This includes *motor caravans* irrespective of MAM. Anything from small family cars to huge American RVs are covered in this class. This same class also covers *goods vehicles* up to 3,000kg MAM (small car-derived van-type vehicles).
■ Class VII tests apply to *goods vehicles* with a MAM of more than 3,000kg, but no more than 3,500kg (most white-van-man-type vehicles).
■ Annual Goods Vehicle tests apply to *goods vehicles* with a MAM exceeding 3,500kg (larger vans and trucks).

decide to do your motor caravan conversion *before* initial registration then be prepared: the Statutory IVA test is a substantial hurdle.

If you've been undaunted by the 'M' class IVA manual's sometimes technically heavy 300 pages and committed to this route, before application for the test you'll need to:

- Make sure your vehicle complies with all of the IVA requirements regarding roadworthiness.
- Ensure you've satisfied the criteria for classification as a motor caravan, i.e. you need to have bed(s), cooking facilities, storage etc.
- Obtain appropriate insurance before driving to the test centre.

If you're confident that you're ready for the test then the application should be made to the DVSA using form IVA 1C following the advice on the form's accompanying guidance notes. You'll also need to include any supporting documents the guidance notes call for, plus the inevitable fee.

The test itself is very comprehensive and takes several hours, during which time patience and humility will be good companions. If you're both extraordinarily talented and haven't fallen foul of any very-last-minute changes to legislation (they happen), your vehicle will pass first time. If you're a mere mortal, the second or third trip to the test centre will hopefully result in a pass and the issue of an Individual Approval Certificate. Treasure this document in the knowledge that it's *very* hard won.

The main reason that the IVA test is so difficult to pass is that you'll very likely be submitting a home-made habitation box mounted to a vehicle that may itself be two decades or more old. Even if your base vehicle is quite new, since it was built, it's almost guaranteed that a raft of European directives will have been enacted by domestic legislation aimed at improving vehicle and road safety standards. The IVA scheme does not recognise the age of your vehicle; it's simply an up-to-the-minute standard that all vehicles must reach. The past decade or two has seen a quantum leap in the safety and environmental impact standards of all motor vehicles and it's against these (now) very high standards that your old van or truck will be measured. What was perfectly acceptable a few years ago, such as exposed nuts on windscreen wiper arms, is now – at the legislative level – utterly frowned upon.

There is a paradox here that you may have already realised but about which you can do precisely nothing. *The very same vehicle* that will hopelessly fail an IVA test might well be perfectly road legal if first tested and registered as a goods vehicle and then converted, *by paper exercise only*, to a motor caravan. It's quite simply the case that the standards required at the first test of a goods vehicle are not as exacting as those applicable to the IVA scheme. This

▲ **More IVA requirements: this plastic hinge had to have its formerly 'sharp' edge radiused (evident by the dark edging). Additionally, plastic covers had to be added to many exposed nuts such as the windscreen wiper spindle also in shot.**

▼ **Other sharp edges required different solutions. For example, these steps required heavy treatment with rubber edging strip.**

situation may well (and arguably *should*) change with the inevitable advent of future legislation.

Following success, and the issue of an Individual Approval Certificate, you can apply to the DVLA for registration and a road fund licence in much the same way as outlined in the earlier part of this chapter by submitting a completed form V55/5 (following the guidance notes carefully) and accompanying it with:

- Your newly issued Individual Approval Certificate (IAC.)
- A Certificate of Insurance (issued against chassis number).
- Personal identity documents and proof of address.
- Supporting documents. These might include, for example, proof of date of first manufacture (usually obtainable from the vehicle manufacturer or a recognised owners' club etc.). Again refer to the V55/5's guidance notes.
- Appropriate fees for registration and vehicle excise duty.

▲ This is exactly the same make and model of truck as the one in previous images and has just passed its First Test of a Goods Vehicle test in spite of the dozens of points it would have failed on if submitted for an IVA test.

If all goes well you'll receive a registration document (V5C) and will be able to get registration plates made and drive off into the sunset in your fully road-legal motor caravan.

A brief consideration of imported vehicles

Following the formality of a declaration to HM Revenue and Customs (HMRC), there are various rules for registering imported vehicles depending on their MAM, whether they're new or used, their date of manufacture, their current registration status and their country of origin. If dealing with an import it's best to contact the DVLA directly, explain the full circumstances of your acquisition and then carefully follow the agency's advice. *Sometimes* vehicles can be brought in with little more than paper shuffling, but don't get your hopes up: it will almost certainly be the case, given our particular context, that you'll be discussing a vehicle that will be deemed a used goods vehicle, and which will, in all probability, be over 3.5 tonnes MAM, in which case it's almost certain that there'll be no option but to submit the vehicle for initial test via the Individual Vehicle Approval scheme.

Unless you're very fortunate and your import meets very specific requirements, your options will almost inevitably be either:

- ■ To initially submit the freshly imported vehicle for the IVA test as an 'N' class goods vehicle, register it as such and then, post conversion, apply to change body-type classification to motor caravan.
- ■ To do the conversion work first, present the completed article for the 'M' class IVA test as a passenger vehicle with the body type motor caravan and, assuming a successful test, register it as such.

A brief consideration of new vehicles

If you're in the enviable position of using a brand-new vehicle as a base for your conversion then the chances are it will be registered by a dealership as a goods vehicle before you take delivery. In this case, you'll simply need to follow the advice as outlined earlier in this chapter for changing body type to motor caravan upon completion of your conversion.

If, on the other hand, the vehicle is for some reason not initially registered and you complete the conversion first, you'll almost certainly need to submit to the 'M' class IVA test and then apply for registration using the relevant version of form V55, most likely the V55/4, which applies to privately registered new (rather than used) vehicles.

Tachographs

The simple part first: *if* your body-type classification is officially recognised on your V5C as motor caravan (and assuming you're not carrying goods or passengers with any commercial interest), you simply don't need a tachograph to be fitted to your van or truck at all, irrespective of the vehicle's weight.

If your classification remains one of the sub-types of *goods vehicle* then be aware that fully calibrated tachographs are required to be fitted where the vehicle (or combination of vehicle and trailer) has a MAM of over 3.5 tonnes. As usual with legislation though, there are exceptions. In two situations that may be particularly relevant to overlanders, it *is* possible to obtain a tachograph exemption *even if* your van or truck still carries a goods-vehicle classification. Full details of all exemptions can be found on the GOV.UK website but briefly, if your vehicle is over 25 years old, *or* has a MAM of no more than 7.5 tonnes, *and in either case it is not to be used for the commercial carriage of goods*, then it's possible to declare a tachograph exemption. This is done by downloading the relevant form and declaring, at the time of your goods vehicle test, the exemption that applies in your circumstances.

If you're not yet thoroughly confused, this might do the trick: just because your vehicle may be required by law to have a tachograph fitted, it will ordinarily be the case that, as a non-commercial driver, you don't need to actually use it. As long as you're not in any way concerned with carrying goods or passengers *in the course of your employment* then drivers' hours' rules and regulations do not apply.

In a nutshell then, if your vehicle is registered as a motor caravan, you simply do not need a tachograph at all. If your vehicle remains a goods vehicle and is over 3.5t MAM, you'll usually require a tachograph to be fitted *unless* you can claim one of the specific exemptions. Even if you can't claim exemption and the vehicle *has* a tachograph fitted, as long as you're simply overlanding and not carrying goods or passengers as part of your work, you do not have to use it. For now…

Driving licences

As with the above section dealing with tachographs, the following is a hugely simplified overview of the legal requirements relating to driving licences and larger vehicles.

If you passed your test to drive a car before 1st January 1997 then you're already entitled to drive rigid vehicles (i.e. vehicles without a trailer) of *any* classification that have a MAM of up to 7.5 tonnes. If you passed your test to drive a car on or after 1st January 1997 you're already allowed to drive rigid vehicles up to 3.5 tonnes, but will need to pass a category C1 test to be able to drive vehicles up to 7.5 tonnes.

No matter when you passed your test to drive a car, if

THE LGV TEST

It may be tempting to take advantage of driving a 7.5-tonne truck on a car licence, but bear in mind that the difference in driving a family car compared to a downrated heavy goods vehicle is substantial. Even if it isn't technically required, a class C LGV licence course would be a hugely beneficial experience and would go a long way to furnishing the skills and experience required.

---

your vehicle has a MAM of more than 7.5 tonnes, you'll need to pass a category C test to be able to drive it. It does not matter whether your vehicle is classified as a goods vehicle or a motor caravan; the MAM is all that the law is concerned with for driving licence purposes. Bottom line: if your MAM is over 7.5 tonnes, you need to pass the class C LGV test.

As an aside, you'll ordinarily be able to pull a trailer of up to 750kg MAM behind your 3.5 or 7.5 tonne vehicle without the need to pass a further test.

Downrating a mid-sized truck to 7.5 tonnes

As will be obvious from the preceding sections, the 7.5-tonne limit is significant in tachograph and driving licence terms. If, alongside this, you consider all that's so far been discussed regarding the advantages of keeping weight low,

▼ **This former 10-tonne truck is downrated and – in spite of its comparatively large overall dimensions – when ready to travel weighs in at less than 7.5 tonnes. This can be a very difficult thing to achieve. The owner/builder took great care to keep weight down during construction.**

you may well already have had a 'light bulb' moment and concluded that any truck that has a manufacturer's design weight in the region of 10 tonnes may benefit from being legally converted to, and used at, the 7.5-tonne MAM point.

The specific benefits of legally downrating a mid-sized truck to 7.5 tonnes (and using it at that weight point) are many. They include:

- The possibility of tachograph exemption (if still classed as a goods vehicle).
- No need to pass a class C driving test (if car test passed prior to 1997).
- Access to roads subject to 7.5-tonne legal restrictions.
- Possibility of lower tolls and taxes.
- Minimising stress on all mechanical components leading to better longevity and reliability.
- Better fuel consumption.
- Better acceleration, braking, cornering and hill-climbing performance.
- Easier on rickety bridges.
- Less likely to bog on soft terrain.
- Easier to recover if bogged.

Of course, this assumes that a downrate actually fits with your intended use and that you can realistically aspire to

▼ **Tricky recoveries are easier if the vehicle is lighter. This would be much more troublesome at 15 tonnes.**

actual travel at the 7.5-tonne mark. Achieving a MAM of 7.5t might mean, for example, that you'll have to limit your fresh-water capacity or shelve plans to carry motorcycles, a large generator, or more than one spare wheel. Most overland camper builds based on trucks with a MAM of 10 tonnes *can* be successfully downrated, but lightweight build techniques *will* be required and the amount of payload left for personal effects and supplies *will* be limited. Trips to a weighbridge with your 10-tonner at various stages of build will give you an idea if the prospect is feasible in your individual case. Do *not* be tempted to put on a show for 'weigh day' and artificially lighten your vehicle in order to squeeze under the 7.5-tonne mark. If you can't comfortably travel at 7.5 tonnes, with all tanks full and everything loaded, this route is not for you. Driving a vehicle whilst in excess of its legal weight limit can have legal repercussions.

If you decide that downrating *is* something that you can realistically achieve and would like to pursue then, as with many other aspects of the legal process, life will be much easier if your vehicle is already officially recognised by the DVLA as a motor caravan. If it is, you can apply to downrate using form VTG10, available (with guidance notes) from the GOV.UK website. When completing this form, be sure to tick the 'Design Weight Certificate' (DWC) option. You'll see that the VTG10 states, in the DWC section, that you need to send evidence from a manufacturer or converter to support the application. This is *not* actually required *providing* you already have motor-caravan status. All that you do need

▲ **The heavier your vehicle, the more worrisome crossings like this become.**

to do is obtain a blank VIN or Manufacturer's plate – these are readily available online – stamp it with your vehicle's details plus the overall and axle weights with which you wish to be allocated, and then send a photograph of this plate together with your application, the appropriate fee, and an authorised public weighbridge ticket proving your overall *and* individual axle weights to the DVSA. Assuming there are no complications, the DVSA will then issue a Design Weight Certificate, which you can then forward to the DVLA, together with your Registration Document to request that section [Y] of the V5C Document (the 'Revenue weight' section), is updated to 7,500kg. Don't forget to attach your newly made VIN/Manufacturer's plate to your vehicle somewhere readily visible for inspection, and ideally near to the original manufacturer's plate.

If your vehicle is registered as a goods vehicle, or isn't registered in the UK at all, then it *is* still possible to downrate but may well require some physical inspection by DVSA. This process *can* still be self-managed and the DVSA's Technical Officers will offer advice relative to your exact circumstances.

If the prospect of getting stuck in bureaucracy doesn't appeal, no matter what status your vehicle currently has with DVLA, there are specialist firms that will, on payment of a reasonable fee, manage the whole downrate process for you.

ROAD FUND LICENCES / VEHICLE EXCISE DUTY / CAR TAX

There is often some confusion regarding the official 'Body type' designation shown at point D.5 on a V5C registration document and the 'Taxation class' designation shown at point [X]. These two classifications *are entirely separate entities*. The vast majority of overland campers will fall into the taxation class of Private HGV (Tax Class 10), which is something of a 'catch-all' class for *all* vehicles over 3.5 tonnes MAM that are not used for commercial purposes. Do not worry that the designation 'HGV' appears in the taxation class section of the document: this will not affect your official body type designation of motor caravan in any way. Happily, at the time of writing, the Private HGV tax class is perplexingly inexpensive and it will almost certainly be a mistake to try to pay your vehicle excise duty in any class apart from this one.

CHAPTER 7

Procuring or building a habitation box

- Ready-made boxes / box-and-vehicle combinations
- Having a box professionally made
- Building your own box
- Thermal bridges

Ready-made boxes that might prove suitable for conversion into a habitation area can be obtained as a stand-alone entity or as an intrinsic part of a box-and-vehicle combination. Other options for living quarters include having a habitation box professionally made, building one yourself, or making use of a commercially available, fully fitted demountable 'truck-camper' or caravan.

Ready-made boxes / box-and-vehicle combinations

As a basis for a habitation-area structure, ready-made boxes – whether already attached to a vehicle or free-standing – are a fairly popular choice amongst overlanders and with good reason: the convenience of a (hopefully) watertight starting point, often obtainable at very reasonable cost, should not be underestimated. Boxes come in all manner of sizes and forms and can be purchased new or second-hand.

The following short and by no means definitive section is designed to highlight a few potential options that lend themselves particularly well as a starting point for a build.

▼ **Large personnel-carrying all-terrain vehicles occasionally come up for sale.**

Utility company personnel-/equipment-carrying all-terrain vehicles

Occasionally, ready-made personnel- and/or equipment-carrying all-terrain trucks used by utility/telecommunication/railway/quarry/forestry companies come up for sale. This kind of box-and-vehicle combination is an appealing starting point for the simple reasons that the base vehicle, the box, and the subframe mounting method *should* all have been designed from the outset to carry payload over rough terrain.

In the case of smaller, van-based vehicles in this genre, GRP-based monocoque boxes are worth looking out for. With this kind of structure, the entire 'pod' is effectively fabricated as a one-piece moulding and makes for a rigid and highly weather-resistant structure. From time to time such monocoque-style pods can also be purchased as a brand-new separate entity although, in the UK at least,

▲ Monocoque boxes are popular with utility companies and form a solid base for a living area. A popular route is to graft a box like this on to a larger 4x4 chassis and build an additional compartment underneath the Luton over-cab section for bulky-item storage.

▲ A former cash-in-transit truck in the process of conversion. Security is a notable feature.

▼ This specialist bus would make a good base for an overlander with the potential for some very panoramic views.

tracing a manufacturer or trade consumer willing to sell one can be quite some task.

Refrigerated vehicles

Like monocoque shells, refrigerated boxes are usually sturdy structures. Additionally, and very usefully, they're well insulated and, because they're generally built with the fewest apertures possible, offer good flexibility with regard to layout and window placement. On the negative side, as refrigerated vehicles tend to be purely road-going, you would almost certainly have to take into account issues around torsional stress. If an entire box-and-vehicle combination is being considered (as opposed to a stand-alone box) it would be highly likely that modifications to, or replacement of, the existing box mountings and subframe would be required.

Cash-in-transit/security/bullion trucks

The boxes on vehicles of this type are, by their very nature, *extremely* tough and can provide reassuringly secure living space. Rarely will this kind of vehicle be intended from the outset for multi-terrain use, but the chassis on such vehicles tend to be quite short and the boxes very strong. Accordingly, incorporating just enough torsion relief to protect the chassis from breaking in repeated bad-road conditions should be a fairly easy matter to resolve. Indeed, in some cases, if the vehicle is built in such a way that the cab is rigidly bolted to the security box *and* the box rigidly bolted to the chassis, normal rules regarding torsional stress do not apply. More about this 'super-rigidity' anomaly appears in Chapter 5.

Tourist buses specifically designed for multi-terrain applications

Rarely, commercial passenger-carrying vehicles specifically designed for multi-terrain applications can be obtained. Such vehicles are reasonably common in developed countries that have large tracts of unsealed roads, especially where tourism is a major industry.

Military or other specialist organisations' ambulances, rescue/communications vehicles and mobile workshops

Just about any existing box-and-vehicle combination used by military or other specialist organisations as an ambulance, rescue vehicle, communications unit, or mobile workshop etc. should prove a worthwhile candidate as a base. In common with 'utility company' vehicles outlined above, the combination will ordinarily have been designed from the outset to deliver reliable personnel- or equipment-carrying multi-terrain service.

In the event that you already have a base vehicle, modular, demountable boxes are extensively used by military forces and the larger military disposal concerns will usually have a good

▲ Communications units make for relatively easy overlander conversions.

◣ A popular ready-made box-and-vehicle combination: a modified NATO 'comms' shelter on a Leyland DAF T244 flat-bed.

▶ Twist-lock fixing method. These fixings are common on demountable boxes and make for very simple box removal and transfer.

stock lurking in their sprawling yards. Such demountable boxes are well proven in multi-terrain situations and are generally designed to enable a relatively rapid change between vehicles. Some even benefit from 'shipping-container' type twist-lock casting that can make mounting a comparatively simple affair. Products utilised or constructed by NATO, KUNG, LAK, Dornier and Zeppelin tend to be amongst the more popular and underpin many successful self-builds.

▼ A demountable Dornier shelter fully detached and in the workshop.

▼ The interior of the same Dornier shelter. Because of their construction method, these shelters lend themselves well to modification. In this case the perforated framework and duller aluminium skin are all original whereas the unperforated framework and shinier metalwork have been added by the owner to extend the living space.

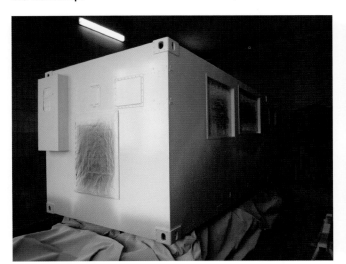

▲ A typical demountable truck-camper on a Ford F–450.

DESIRABLE ATTRIBUTES

Of the ready-made boxes that *could* be pressed into service, there are so many different types that it's difficult to make general recommendations. Materials, build quality, specification and structural integrity are hugely variable. Nonetheless, in an effort to assist to at least some degree, here are some desirable attributes to look out for:

- An outer skin of abrasion-resistant material that is able to take knocks. Fibreglass (GRP) is well proven in this regard.
- Monocoque construction. One-piece GRP type 'pods' are very strong and do not suffer from water ingress. Conversely, boxes with many seams or mechanical fixing methods that puncture the outer skin can (especially over time) be prone to leaks.
- A subframe. Any intrinsic steel or similar structure built into the base of a box might save time and effort if it could be utilised as the basis of a mounting system.
- Intrinsic strength. Any box that visibly flexes is probably not going to be strong enough.
- Insulation. If the box comes with *good* insulation or insulative qualities, significant time and expense could be saved later into the build.
- Obvious high build quality and attention to detail. Tell-tale indicators are the quality of welds and how much care has been taken with the application of adhesive sealers etc.
- High-quality materials. Stainless steel and hardwoods etc. tend to indicate a quality product.

Demountable 'truck-campers' and caravans

Commercially available demountable 'truck-campers' are very popular in some parts of the world (particularly North America) but enjoy only a niche following in others. Although variations exist, they're most commonly fully pre-fitted with all domestic equipment and are designed to be mounted directly into the load bed of a pick-up truck. If the prospect of a fully-fitted 'pod' is appealing, this route may be worthy of consideration. Of course, choices regarding layouts, and equipment and systems will usually be somewhat limited to the production models available and it will almost certainly be necessary to look at ways to improve fresh water carrying capacity at the very least.

In a similar vein, some very nice overlander builds have been achieved by – very simplistically – grafting a caravan on to a suitable base vehicle. Again, layout and capacities may be an issue and because the vast majority of caravans are not generally intrinsically robust (though some specially prepared rough-road units *are* available), a well-thought-out

▼ This modified caravan (a Bigfoot 1517) and Fuso 4x4 combination was famously built in an extremely short period of time, yet proved reliable across Asia and the Americas.

subframe plus a great deal of strengthening and patient improvements to the structural integrity of fixtures and fittings may be necessary.

Panel vans

Panel vans are an obvious example of a vehicle with a ready-made box and it's worth bearing in mind that vehicles in this class also have the distinct advantage of intrinsic structural integrity. That said, torsional stress, though in most cases falling short of causing *structural* damage, *does* still affect the shell and this most often becomes apparent with the ingress of dust. In dusty conditions, a particularly vulnerable

▲ **Of the very many suitable panel vans available, Mercedes Varios are a very popular choice and with good reason – both two- and four-wheel-drive versions are well proven on full round-the-world trips.**

point is the rear door area. When driving, eddies in air flow relentlessly 'suck' dust into this area and, if driving on very uneven terrain, torsional stress can easily cause the rear doors to move independently of the surrounding bodywork. This can play havoc with any rubber sealing system and may lead to unfathomable quantities of dust covering the entire interior. Do not underestimate this potential problem…

PROS AND CONS OF READY-MADE BOXES

Pros
- Much time, expense and effort can be saved with the purchase of a ready-made box or box-and-vehicle combination.
- Many boxes and box-and-vehicle combinations, particularly those utilised in all-terrain applications, will already be field proven – offering some peace of mind that the structure is unlikely to fail catastrophically.

Cons
- Weight. *Some* types of box are very heavy and could make adherence to the 80% rule totally unattainable, compromise payload or make the prospect of a 7.5-tonne downrate impossible.
- Dimensions. These will be fixed unless you're prepared to undertake extra structural work, some of which may be significant.
- Doors, access lockers and window positioning will often be predetermined; again, unless you're prepared to take on structural modifications.

- The frequent reliance upon aluminium as an outer-skin material. Aluminium sheet is readily damaged upon moderate contact with branches or if otherwise knocked.
- Excess original equipment, particularly with military communications shelters. Much very interesting but ultimately useless equipment and wiring may need to be stripped out and panel work made good.
- Torsional stress. With a box-and-vehicle combination – unless specifically designed from the outset for all-terrain use – some modification of existing mountings or the fabrication of a completely new mounting system may be required.
- Demountable campers and caravans will usually have fixed layouts and limited water and LPG capacities. Additionally, caravans in particular *tend* to be intrinsically very flimsy.
- Some boxes will have seen better days and may be *very* shabby at the point of acquisition.

Having a box professionally made

If your preference is for new and bespoke, it's entirely possible to have a habitation box professionally made to any stage of completion and to your own exacting specification. There are companies specialising in building overland campers that understand well the issues involved and who will, at a price, be willing to do business. This can be a time-consuming process, but providing you have chosen your professional well, you're almost guaranteed a quality and fit-for-purpose product.

Aside from professional overland camper builders, there is also the possibility of persuading a commercial coach building entity such as a horsebox or race-truck builder to become involved with your project. Bear in mind though that companies specialising in such vehicles may not fully appreciate how the issues of structural integrity and torsional stress are crucial concerns in the overland-camper context.

When building a box of any description that's intended for use on a vehicle, most professional builders will, by default, gravitate towards tried-and-tested coach building methods. Not all, though: a few specialist companies are now building boxes utilising very lightweight structural-honeycomb panels that, when plastic-welded together, form a very stiff but incredibly lightweight and highly bespoke structure. Such are the possibilities of this material that it's even possible, for our purposes, to weld into place interior partitions to make, for example, things like seat bases and watertight shower rooms.

The panels used in this construction method comprise a honeycomb polypropylene structure sandwiched between glass-fibre-reinforced polypropylene 'skins', which, when all thermally compressed and bonded together as a composite panel, are not only very light but are also claimed to possess good abrasion resistance and very good insulative qualities. All individual components of the composite structure are available in a choice of thicknesses and colours and, using the specialist welding process, are highly workable. Though the use of this material is reasonably well established in the road-transport industry, it's in its comparative infancy in the overlanding context. Some intrepid builders have already gone down this route though.

The material is intended to be put to use exactly as supplied, but if you have designs on adding further elements such as more inner insulation or a protective outer skin, you'll need to ensure any material you add will expand and contract at a very similar rate (or otherwise be able to yield) to the structural honeycomb. 'Warping-skin' issues are known and there's a good argument for using the panels exactly as supplied, or otherwise taking close heed of advice from the panel manufacturer in this regard.

▲ **A non-laboratory-conditions stress test of a structural honeycomb panel.**

Building your own box

Building your own box from scratch may initially seem daunting but it has many attractions, including:

- The freedom to exactly specify all materials.
- Complete control of overall dimensions and the locations of doors, windows, lockers and hatches.
- Greater quality control.
- Cost savings over a professional build.
- The ability to control weight.

If you think that building your own box is the right route for you, you'll need to decide how you're going to tackle the job. Though many self-build techniques have been successfully employed (some of which are briefly considered later in this section), the two most tried and tested involve either:

- Assembling professionally made composite panels.
- Creating a skeletal frame in steel or aluminium and then skinning, insulating and lining the framework structure.

Self-building a composite panel box – the basic principles

Laminating composite panels involves specialist adhesives, equipment and, ideally, a temperature-controlled environment. It is *not* a DIY job – not if you want your panels to stay together anyway. Fortunately, specialist companies will make individual composite panels to your own specification. Though many different combinations of materials of varying thicknesses have been utilised, a composite wall panel for an overland camper might *typically* comprise a 1.5–3mm outer skin of GRP, a 5–10mm layer of plywood, a 40–50mm layer of expanded polyurethane or extruded polystyrene foam, a further 5–10mm layer of

▲ A cut-off from a typical five-element composite panel showing a full-width timber inlay.

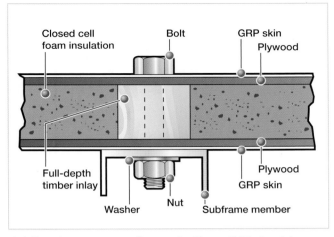

Closed cell foam insulation — Bolt — GRP skin — Plywood — Full-depth timber inlay — Washer — Nut — Subframe member — Plywood — GRP skin

▲ A five-element composite panel with a solid timber inlay positioned directly over a subframe member. Arrangements like this allow for solid through-bolting without damaging panels.

plywood and a final sub-1mm layer of GRP to provide a smooth, clean, waterproof interior finish. Roof and floor panels largely follow the same pattern, but floors particularly are often specified with a thicker layer of 'inner' ply to protect the foam layer by dissipating the stress of constant footfall. Note: some floors on conventional motor caravans have been known to delaminate because the floor was insufficiently stiff and allowed too much 'give' under the point-load of footsteps. Repeated footfall can lead to eventual degradation of the adhesives and foam core in these circumstances.

As well as specifying the overall composition of the panels, it's also possible to commission different structural inlays. If, then, you have designs on fixing a push-bike rack or will need to add pneumatic struts to support a heavy locker door, it's logical to get timber (or other material) inlays placed within the composite structure in the appropriate locations in order to deal with the associated stresses and to accommodate appropriate fasteners. As well as inlays to deal with specific items, it's also wise to have the occasional inlay inserted to help with overall structural integrity. Your specialist company of choice should be able to help with specific advice given the size, composition and intended use of each panel. Something else to consider is a specialist series of inlays that together effectively create a full peripheral frame for each and every individual panel. This option is highly recommended as such frames confer a very strong and highly suitable surface for subsequent panel-to-panel bonding, especially if the frame is also appropriately rebated. Don't worry if some of this is proving difficult to visualise at this introductory stage; you'll be able to view examples of inlays and peripheral frames being incorporated into builds in the 'Composite panel build techniques' section that follows.

There's nothing revolutionary about laminated composite panels; indeed, it's the kind of panel that's been the

component member of professionally made overlanders and refrigerated vehicles for many years. Conventional motor caravans, too, often make use of such composites, though they're ordinarily only three-element panels comprising a thin layer of aluminium as an outer skin, a 30mm-or-so insulative core and a thin layer of decoratively veneered ply as an inner skin. There really is no hard and fast rule regarding the

THE PROS AND CONS OF COMPOSITE PANELS

Pros
■ The finished product can be comparatively light, especially if the wood content is kept to a minimum.
■ High-quality insulation and few internal frames mean thermal bridges can be minimised.
■ Very professional finish.
■ Assuming you've specified appropriate panel elements, fixtures, furniture and fittings can very easily be screwed or bonded directly to the interior walls.
■ GRP-skinned composites are resilient to knocks and tangles with vegetation.

Cons
■ The finished box requires effective protection from torsional stress.
■ The panels themselves require specialist manufacture.
■ Expensive.
■ Require extra engineering and the construction of separate supporting structures to be able to carry very heavy-duty racks, motorcycles etc.

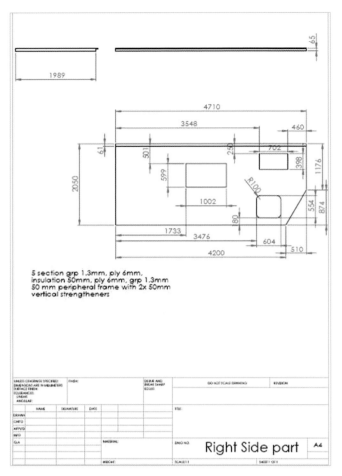

5 section grp 1.3mm, ply 6mm,
insulation 50mm, ply 6mm, grp 1.3mm
50 mm peripheral frame with 2x 50mm
vertical strengtheners

Right Side part

number and composition of elements, but, depending on the climates in which the vehicle will be used, somewhere between three and five elements and a total thickness of 45–65mm is loosely representative.

If you think this method of construction might be for you then the first and most crucial step is to design each panel according to your exact needs. Particular attention needs to be paid to the placement of inlays and the position and size of any door, window and hatch apertures you would like the manufacturer to cut during the production process. Whilst considering inlays, if you ultimately intend to through-bolt the floor panel to a custom-made subframe, you may wish to incorporate suitable full-depth members in the floor – these will stop the floor being compressed and potentially damaged when the panel-to-subframe bolts are tightened.

Once you're happy with your design, it's vitally important to convey your exact plans to the panel manufacturer. This may sound obvious, but any misunderstanding *will* result in expensive errors and potentially long delays. Once the individual panels are completed to your specification, all that remains is to arrange delivery and assemble what will probably be the largest flat-pack you've ever taken on.

◀ **It's vital to be very precise with your brief to panel manufacturers.**

▼ **Panels made and collected.**

3 Knowing the front wall and floor panel are square makes for quick progress with the sidewalls. Note how the sidewalls are 'locked' at their base between the just-visible already-bonded-down floor panel and the aforementioned steel angle perimeter lip (see illustration for details).

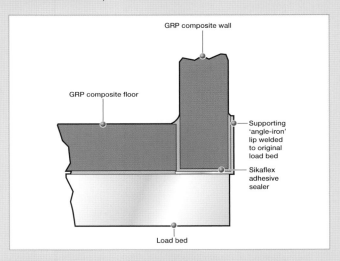

GRP composite wall

GRP composite floor

Supporting 'angle-iron' lip welded to original load bed

Sikaflex adhesive sealer

Load bed

1 This particular composite-panel box is destined to be built directly on to a (stripped) manufacturer's flat-back load bed. Note the 3mm-thick steel angle 'lip' welded to the perimeter of the bed. This will eventually act as a locator for the whole base of the box structure and prevent any lateral movement or shearing stress that might otherwise compromise the adhesive sealer used to bond the floor panel and sidewalls to the load bed. In other words, it prevents any possibility of the box tearing from its bond and sliding off!

4 A different build but utilising the same methodology. The floor panel is already Sikaflexed and in this case also bolted to the subframe (again to prevent shearing forces from compromising the adhesive), and copious amounts of Sikaflex 252 are being applied in preparation for dropping the temporarily supported sidewall into place. Note the inlays forming a peripheral frame and the deep rebate in the floor panel's frame – this will neatly butt up to the sidewall panel.

2 To ensure everything ends up square it's important to set the first panel correctly. In this instance the truck's original headboard stays were known to be absolutely vertical so were utilised as a datum point.

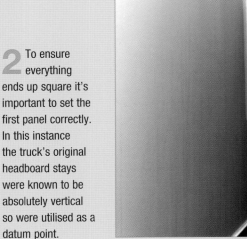

7 The very same joint but now back-filled with Sikaflex 221. The idea here is to fill any gaps in the original adhesive sealer application and to seal all the exposed wood. The joint will eventually be capped and should be watertight but if any water were to find its way past the capping, thanks to the 221, at least the integrity of the panels will not be compromised.

5 The top of a sidewall elevation, again complete with a rebated peripheral frame that will, in this case, eventually accommodate the roof panel. When bonded, the increased surface area and 'interlocking' effect afforded by the rebating technique make for a very strong finished structure. Note the screws (which are also evident in the previous image). These have been added as spacers to prevent the panels registering too closely and thereby squeezing all of the adhesive sealer out of the joint. Follow manufacturers' instructions carefully regarding the minimum adhesive sealer bead dimension required to achieve full bonding strength.

8 Upper rear panel bonded into position. Note the two just-visible hex-headed screws either side of the panel; these are only temporary and are holding the panel in position pending full curing of the adhesive sealer. This image also demonstrates how each panel on this particular build has timber peripheral frames and timber inlays around all window and door apertures.

6 Two rebated wall panels fully bonded together with Sikaflex 252. Note the bead width of the adhesive sealer.

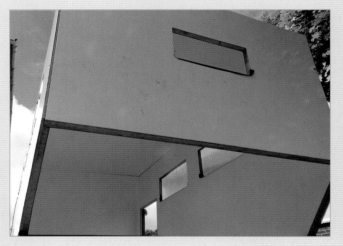

9 There's an easy way and a difficult way to lift a typical composite roof panel into position. The difficult way involves at least six strong people and a good deal of grunting. All of the apertures in the panels shown were very accurately cut by the panel manufacturer. Using the manufacturer ultimately saves time and the potential for panel-ruining disasters. CNC-driven routers are immeasurably more precise than self-builder-driven jigsaws!

10 As soon as panels are bedded on the structural bonding, any excess adhesive sealer squashed out of joints can be removed and, if required, all panels can later be neatly back-filled. Large amounts of Sikaflex can be removed with a blunt scraper and the product is fairly easy to smooth with a wet finger. Patient work with white spirit or a proprietary remover can help clean up any drastic errors, but in all cases you don't get long to tidy up a sealer run before it starts to cure to the point of becoming unworkable. Dealing with one seam at a time and using masking tape to ensure very neat edges helps produce a well-finished job.

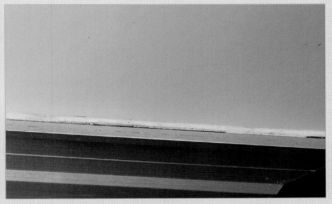

11 When all panels are assembled, capping should be added to finish and protect the joints. Different styles are available and simply bond into position – in this case with Sikaflex 521. Do not be tempted to screw capping into position. The holes will almost certainly, given time, become a point of water ingress. The Sikaflex-filled gap at the meeting point of this capping is to allow room for slight expansion of the aluminium in very hot conditions. Note the aluminium finishing strip covering the joint of the upper and lower rear panels. This is just a strip of 3mm aluminium flat bar that was pressed to the required angle by a local engineering firm.

12 Check joints frequently. Good quality adhesive sealer is a genuinely impressive product and brings self-building within reach of those without time-served fabrication skills. However, it is not infallible and if incorrectly applied, or if subjected to too much stress, it can fail. This seam originally sealed a capping piece that had probably not been cleaned properly prior to application. Surfaces need to be clean, dry and free from contamination – follow manufacturers' instructions carefully

in this regard. Proprietary surface cleaning products are available if you don't trust your own preparation techniques. ▲

13 Following laborious and very careful gouging with a series of knives and scrapers, the affected panel and all old adhesive was removed, everything was cleaned and degreased, and the capping reset with Sikaflex 521. All has been well since…

If you have decent metalworking skills, or ready access to someone who does, this method of building is one over which you have a great deal of control. In its simplest form, a skeletal structure is built, an outer skin is added, insulation is positioned and a final inner skin is affixed to create a nominal three-element structure. Naturally, the exact materials and number of elements utilised can (and do) vary but *typically* comprise:

- A steel frame.
- An outer skin of sheet aluminium.
- An insulation layer of expanded polyurethane or extruded polystyrene foam, or alternatively a glass or mineral wool based material.
- An inner lining of good-quality stable plywood (sometimes faced with a decorative laminate).

As is the case with composite panel boxes, floors tend to be thicker and incorporate a more substantial layer of marine ply or similar to assist with insulation and structural integrity.

Naturally, as you have complete control over materials, it's a matter of choice regarding the exact composition of elements and some builders elect to use different materials or incorporate extra layers of insulation, inner-skin mounting battens or impermeable membranes designed to ward off any potential condensation issues. Whether such membranes are absolutely necessary with a skeletal box is not widely agreed upon but adding them is unlikely to cause any harm.

If you decide on this method of construction then once again thoughtful design will pay dividends. Careful positioning

THE PROS AND CONS OF SKELETAL FRAMES

Pros
- No requirement for any major third-party involvement (if you can weld).
- Very strong finished structure.
- Resilient to torsional stress.
- Able to self-support very heavy-duty external racks and equipment.

Cons
- Comparatively heavy unless special materials or construction techniques are used.
- Can be difficult to prevent water ingress over the long term (depending on how the outer skin is affixed).
- Thermal bridges *may* be more difficult to overcome.
- Reliance on aluminium sheet as an outer skin (other solutions *are* possible but can be difficult to use in practice).

of the structural steel members will be necessary in order to accommodate the subsequent fitting of doors, windows, hatches and so on, and to accommodate any heavy-duty external racking that you may be planning to build. If you intend to carry the 300kg+ weight of a two-spare-wheel-and-tyre combination, or equipment like a motorcycle, then this is the time to ensure structural members and any necessary brackets are suitably incorporated.

INNER SKINS COMPARED

For the final lining-out job in a skeletal structure, many materials have been successfully employed. Here are just some of the more commonly used sheet materials, complete with a few general pointers:

- **ABS**: Waterproof and resistant to heat and moisture. Easy to clean, high-gloss finish and stable in widely varying temperatures. Reasonably reliable to bond.
- **Polypropylene**: 'Warm' to the touch, easy to clean. High-gloss finish but prone to scratching. Expands/contracts at a far greater rate than most other similar materials, which can lead to bulging and warping. Resistant to moisture. Very difficult to bond. Inexpensive.
- **PVC Foamboard**: 'Warm' to the touch, very easy to work, available in many colours. Moderately stable across a wide temperature and humidity range. Reasonably reliable to bond.
- **GRP**: Easy to work and repair, moderately stable across a wide temperature and humidity range. Available in different colours. Very easy to bond.
- **Marine ply**: Stable across a wide temperature and humidity range, easy to work, adds to structural integrity and will hold screws firmly. Very easy to bond. Requires some work to produce a nice aesthetic finish.
- **Decoratively veneered ply**: Quality of ply can be variable. With budget products, veneers can be fragile and prone to peeling, especially if utilised in a position prone to variable temperature and humidity. Easy to work and attractively finished. Can be expensive.

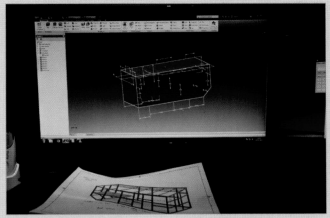

1 Though the use of computers is entirely optional, to ensure an efficient and successful build a good plan is pretty much obligatory.

4 Rear view of the frame after being epoxy coated. The floor panels are now bolted in. Note the two large RHS members and the bracing brackets in the centre section of the rear elevation…

2 Work well underway. To maximise rigidity, the base of this box (currently upside-down) was constructed in 100mm x 50mm x 3.2mm wall rectangular hollow steel (RHS). The wall members are 80mm x 40mm x 3.2mm and the roof spars 40mm x 40mm x 3.2mm. Thanks to thoughtful design, the frame members are placed at centres that will allow the easiest and most economical use of aluminium sheeting. This is an incredibly sturdy frame.

5 …they are fixing points for a hoist and spare-wheel carrier. A major advantage of this build method is that heavy-duty racks/carriers for items like spare wheels and motorcycles can easily be accommodated.

3 Floor panels being prepared. In this case 25mm marine ply was augmented by an approximately 3mm-thick skin of fibreglass which was then flow-coated. This treatment will ensure the underside of the floor remains totally protected from weather and road spray.

6 Another advantage is that if plans change, alterations are relatively easy – given the necessary skills and equipment.

7 Preparation for final skinning. By this stage, all aluminium skins have already been mocked into place, all rivet holes have been drilled (at centres of 60mm), and the skins then taken back off to allow the job to be cleaned of all swarf and fully degreased. At this stage 3M VHB double-sided tape is being added to all members in preparation for the skins' final fit.

8 Following a bead of Sikaflex 252 run parallel to the VHB tape, the skins are carefully refitted using locating pins and the riveting operation begins. The double-sided tape and adhesive sealer serve the purposes of bonding/sealing the panel and simultaneously minimising physical contact with the mild steel RHS frame. Even though the frame in this case is epoxy coated, galvanic corrosion needs to be headed off at all costs.

9 Rather than use aluminium to skin the roof, the owner decided to use a GRP-based composite panel. Here, it's being weighted-down whilst adhesive sealer cures.

10 Once skinned, window apertures are cut, and battens to accept the windows are bonded into place.

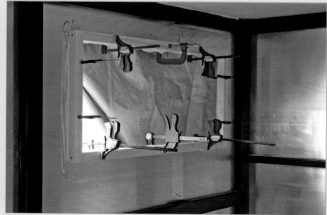

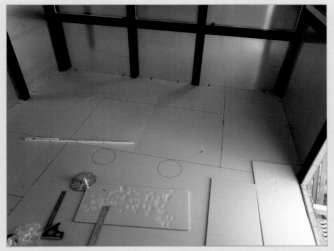

14 Lining material finally being supported/bonded to the 10mm foam layer. This box is now approaching the fit-out stage.

15 The earlier-mentioned spare-wheel hoist and carrier, completely supported by the steel framework. This kind of carrier cannot easily be incorporated directly to the rear panel if utilising the composite panel build technique.

11 Closed-cell foam insulation added over the marine-ply floor and location of furniture carefully marked.

12 40mm-thick RTM foam is bonded to the aluminium skin. Note the extra wooden battens also bonded to the skin: these are to provide a suitable substrate that will later provide attachment points for furniture etc. Note too that the bespoke windows are now bonded to the battens that were attached earlier in the process.

13 Internal lining of choice being cut to size. Note that a further 10mm layer of insulating foam has wisely been bonded to the underlying steel/wood/RTM foam (easily visible on the roof section). This is primarily to help to avoid any thermal bridging issues.

If using mild steel, rust-proofing of the frame will be required and some builders even go to the trouble of galvanising or powder coating the structure, and also spraying rust inhibitor into the hollow members themselves. Aluminium panels are usually attached with a combination of strong double-sided tape, adhesive sealer and rivets. As steel and aluminium are being joined, you'll need to be mindful of galvanic corrosion, hence the reason for the use of tape. This medium separates the two dissimilar materials of the frame and outer skin and if used along with sealed-head aluminium rivets with stainless-steel mandrels (especially if these are also dipped in a rust inhibitor before application), will help to ward off potential problems. The bead of adhesive sealer run adjacent to the

tape acts as an effective bonding safeguard in the event of rivet failure and furthermore helps to ward off any water-ingress issues.

Insulative material can be bonded or simply interference-fitted into place between structural frame members, but if using material that could be prone to 'slump' then it will be useful to ensure the top section at least is firmly attached to prevent any settlement and subsequent loss of insulation performance. A further, and potentially labour-saving, option is to have a professional company supply a spray foam application. Finally, following the insulation process, the internal skin can be bonded or fastened into position. If riveting, screwing or similar, again be mindful of potential corrosion issues. Using non-metallic fasteners or thin strips of wood bonded perpendicular to the skeletal frame as an interface to which to screw are just a couple of simple ways of sidestepping any potential problems. The latter will also usefully help to minimise thermal bridging.

Alternative approaches

Though the laminated composite panels and aluminium-skinned skeletal frames methods already discussed are the most conventional options for a self-built box, you're by no means tied to these. Indeed, creativity abounds. Here are just five examples of less-than-conventional or hybrid-build methods.

A NOTE ON PANEL VANS

The basic principle for lining out panel vans is similar to adding insulation and interior panels to a skeletal frame box. In steel vans, wooden battens are fashioned and bonded to the inside of the van's shell; then insulating material is placed within the framework created before a waterproof membrane is added and, finally, an interior skin is fastened to the battens to complete the 'composite'. Materials *usually* comprise:

- The van's original outer shell.
- The insulative material of choice. This is usually pliable glass/mineral-based wool or spray foam as opposed to the rigid sheets of material most often employed in skeletal steel structures. This is because rigid sheets of closed cell foam are not easy to form around the various curves and pressed steel members found inside panel vans.
- A waterproof membrane like, for example, sheet polythene. Because the outer shell and all the van's structural components will almost certainly be steel, some of which (especially if out of sight) may not benefit from the best rust-proofing, there is a high probability that water vapour produced by occupants could reach the inner surface of the cold outer shell and settle out as condensation: ultimately leading to corrosion issues. No matter the quality of insulation, to prevent any vapour passing to the outer shell, the waterproof membrane is generally accepted as a wise precaution in the case of steel panel vans.
- The finishing inner skin. High-grade ply is frequently pressed into service but numerous other materials can be used to good effect. Just some of these are outlined in the 'Inner skins compared' box on page 96.

▼ **A wooden wonder. This box was totally home-made using an ash timber frame, a plywood outer skin, Celotex insulation and a plywood inner skin. Note the clever radius to the upper sidewall sections, which increases strength, avoids potential water-pooling issues and gives a few more centimetres of clearance for overhanging vegetation etc.**

▲ A very individualistic approach – this box is based on a very lightweight 30mm box-section steel framework and has a 3mm marine ply outer skin. Insulation is courtesy of extruded polystyrene foam and the inner skin is handcrafted in a combination of tongue-and-groove pine with attractive cedar highlights. The roof is probably unique as it's formed using sheets of zinc.

▶ Conventional composite upright panels are complemented by an unusual and highly individual roof. This was formed by curving a plywood base over an underlying frame and then hand-laying several layers of fibreglass matting/resin on to the plywood. This effectively forms a very strong one-piece roof section that is utterly impervious to rain and heavy snow. The copings at all panel junctions are similarly formed by hand-laid fibreglass matting/resin.

▲ This box comprises sheets of structural honeycomb. This section is being prepared for a shower room panel to be plastic-welded into the rebate.

▼ The interior of the same box showing the fully waterproof shower room welded into the structure.

▼ The overall structure is extraordinarily lightweight.

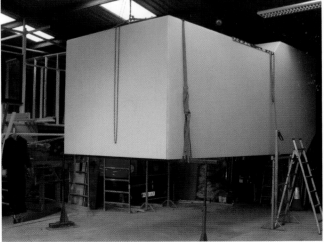

▲ For this particular build it was deemed the polypropylene honeycomb panels themselves would not offer sufficient insulation so the entire structure was lined using these professionally laminated RTM foam/ply/GRP sheets – a very time-consuming job.

▲ Another exponent of structural honeycomb. On this highly innovative build, a framework of heavy-gauge aluminium was fabricated...

▼ ...into which panels of 40mm NidaCore (complete with inner and outer fibreglass skins) were bonded. The interior was later insulated with sheets of 10mm closed-cell foam and trimmed with a skin of Formica.

Thermal bridges

When the inner and outer surfaces of any type of habitation box are bridged by anything other than an efficiently insulative material then the phenomenon known as thermal bridging can become an issue. Steel members from a skeletal frame, wooden inlays from a composite box and the steel structural pressings of panel vans are all capable of very efficiently thermally connecting the extremity of the outside surface to the extremity of the inside surface. There are many other fixtures and fittings that efficiently conduct heat and

▼ Thermal bridging at work. The heat inside this habitation box has been conducted via timber inlays in the composite panels to the exterior where it can clearly be seen to have affected where condensation has formed. Of course, on the interior, the exact reversal of this effect can occur.

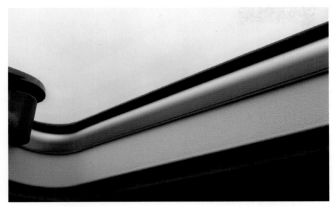

▲ **The aluminium frame of this marine hatch is a very efficient thermal bridge and if placed over a bed would, in the right climatic conditions, very readily drip condensation on to sleeping occupants. A cure for this specific issue features in the following chapter.**

some of the more obvious culprits are window, door and hatch frames, and through-fixing bolts.

Thermal bridges result in many undesirable consequences such as unpleasant cold or hot spots and in some circumstances can lead to the very unwelcome presence of a heavy build-up of condensation. It will pay to bear this

▼ **Two solutions to combat thermal bridges resulting from the wooden peripheral frame in this composite panel box. The upright beech corner trim not only isolates the thermal bridge but also conceals a wiring run. Meanwhile, the grey Foamboard strips are affixed using hook and loop tape (and then sealed for a neat finish). The extra air gap conferred by the hook and loop tape adds to the board's already-good insulative qualities.**

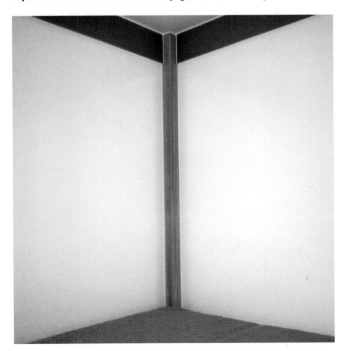

phenomenon in mind and to design structures and choose materials wisely to avoid, wherever possible, allowing any kind of potential thermal bridge into your build.

Even the most thorough designs and the wisest of material choices will be unlikely to avert the issue altogether and if you find an area that causes a problem, creative solutions may be necessary. Ensuring particularly troublesome areas are enclosed within or behind internal lockers or furniture is a useful way round the problem, but in cases where this is not possible extra insulative measures may be required. Popular amongst professional panel-van converters is good old-fashioned lining carpet. Carpeted walls seem to excite opinion but however you feel about them, the simple truth is that they serve their insulative purpose pretty efficiently. If you're no fan of lining carpet then there's huge scope for creativity. There are no hard and fast rules; anything goes to combat the problematic area(s).

GENERAL GOOD PRACTICE

Whichever method of box construction you choose, here are some overall considerations that may be of assistance:

- Plan carefully. At the risk of overstating this point, it really is vital. Plan particularly well for door and window apertures, inlays and for any structural members required to support heavyweight racks.
- Floor strengtheners. If you intend to mount the base of your box on to a custom-made subframe then it will be vital to ensure you build sufficiently strong members into the floor to permit through-bolting.
- Walk-on roof. If you plan on using your roof as an observation platform, a secluded sunbathing area, somewhere to carry equipment, or if you plan on walking on it for any other reason, you'll need to ensure that it will be able to support your point-load weight. Cross-bearers in a composite panel or a suitably thick layer of marine ply built into the structure will do the trick.
- Water pooling. It's surprising how much water will collect on a roof and if it can pool, it's often only a matter of time before ingress becomes an issue. Drain channels or run-off points are recommended.
- Capping. In order to neatly finish a self-made box, and to protect the panel joint seams from water ingress, good-quality capping should be used and secured with a properly applied high-quality adhesive sealer.
- Perforations. *Any* hole made in a shell is a potential water ingress point: keep them to a minimum.

Colin Woollard

1   Name
Colin Woollard.

2   Base vehicle
Gaz-66 – 1970.

3   Drive
Part-time four-wheel drive.

4   Fuel capacity
40 litres LPG / 105 litres petrol.

5   Weight when loaded and ready to travel
5.8 tonnes.

6   Reason for base vehicle choice
Competent off-road capability; simple, robust engineering; and the habitation box was already built to a high standard.

7   Subframe solution
The subframe is located with rubber bushes either side of the rear axle and with opposing springs at the front.

8   Habitation-box construction
This is an ex-military radio box that seems to have originally been used as an electrical repair unit. It has aluminium skin, a foam core, and plywood inner skin.

9   Habitation-box insulation material
High-density foam.

10   Habitation-box manufacturer
'Kung' body – this is a standardised design used in many Russian military vehicles.

11   Habitation-box windows
Standard Kung: insulated / double glazed.

12   Habitation-box door(s) and locker(s)
Standard Kung.

13   Fit out done by
Self.

14   Furniture construction
Welded aluminium frames with plywood skins. The original Russian-built interior cabinets were of a high-quality construction so I re-used them. Some aspects of the layout were compromised as a result, but the cabinets were of such a high standard it would have been crazy not to leave them in.

15 Fresh water

2 x 70 litres – to be changed for 1 x 200 litre tank. No filtration fitted at present.

16 Refrigeration

Waeco 50-litre chest fridge freezer, compressor type, strapped down to cabinet top.

17 Space heating

Blown-air LPG (propane) 1,600W Propex heater plus a 4kW petrol-fired Eberspächer Hydronic furnace supplying one wet radiator and one heated towel rail.

18 Water heating

We have a calorifier heated by the above Eberspächer Hydronic furnace.

19 Cooking facilities

Three-ring LPG (propane) hob.

20 Habitation-box cooling

None, but air circulation is good through the box when driving. Air flows from the cab, through the crawl-through, and out from the rear vent.

21 Leisure-battery charging

Charging is primarily by a 270W solar panel. I also have a Mastervolt battery charger for when on mains and a 1000W petrol inverter / generator.

22 Things to do differently next time

Maybe spend a little more time on build quality. The truck has evolved as a series of last-minute efforts before trips away; it would have been nice to have set aside a proper build period and spent more time on various aspects. Some finer details of the layout could be better, but I am not averse to ripping out some parts and redoing them in the future. Specifically, it seems that we never really have much use for the two tables I originally provisioned and that a large seating area, which doubles as a semi-permanent bed, is more useful. The truck habitation box layout was primarily dictated by having to safely carry five children in forward- and rearward-facing seats with belts.

CHAPTER 8

Hatches, windows, doors, roof lights and ventilation

- Connecting the cab to the box
- Windows
- Doors and lockers
- Roof lights, hatches and vents
- Ventilation

If you're now able to stand contemplatively in an empty box, congratulations! You've passed a significant milestone.

Connecting the cab to the box

Crawl-throughs, as they're commonly known, allow occupants to pass between a truck-style cab and the habitation box. They're a very popular modification but not an addition that all owners choose to make; here are some arguments for and against:

Pros:
- No need to leave the vehicle to pass between front and rear.
- Give more light and a more spacious, open feel.
- Confer a view forwards from the habitation box.
- Allow for quick getaways.

Cons:
- Can be difficult to engineer and an ongoing source of niggles.
- Cutting a large hole in the back of the vehicle's cab could, unless appropriately strengthened, compromise its structural integrity.
- If poorly engineered/fabricated, can allow water/dust ingress
- Can make tipping the cab for maintenance a time-consuming affair.
- Increased engine/transmission/road noise.
- May present a security issue (especially during shipping).
- If a cab-to-box cowl is built to help weatherproofing, this can prevent heat escaping from the engine/transmission and potentially lead to heat-soak issues for both mechanical components and occupants.

Many different approaches have been used in the creation of crawl-throughs and results have met with greater or lesser success. In general, they're more difficult to successfully fabricate if the habitation box mounting system permits a large degree of articulation between the cab and the box. Indeed, the difficulties encountered in engineering a crawl-through is one reason that some builders choose a fixed front cross member in a three-point pivoting subframe; notwithstanding the potentially problematic load-point issues such an arrangement can introduce.

▲ **Good for keeping out the weather and dust, but cowlings can lead to heat soak.**

If you're thinking of making a crawl-through, you'll need:
- A framework built into the rear of the cab aperture, constructed in such a way as to reliably accept your flexible joining material of choice. This frame will need to be well engineered in order to replace any structural integrity lost when cutting an aperture in the rear of the vehicle's cab. If you have to cut through *any* reinforced or ribbed sections of cab, this should only be done following consultation with the vehicle's manufacturer.
- Some flexible joining material.
- A framework built into the front of the habitation box, again constructed in such a way to reliably accept your joining material of choice.
- Partitions. No matter how well engineered, to address noise and security issues, a final stage in creation ideally involves building a lockable door or some other solid partition in both the back of the cab and in the front of the habitation box.

No matter what materials or methods you use, you'll need to bear in mind that the crawl-through is an easy one to get wrong. Many a builder has spent frustrating hours remodelling various components in order to ensure reliability. Water, noise and dust will find any weak spot in design and construction with alarming efficiency.

CREATING A CRAWL-THROUGH

Though by no means the only way to build a successful crawl-through, the basic design featured in this sequence has proved reliable.

1 The crawl-through aperture required is marked on the back of the cab.

2 Following half an hour with an angle grinder, some of the now-removed steelwork is marked out for re-use.

3 A strengthening frame is fabricated and temporarily clamped into place.

4 The by-now-cut halves of the cab's original window-frame steelwork are re-sited at either side of the freshly-cut aperture.

5 The strengthening frame and original window-frame steelwork is then all welded together and sealed.

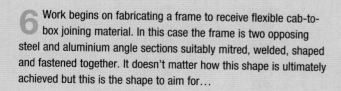

6 Work begins on fabricating a frame to receive flexible cab-to-box joining material. In this case the frame is two opposing steel and aluminium angle sections suitably mitred, welded, shaped and fastened together. It doesn't matter how this shape is ultimately achieved but this is the shape to aim for...

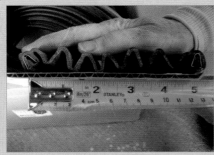

7 …because this rubber accordion-boot material is the key to the whole operation and its inlaid sprung metal attachment clips demand the frame-shape pictured.

8 Push-fitting the boot to the frame.

9 A different project but the same principle. Here a bespoke frame is riveted and bonded to the habitation box.

10 A custom fabrication for the cab-mounted frame section takes shape.

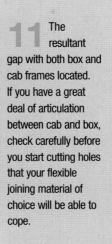

11 The resultant gap with both box and cab frames located. If you have a great deal of articulation between cab and box, check carefully before you start cutting holes that your flexible joining material of choice will be able to cope.

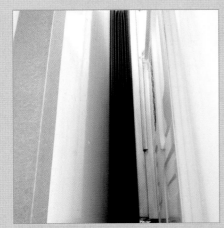

12 Yet another project but again adopting the same principle. Here the accordion-boot is fully fitted and joined at the bottom of the aperture assembly with superglue.

13 Many alternatives are possible and dozens of individual approaches are utilised. Here some PVC 'curtainsider' style material bonded to interlocking wooden frames is employed; weatherproofing is helped by the custom-made cab cowl. Note the seals attached to the rear of the cowl to help keep water and dust out.

14 Depending on the individual truck and your intended use, lockable partitions may be desirable to help with security, temperature and noise – here's one such partition during the early stages of construction.

CUTTING HOLES IN HABITATION BOXES

If using a jigsaw to cut through habitation area walls, be very careful, especially if the panel is a thick one. Jigsaw blades readily bend whilst cutting and thereby fail to cut perpendicular to the jigsaw's plate. You may be following a line to the millimetre in an outside wall, only to find when you complete the cut that the blade has run alarmingly off true and that your inner wall, and all of the material in between, resembles a work of modern art. It can be better to use a very short blade and make the cut twice: once from the outside and once from the inside using carefully drilled pilot holes to mark out the proposed aperture. If the blade runs off, at least it will only be the inner insulating material that has to be dressed. Additionally, when cutting with a jigsaw, always lay some masking tape adjacent to the cut line to prevent the tool's plate from scuffing or scratching your expensive panels.

▼ **Protect panel surfaces from jigsaw plates with masking tape.**

Windows

It's undoubtedly the case that *most* existing self-builders have followed the route of the conventional motor caravan industry and fitted Seitz brand pre fabricated window systems. Though these work well, they are not without problems, nor are they the only option.

Seitz brand windows

The Seitz window system, particularly the S4 derivative, is a very popular choice. The windows are supplied fully complete and are assembled by simply sandwiching the wall of the vehicle between the inner and outer frames of the window assembly and then screwing the frames together. There is absolutely no need to screw into the vehicle's wall itself. The inner frame contains a roller fly screen and a black out blind combination and the window itself comprises a double-glazed acrylic unit. Two different styles of opening mechanism are available: top-hinged and sliding. The frames are engineered to fit a 26mm-thick wall section as standard but by adding home-made spacers to different parts of the assembly (the supplied instructions advise how) and by using different length screws, the manufacturer advises that wall thicknesses of between 1 and 53mm can be catered for. In practice, even greater wall thicknesses can be accommodated.

If your habitation-box structure has a foam core but is intrinsically sturdy, it's not necessary to incorporate battens within the receiving aperture to mount these windows. Battens, for example, would *not* be required in a professionally laminated GRP-ply-Styrofoam-ply-GRP composite structure; the force required to sandwich the two parts of the window frames together is comparatively light and will not cause even the slightest distortion in such a panel.

▼ **31.8 x 3.2mm aluminium flat bar being bonded to the outer frame of a Seitz S4 window to allow fitting into a 54mm-thick wall.**

Pros:
- Lightweight.
- Self-contained inner and outer frames complete with integral blinds and fly screens.
- Easy to fit and reliably watertight if fitted correctly.
- Easy to remove, reseal and replace.
- Vast choice of sizes.
- Reasonably efficient in terms of thermal performance.
- Available with sliding or top-hinged opening mechanisms
- Readily available.

Cons:
- Build quality issues are frequently reported.
- *Very* prone to scratches and damage.
- Relatively expensive.
- Fly screen system does *not* prevent insects passing through ventilation ports.
- Offer virtually no resistance to would-be thieves.
- The acrylic window profile is not flat throughout which can result in a distorted image depending on your viewing angle. This phenomenon is more pronounced in the sliding versions.

KCT windows

These windows are purpose-made for automotive applications and are often the choice of the high-end professional overland-camper manufacturers. They are, though very expensive, undoubtedly of outstanding quality. They comprise double-glazed tempered safety glass complete with an inert gas filling and utilise the highest quality steel reinforced plastic framing, which is constructed in such a way to combat thermal bridging. All metal fixtures and fittings are of high-quality materials specified both to prevent corrosion and to provide the highest possible levels of security. In this regard, a separate stainless-steel shield is also available, which can quickly be fixed or removed without the use of tools (from inside of the vehicle only). Integrated blinds and fly screens can also be purchased and, again, no expense is spared in materials and construction. As standard, the window units are available in five sizes and for walls of 60mm thickness but can also be made to bespoke dimensions to order. Fixing is by permanently bonding the whole unit in situ.

Pros:
- Superb build quality.
- Extremely tough and scratch resistant.
- *Very* secure.
- Exceptional thermal performance.
- Efficient venting positions, even in heavy rain.
- Complementary blinds and fly screens available.
- Undistorted views.

Cons:
- Extremely heavy.
- Very expensive.
- Can be subject to long lead times.
- If flush-fitted as intended, they require different-sized apertures in the inner and outer walls, which might prove difficult to cut in a pre-laminated composite shell. Some *very* careful routing may be required.

Windows based on domestic double-glazed units

Traditional double-glazed units designed for use in domestic applications may well – unless suitably modified – prove unsuitable for the rigours of overland-camper use. Conventional uPVC frames and the structural integrity of the entire assembled unit, though fine if sitting in a dwelling house, can suffer in the overland-camper environment. Apart from the potential problems caused by incessant vibration and road-induced impact, a major issue is the fact that most *standard* double-glazed units are not designed to deal with the constant changes in pressure associated with changes in altitude. Unless the units are built to account for this, then the changes in ambient air pressure at high altitude could result in the glass failing.

In spite of the potential for problems, some builders *have* successfully used domestic-based double-glazed units (see John Brooks' case study feature on page 132 for a particularly impressive example) and if going this route, frames with slimline aluminium profiles, very rugged construction, some kind of pressure compensation arrangement and very heavy-duty glass are useful features to aim for. Fixing will ordinarily be by permanently bonding or screwing the frame into place

▼ **Battens bonded to this aluminium skinned overlander provide a secure mounting substrate for these bespoke double-glazed units.**

and, if screwing, wooden battens or similar will need to be incorporated within the box's window apertures in order to securely hold the fasteners.

Pros:
- ■ Scratch resistant.
- ■ Good security.
- ■ Good thermal performance.
- ■ Undistorted views.
- ■ Glass should, theoretically, be easy to replace in most countries.

Cons:
- ■ Comparatively heavy.
- ■ Depending on construction and materials there is the *potential* for: structural integrity issues, failure of glass at altitude, thermal-bridging issues.
- ■ Requirement to fabricate inner finishing trim and source suitable third-party blinds and fly screens.

Other possibilities

Specialist automotive glazing companies have, for years, been making single-glazed units for panel vans, horseboxes and similar vehicles, but, because of the heat-conducting properties of the glass used in these traditional units, they're arguably less than ideal for any kind of campervan. The same applies to windows traditionally made for boats. Nowhere is this more apparent than with their tendency to produce large quantities of condensation. However, with the advent of heat-reflecting glass, some newer panel vans are now supplied with single-glazed windows that are supposedly very thermally efficient. Very briefly, glass can be coated with thin layers of metal or metal oxide, which does not significantly affect light transmission but which *does* efficiently reflect heat. This means that the worst effects of direct sunlight are reflected back out but, conversely, when it's cold outside, any heat produced within the vehicle will be reflected back in. The possibility of using high-grade heat-reflecting glass, though not currently popular, may be worth considering in some installations.

Finishing trim

If pursuing a less-than-conventional option such as domestic-based double-glazed units, you'll almost certainly need to fabricate some kind of finishing trim to make the interior of the box's window apertures look presentable. You'll also have to come up with an aftermarket solution for fly screens and blinds. Fortunately, there are a number of companies that market self-contained cassette-style units that fulfil these functions and which are easy to fit.

Doors and lockers

Whereas it's possible to *completely* self-build major lockers and doors, obtaining the requisite frame profiles, not to mention locating appropriate sealing rubbers, means that it can be a time-consuming and frustrating job that all too often ends in only partial success. By far the easiest and potentially cheapest door and locker solutions are: to buy prefabricated frames, to have doors professionally made, or to utilise ready-made caravan-style doors.

Prefabricated frames

These can be purchased from larger caravan and motorhome accessory stockists and basically take the form of a one-piece unit comprising a pre-assembled aperture frame, hinges, seals and door frame. They also, in some cases, include a rudimentary lock. The aperture frame bonds

◀ **A prefabricated frame ready to receive your door-panel material of choice.**

or screws into an aperture you've created and it's then up to you to add a suitable panel into the door frame. This is, handily, usually based on the material you originally cut from the aperture. The range of frame sizes is quite limited and the finished assemblies are usually fairly insubstantial structures so this solution is probably best reserved for smaller locker doors.

Having door units made

Though primarily servicing the horsebox and road-transport markets, many companies routinely make ready-to-fit doors and lockers that can be pressed into service in overlanders. One advantage of having doors professionally made is that exact sizes, plus the specifics of hardware such as handles, locks and hinges can be built to your bespoke requirements. It's also a particularly useful feature to be able to choose locks that can be 'suited' – so one key will operate each and every door and locker that you choose to fit. Professional

◀ A professionally made habitation box door ready to simply bond/screw into a suitable aperture.

▶ An example of a small professionally made locker door. Note the drainage channel section bonded in place to divert water from the frame.

manufacturers have ready access to suitable frame profiles, seals and other associated hardware, plus they have the capacity to make composite panels in-house. These resources are not ordinarily available to self-builders, which is why self-building doors and lockers from scratch can be so problematic.

With most horsebox-style constructions, the door panels themselves are *usually* based on a block of closed-cell foam of about 30mm thickness, which is bonded between an inner and outer skinning material of choice to form a three-element composite panel. Matching the door to your box's existing inner and outer skinning material is therefore

▼ Essentially a top-hinged, professionally-made locker door with a Seitz window inset into the panel. Substantial fixing points and sturdy aperture frames would ideally be required to support the gas struts on such fabrications.

a relatively straightforward matter but may mean you'll need to supply the company with the appropriate material if it's anything other than a sheet of plain aluminium. One thing to bear in mind: overall door-panel thickness will be determined by the profile of the (usually extruded aluminium) door frame the company uses so you may have to take advice from the manufacturer regarding the thickness of inner and outer skins they can accommodate.

Once fully assembled, the door is delivered as a completely self-contained unit and this is then simply bonded or screwed into position. An important point to note is that until the aperture frame is firmly attached to the habitation box, the frame is quite a flimsy structure that will easily assume a diamond shape if allowed. It is *vital* to set the frame square into the aperture to ensure the door will sit and seal properly within it. Do *not* bond the frame into the aperture until you are happy all is well.

The large – often windowed – gas-strut-supported hatches that many overlanders sport that open up to provide authentic al fresco experiences are essentially no more than top-hinged horsebox locker doors. Worthy of note is that *all* doors of this type may need some extra work in ensuring rain is channelled away from the top edge otherwise water ingress can be an issue. Luckily, a purpose-made drainage channel is available if you have no home-brewed solution.

Off-the-peg doors

Usually constructed by very large industry-only suppliers and intended for use on caravans, motorhomes or horseboxes, this kind of door can fairly readily be picked up at dealers that specialise in selling the surplus or redundant stock of professional manufacturers and converters. Doors of this type are complete and ready to fit, and sometimes even

◄ **Interior view of a self-contained off-the-peg caravan door complete with decent insulation and window etc.**

come with such niceties as built-in waste bins and fly screens. You are, however, stuck with the supplied interior and exterior finishes which, unless you are willing and able to colour-match, may not blend so well with the remainder of the vehicle. Quality is also a mixed bag – some are very well made, others not so.

General notes on fitting doors

The above types of doors are frequently employed but are not the only options; many other self-made solutions, or unconventional ready-made doors, have been utilised and if you find something that works for you, that's all that really matters. Whichever doors you eventually choose, you're likely to be faced with the common tasks of physically affixing the door frame to the box's aperture and finishing off the interior framework to present a neat installation. How to fix to the aperture will depend greatly on the structural integrity of

◄ **This is only a locker door so the interior trim didn't have to be elaborate. Nonetheless, the mitred aluminium angle bonded into place looks quite neat. The white strip between the mitred aluminium trim and the door-aperture frame is simply a skim of patiently applied adhesive sealer.**

your habitation box. In most cases battens inlaid into the periphery of the aperture will be desirable as these will supply a very solid framework to fully support the sometimes-quite-weighty finished door structure; plus, they will provide a suitable mounting point for gas struts and extra security locks. Battens also allow door frames to be screwed into place rather than permanently bonded, which will facilitate later removal in the event of damage. If, however, your habitation box panels are *intrinsically solid* and permanently bonding does not deter you, there's no reason why frames – particularly in the case of smaller and lighter lockers – can't be bonded in situ without the need for a supporting frame.

Finishing off the interior of the aperture can be done in a number of ways but will usually involve fillets and/or angle sections of a suitable material, cut and mitred into shape before being attached to the inner aperture facings.

Door frames generally can be prone to thermal-bridging issues. Door handles can also be a problem in this regard. Doors that are purpose-made for caravans and motorhomes are perhaps the least likely to present problems whereas the deep aluminium frames usually found in horsebox-type doors are *very* efficient conductors of heat. How to get round any bridging problems will be determined on a case-by-case basis, but be aware that some creative remedial steps may need to be taken.

◄◣ **This door frame was a real problem in terms of thermal bridging so a bi-folding 4mm polycarbonate shield was fabricated to prevent warm air from reaching any part of the door or frame. This cured the problem completely. As a bonus, the shield can also be deployed in its own right to let in light but keep out the weather or winged insects.**

Roof lights, hatches and vents

Roof lights, hatches and vents perform a number of useful functions: they let in light, provide ventilation and, in some cases, allow access to the vehicle's roof from the interior. Differentiating a hatch from a vent is somewhat arbitrary but for our purposes the following distinctions are made.

Roof lights

Roof lights are transparent, opening structures of a comparatively large size that are primarily manufactured for the leisure-vehicle market for use in caravans and motorhomes. They are designed to both let in light and provide ventilation. In order to provide ventilation, they can be opened to a greater or lesser extent and in some cases even incorporate a tilt and slide function. However, they're generally poorly suited as an access point for climbing on to the roof as they rarely open past around 80°. They also tend to sit very proud, high above the roofline and – as they're also comparatively flimsy items – are vulnerable to overhanging branches and wires etc. On the plus side

▼ **Typical motor caravan roof light.**

they're usually quite well insulated and so not particularly prone to thermal bridging. They're also generally neatly finished and more often than not come supplied with integrated fly screens and blackout blinds.

Hatches

Hatches are fully opening, usually transparent structures, which, notwithstanding their marine roots, are very popular amongst overland-camper builders. They tend to be altogether tougher than leisure-vehicle roof lights – indeed some can safely be walked on – and of a lower and sleeker profile. Accordingly, they're less vulnerable to damage if caught by objects sliding along the roof. They're also comparatively inexpensive and often open up to at least 170°, so provide unrestricted access to the roof. On the negative side, they *tend* to be less refined than motorhome-specific roof lights and can, depending on the model chosen, be far more prone to thermal bridging. A further issue is that hatches are less likely to come supplied with any integrated fly screens or blinds.

Roof vents

Roof vents are generally smaller than roof lights and hatches. Their main purpose is to allow *permanent* ventilation rather

1 As the laminated composite panel in view is quite thick, this hole was carefully cut from inside and out with a jigsaw using pilot holes and pencil marks as guides. In this instance no strengthening battens were deemed necessary as the roof is supported underneath by full height cabinets and the panel's outer layer of ply is thick enough to accept the hatch's locating screws.

2 A good tip in any circumstance where holes are made in the habitation box. Liberally spread sealer over all of the exposed surfaces so in the event that water finds its way past any fittings, at least it won't destroy any vulnerable material.

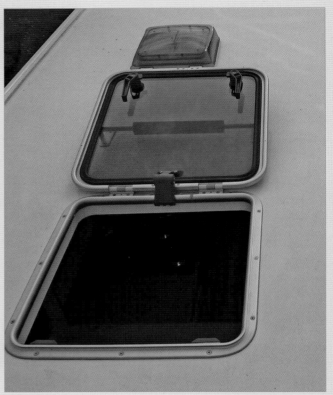

3 The hatch is bedded on Carafax Caraseal IDL 99 non-setting mastic and is accompanied by a very thin bead of Sikaflex 521 round the very perimeter of the hatch's frame. The Sikaflex provides just enough of a bond to prevent the non-setting mastic from bleeding out. Without it, the mastic tends to continue to work its way out of the joint – even after several months. The stainless-steel screws are only lightly nipped down and each screw hole and thread was given a dab of Sikaflex to keep water out of the plywood.

4 Note how low the hatch sits compared to caravan-style roof lights. Marine hatches are also generally more robust, so stand a fair chance of survival if (when) whacked with a tree branch.

5 Full access to the roof from within is easy. Note how the hatch is supported on its plastic handle pivots. This particular model cannot open to a full 180° as the strain would break the hinge and/or frame.

6 The cosmetic dilemma often faced when fitting hatches, doors and windows in cases where the item isn't supplied with a finishing trim kit.

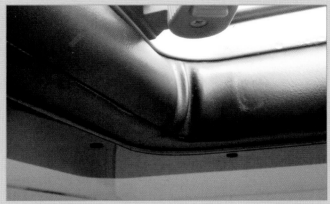

7 This is the same hatch as the previous image: the trim was totally handmade.

8 As it happens a (rather expensive) trim kit is an optional extra for the hatch in question and this comes with turnbuckles as standard that are intended to support…

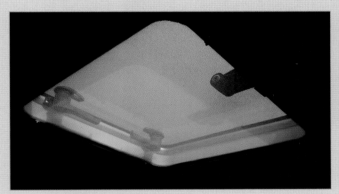

9 …the accompanying supplied fly screen.

10 Devil in the detail. To make fly screen removal/refitting quicker and easier, two custom-made lips were fabricated to replace two of the turnbuckles.

11 These are also far more reliable supports for a custom-made 4mm polycarbonate shield that was cut to exact dimensions by a local supplier. The aluminium frame of the hatch is a very efficient thermal bridge and in cooler/humid conditions condensation would form on the frame at an alarming rate. Now, when travelling in such conditions, the fly screen can be replaced by the shield, which prevents warm interior air from reaching the frame and completely cures the problem. Ideally, the manufacturer would employ a frame material that is a poor thermal conductor, or at least introduce some thermal breaks into the frame's design.

12 If you are going to ship your vehicle, or are worried about leaving it unattended, apertures in the roof leave vehicles vulnerable. Here is one brilliant solution that involved creating a bespoke frame the size of the entire roof and then fabricating a series of lifting / lockable panels and barred inserts. This is definitely not a single-weekend job…

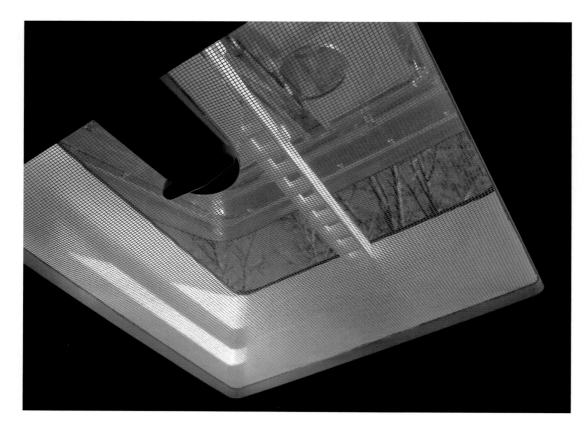

◀ A 280 x 280mm roof vent with built-in fly screen. The two clear acrylic skins are formed in such a way that ventilation is permanent. This particular model cranks open widely to allow excellent air flow when required.

than let in light. They come in a myriad of designs and sizes ranging from the very small 'mushroom' style to quite large and sophisticated items that, visually at least, resemble small roof lights. It is vital to have some high-level permanent ventilation in your overland camper otherwise it *will* suffer from a build-up of stale air and, in some ambient conditions, invite an unpleasant build-up of condensation.

Fitting roof lights, hatches and vents

Holes cut into the roof *will* weaken the overall structure and care should be taken to avoid placing heavy point loads (e.g. standing) too close to apertures unless the roof structure is specifically strengthened to cope.

Roof lights, hatches and vents are all fitted in a similar way. They tend to be bedded on a non-setting mastic and either screw directly to the roof or, in a similar manner to Seitz windows, may be designed with an inner and outer frame that are screwed together and simply sandwich the roof panel. Again, as in the case of windows and doors, battens set into the roof will supply a solid mounting substrate but may not strictly be necessary if your roof is an intrinsically sturdy structure. In the event that your chosen roof light, hatch or vent is one that is designed to sandwich the roof panel, be aware that it's often the case that the entire assembly will be designed to fit roofs up to a maximum of around 45–50mm thickness. So in some instances, unless special versions are available, you may find

the product requires modification to fit the typically thicker roofs of overland campers.

Larger apertures in the roof can present a security risk, especially if shipping a vehicle. If you do fit roof lights or hatches and intend to ship, you'd be very wise to build in some security measures. In the case of roof vents, it's advisable to choose units on the small side to prevent them being used as a point of entry. 280 x 280mm and 400 x 400mm are popular vent sizes. The former should offer reasonable security, the latter probably not.

Locating roof hardware is a matter of personal choice, but you may wish to bear a couple of points in mind. All roof apertures present the possibility of leaks – or at least the build-up of condensation which can then drip – so placement directly over sleeping areas is often avoided. That said, sleeping areas *are* prone to condensation generally and air here can quickly become stale, so a small vent somewhere in the *vicinity* of sleeping quarters will be a useful addition; mushroom-style or 'five-way' vents are good choices in these circumstances. Five-way vents in particular are useful when conditions are very hot. This is because, as the name suggests, they can be opened in five different ways and so can always be angled to make the most of any breeze that may exist and deflect at least a little moving air into the vehicle (or likewise allow some air flow but without letting in rain). When it comes to kitchen areas and shower rooms, good ventilation and extra light are always welcome so vents in these areas are highly recommended.

Ventilation

Ventilation is often overlooked but is a very important issue to get right. Air needs to be able to circulate throughout the entire finished habitation area, including all lockers, furniture bases and storage areas. Adequate ventilation (along with addressing thermal-bridging issues) is the best way to head off the unpleasant and ultimately damaging phenomenon of condensation. In cold and humid conditions, insufficient air flow *will* eventually lead to mouldy clothes and soft furnishings, and can even cause structural issues.

Permanent roof-mounted ventilation needs to be complemented with *permanent* floor vents. These are easily fitted and require no more than screwing or bonding into place in holes bored through the habitation box floor in selected spots around the floorpan. Not only will floor vents promote the free flow of air but they will also act as gas-drop vents in the event of an LPG leak. The butane/propane mixes used in LPG systems are heavier than air and, if a leak develops, will tend to drop out of the vehicle rather than build up within, along with all the consequent risks… Two points are worth bearing in mind when situating and fitting floor vents. First, try to position them away from areas exposed to high concentrations of trail dust, for example directly behind the rear axle. If left exposed, dust will be drawn into the vehicle as it's driven along and can create a real mess inside. If it's impossible to avoid areas of high dust concentration, then some kind of cover or dust deflector will be an asset. Secondly, utilise the method pictured in the 'Fitting a hatch' sequence, and smear a waterproofing layer of silicone sealer in any hole you drill through the floor before affixing the vent. This will ensure that if the very significant road spray thrown up whilst driving in the wet gets past the vent, at least it won't penetrate any of the floor's constituent materials.

Though slightly getting ahead of ourselves, reiterating the theme of free-flowing air, when you eventually get to the point of constructing furniture, ensure that each partitioned section that forms the base of seats, storage areas and so on has *at least* one vent hole of a minimum of 60mm in diameter situated in each face of each compartment. Do not underestimate the need to keep air flowing throughout the interior structures of the vehicle. Without it, as well as condensation and the unpleasant sensation of stale, oxygen-depleted air, components *like compressor fridges and blown-air heaters may* not function correctly. Overheating and air-starvation issues relating to such appliances are commonplace and unwitting owners can spend many frustrated hours incorrectly focusing on perceived internal problems in 'faulty' equipment…

▲ ▼ **Floor vents are simple to fit but make a huge difference to the well-being of the vehicle interior and occupants. For areas near axles etc., partial covers prevent trail dust from filling the vehicle.**

CHAPTER 9

Water and gas systems

PART 1 – WATER SYSTEMS

- Fresh water
- Waste water
- Plumbing and fittings

PART 2 – GAS SYSTEMS

- An introduction and overview
- Design considerations for LPG systems
- Building the system – general hints and tips

Because the hardware associated with water and gas systems is bulky and requires 'first-fix plumbing', it's best, whilst still at this stage in the overall project, to fully plan each utility system and to fit at least the major components of each; *before* building furniture.

PART 1 – WATER SYSTEMS

At one kilogram per litre, too much water can be a liability in terms of sheer weight: too little means that a trip can be dominated by an almost constant and stressful quest for supplies. Though each extreme has its advocates, established wisdom suggests 200 litres is bordering on insufficient whilst anything over 500 litres may begin to prove something of a liability.

Fresh water

Fresh-water tanks are available off the peg or can be fully custom made. Tank attributes that are field proven include:

- An internal baffle system if the tank is over about 150 litres in capacity. This is desirable in order to prevent problems caused by unrestrained sloshing mass.
- A large-bore filler neck to allow easy filling from portable containers in the event that no pressurised water supply is available.
- At least one inspection hatch large enough to allow every corner of the tank to be reached in order to be properly cleaned out. This can also be used instead of a large bore filler neck to allow direct filling from a portable container.
- A dark colouration to prevent the entry of light: this can help subdue biological growth.
- An efficient *permanent* breather tube to allow air to be displaced in rapid-fill situations or in order to avoid problems caused by pressure differentials brought about by changes in altitude or when water is drawn off for domestic use. The breather tube should be free from the potential for blockage at all times, including blockages caused by low spots which could pool water.
- A drain point that will allow a full draindown for cleaning and inspection, or to prevent frost damage if the system is decommissioned in times of freezing temperatures.

When it comes to placement, consider very carefully the weight distribution of the vehicle in general and try to avoid placing the tank in a position that may jeopardise good overall balance. If possible, a point somewhere close to the centreline of the vehicle and just ahead of the rear axle is recommended; placement *behind* the rear axle is generally best avoided. Wherever you manage to accommodate the fresh-water tank, it will need to be secured very comprehensively and as well as substantial mounts for the tank itself, it's wise to build bulkheads or furniture tight to the tank's outer dimensions to afford further restraint. Placement *inside* the vehicle is highly desirable in order to ward off potential freezing issues, but if you must place it outside, insulation and/or a heating source will be a necessity: unless of course you'll only ever use the vehicle in warmer climates.

▼ **100mm x 100mm x 3.2mm aluminium angle screwed and bonded to the floor to provide a ground-level restraint for a large water tank. Additionally, furniture was subsequently built tight up to the tank to totally constrain movement in any direction.**

▲ **Beneath this furniture is a 345-litre tank supplied by CAK. Unfortunately, the tank is un-baffled and on one trip the force of sloshing water was so great that it blew the just-visible inspection hatch cover clean out of the threads leading to a serious flooding problem. The pictured 'restraint' was fabricated to lock the inspection cover down to prevent a repetition.**

▼ **A 30psi Shurflo diaphragm pump feeding into an accumulator tank. Note how the supplied rubber-isolator-feet of the pump are not mounted direct to the floor but instead on hardwood battens, which are themselves bonded down with a large bead of Sikaflex. This provides an extra layer of isolation to combat the not-insignificant disturbance caused by pump resonance.**

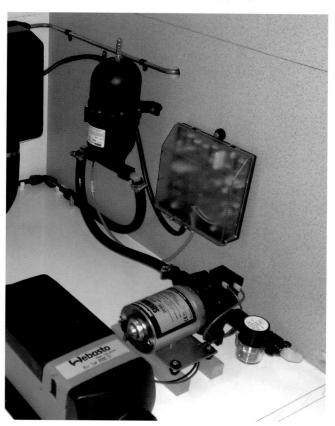

Don't underestimate the effect of half a tonne or more of water moving around: sloshing water can create enough force to cause very real problems. It has even been known to tear tanks away from poor mountings. If internal baffles can't be obtained in larger tanks, it's worth considering a twin-tank system.

Filling

Filling, ideally, will be from a clean tap and via a food-grade hose. Food-grade hoses are readily available through leisure vehicle and marine suppliers and can even be obtained in a fold-flat design. Though these are attractive in terms of storage, it sometimes happens that insufficient supply pressure is further inhibited by the constricting effects of the structure, meaning fill times can be painfully slow. In circumstances where there is no mains supply and reliance may be upon a spring, trough, stream or well etc., the use of a submersible pump and/or a portable container is the norm. Pre-filtering water from such sources is desirable and a decent strainer will prevent larger foreign objects from finding their way into your water tank.

Pumps

Water pumps are generally of two kinds: submersible or inline diaphragm. Submersible pumps sit within water tanks and are electrically triggered by micro switches built into every single tap in the plumbing system. Though such pumps are frequently used in small conventional motor caravans, they tend to be less powerful than their inline diaphragm counterparts and, because of the reliance on numerous micro switches, the system as a whole tends towards complexity and unreliability. Inline diaphragm pumps are comparatively powerful and are automatically electrically operated by one solitary internal switch, which is triggered following a lowering of internal water pressure. When you open a tap, pressure within the system drops and the internal switch closes and supplies power to the pump motor. Diaphragm pumps are generally self-priming and capable of lifting water to a degree so their placement can be flexible. Ideally, they should be internally mounted and benefit from a residual heat source to prevent freezing issues. They should also be sited so they're easily accessible for maintenance – they frequently come with a course-filter bowl attached and this requires sporadic attention. Diaphragm pumps can be noisy and resonate heavily in operation so if it's possible to build them into well noise-insulated areas then so much the better.

If your system is large and complex, or if you're going to install water filters, a high-pressure pump (capable of at least 30psi) is recommended as the resistance offered by large systems and filters can restrict flow significantly. A vital addition to any diaphragm pump is an isolation switch that should be used to cut all power to the pump whenever the vehicle is in

Accumulator tanks are basically a diaphragm-equipped chamber that allows space for the head of pumped water to expand into before being distributed around the system. They essentially absorb surges and reduce the fluctuation of pressure within the system thereby smoothing flow from taps and reducing pump cycling. Though not absolutely necessary, they're a cheap and simple addition that works.

motion, left unattended, or even whilst attended but during sleep. Without isolation, if any leak develops in the plumbing system, the pressure switch in the pump would trigger and pump the entire contents of your water tank into the habitation area. This is not a situation you ever want to encounter.

Filtration and purification

Such is the potential for serious illness from waterborne toxins and pathogens that it makes good sense to treat, at a minimum, your drinking-water supplies. In *most* overland camper applications, treatment can take three basic forms:

■ Chemical treatment of the entire contents of the fresh water tank, most usually comprising chlorine- or iodine-based applications.
■ A physical strainer-style filtration process where a semi-permeable medium is used to physically prevent impurities from passing. This kind of filter will not remove bad tastes and smells so if you've treated your tank with chlorine dioxide tablets, for example, this will still be apparent at the point(s) of delivery.
■ A chemical strainer-style filtration process where a medium such as carbon or charcoal is used to not only physically strain water but also to adhere impurities by adsorption. This kind of medium can remove bad tastes and smells as well as physical impurities.

It's possible to employ any combination of these treatment systems and some overlanders go so far as to purify the entire water system by pre-filtering water added to the tank, chemically treating the tank contents with chlorine/iodine etc. and then subjecting this pre-treated water to a series of increasingly fine physical strainer-style filters before finally utilising a carbon-based purifier on each and every tap used for consumption. Though adopting this thorough approach is undoubtedly a very safe option, it's also expensive and requires regular maintenance – filters require frequent replacement.

Not all are convinced of the necessity for whole-system treatments and there are advocates of far less onerous approaches. Some simply treat water intended for

consumption *after* it has been dispensed from the tap and rely upon an 'and/or' combination of boiling, commercially available purification tablets and fully portable backpack-style purifiers to treat small amounts of water on a totally as-and-when-required basis. Still others eschew all treatment and just rely completely on bottled water. The level to which you employ purification systems, then, is largely a matter of your attitude to risk having considered the water quality you expect to encounter.

In the name of compromise, and with a nod towards simplicity, reliability and ease of maintenance, a perfectly viable system might comprise just one spur of the cold water side of the plumbing system into which is first installed a physical strainer-style filter, followed in series by a carbon- or charcoal-based filter, all serving just one dedicated tap used solely for drinking, food preparation and cleaning teeth. In such a system (if well maintained), water *should* be purified to a high standard *plus* be largely free of bad tastes and odours. A further advantage with this approach is that because only a comparatively small quantity of water is subject to full treatment, and because the physical strainer will remove many impurities, the service life of the final carbon-based filter will be usefully improved.

If multiple filters in series and chemically based solutions do not appeal, very simple (in terms of plumbing) but rather more expensive integrated multi-stage filtration systems are also available. These boast a mixture of technologies in just one unit, which claim to strain, adsorb *and* add a further stage of purification by trapping impurities using a process of reverse osmosis. It's fair to say such fully integrated purifiers rarely receive negative comments or poor reviews and are, at a price, a popular solution.

Waste water

Waste (or grey) water tanks are fitted to collect water that's been used for washing, showering, cleaning teeth or cooking. They tend to be of a much smaller capacity than fresh water tanks and are often placed, as is logical for drainage purposes, outside and beneath the habitation area. Placement is not as critical as with large fresh water tanks, but attention will need to be paid to good insulation and/or an external heating source, especially around the drain valve in order to prevent an ice cube of mammoth proportions totally preventing any further use of sinks and shower trays.

In order to get round the issues of complexity, weight and potential freezing, some builders utilise *very* small grey water tanks and drain them frequently, whilst others – especially those that tend towards avoiding areas of human habitation – do away with a tank altogether and simply drain directly to the ground. In all cases it's important to drain responsibly. If draining directly to ground, it's vital to use biodegradable cleaning products, to avoid draining into a watercourse, and to ensure that no harmful contaminants whatsoever are deposited. If you wouldn't pour it on your own patio, don't pour it straight to ground. Also vitally important is public image: there's often a perception of harm even if perfectly clean fresh water is allowed to drain from a vehicle. If you do decide to eschew a fixed grey water tank, the use of a portable collection container is recommended in cases where there might be *any* possibility – or even public perception – of adverse environmental impact. Note well, in some areas, it may even be contrary to law to deposit waste water anywhere other than at authorised disposal points.

Plumbing and fittings

Many motor caravan parts suppliers carry an entire range of plumbing fittings for both fresh and waste-water systems and the use of good-quality equipment is highly recommended; cheap and flimsy fittings are often a source of ongoing grief. Worm-drive style clips especially are a frequent cause of trouble and their use is best avoided. If their use is unavoidable, at least use a high-quality version. On the fresh-water side, 12mm or 15mm semi-rigid plastic

▼ **An example of a fairly typical water system.**

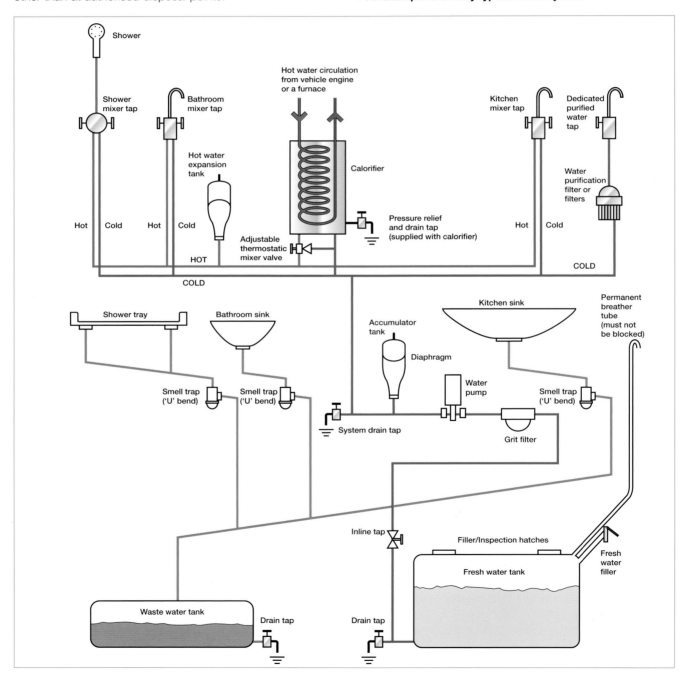

▲ **Push-fit semi-rigid plumbing systems are quick to assemble and generally very reliable. Note that a couple of collets are not yet clipped to the fittings: when clicked into place these prevent accidental decoupling.**

pipe and push-fit fittings are reliable and are very easy to work. Entire systems can be built comparatively quickly and subsequent modifications are easy to make. Each push-fit fitting is fully demountable and can be removed and replaced without issue. On the waste side, large-bore and internally smooth fittings and pipework are recommended.

Slow-to-drain sinks and shower trays are a pain. Avoid any flexible grey water drainage pipework that has spiralled ridges inside, these are slow to drain, can trap food particles and block easily. If you are draining into a grey water tank, the use of smell traps is recommended as it doesn't take long for foul-smelling water sloshing around in the holding tank to make its presence known; indeed, it can even slosh back into shower trays in poorly designed systems … you have been warned! For grey-water drainage valves, choose a sturdy version: flimsy items can readily break.

PART 2 – GAS SYSTEMS

An introduction and overview

If used for cooking duties only, a typical 2 x 12kg Liquefied Petroleum Gas (LPG) cylinder set-up will last for many, many months. A typical burner will consume gas at a *very approximate* rate of 100 grams per hour. A very rough calculation, even accounting for inefficiencies, should give well over 100 'burner hours' per typical 12kg bottle. If, however, you also rely on LPG for heating, consumption will increase dramatically, not because heaters are inefficient (a typical 2,400W blown-air gas heater simply *maintaining* a reasonable room temperature will consume gas at the rate of 100–200 grams per hour), but because in cold conditions heaters tend to be used for *many hours a day*. If, as well as cooking and heating with gas, you also decide to run an LPG-powered refrigerator, the need to replenish gas supplies may start to dictate your trip. Your cooking, heating and refrigeration preferences should, then, help to determine an LPG capacity that will meet your individual needs.

LPG systems are basically divided into three distinct sections:
- The storage side. This includes filler tubes, tanks/cylinders and any pre-regulator pipework. All of this hardware holds LPG in both its liquid and gaseous state at very high pressure.
- The regulator. This is a device responsible for reducing the high-pressure gaseous LPG held in the storage side to a very low-pressure gaseous state for use in the distribution side.
- The distribution side. This includes distribution pipework and appliances that hold low-pressure LPG in a gaseous state ready to be burned as required.

Storage vessels

The most often encountered bulk-storage vessels are:

- Refillable fixed tanks. Fixed LPG tanks are available in many different sizes and are, as the name suggests, permanently fixed to a vehicle, usually to the chassis or subframe. If the country you're in has LPG-powered cars, these tanks can be refilled at fuel station forecourts in much the same way as if taking on petrol or diesel. A filling point mounted on the vehicle (but remotely from the tank) is used to accept a specifically designed nozzle from an LPG-dispensing pump. If the country you are in does not have LPG-powered cars, refills *may* still be possible but are far less straightforward and will usually require an amenable bulk supplier. NB: tanks are specifically of the vapour take-off type, meaning only the gaseous content is tapped off for distribution to the camper's appliances. They are of a fundamentally different design to the type of tank used on vehicles that use gas as fuel for their engines.

■ Refillable cylinders. These are identical in concept to a fixed tank but take the form of a typical gas cylinder. They are, like fixed tanks, available in different sizes but are only *semi*-permanently mounted in a dedicated locker. They have the advantages of portability and ease of substitution if required.

■ Exchangeable cylinders. These cylinders are purchased or hired and simply used until empty whereupon ownership is relinquished or, in the event that you're still in an area supported by the original supplier, may be returned for a refund or traded-in against a pre-filled replacement. They can only (safely/lawfully) be refilled by authorised outlets. Use of such cylinders remains common throughout the world, but their physical design and requisite fittings have absolutely no standardisation. In spite of a myriad of versions and problems surrounding compatibility, exchangeable cylinders have the massive advantage of being comparatively easily obtainable wherever you happen to be.

FILLING REFILLABLE VESSELS

Tanks and cylinders should only ever be filled up to a maximum of 80% of their capacity. More than this can cause vessel failure with predictable consequences. Helpfully, most refillable tanks and cylinders have a stop-cock style of valve fitted internally that prevents overfilling. Vessels simply won't accept more LPG when they reach the 80% point. Check with the manufacturer to ensure the mechanical shut-off device is a feature before purchase.

Where pumped LPG is available on forecourts, different styles of pump nozzle may be encountered. Depending on the design of your own particular filling point, three or four commonly available adapters will be needed to ensure you'll be able to match whichever nozzle you encounter to the filling point on your vehicle. A quick internet search or advice from a refillable system supplier will see you duly equipped.

It's helpful to be able to monitor LPG reserves. Float gauges are fairly reliable indicators of the amount of LPG that remains in a refillable vessel. Gauges that rely on pressure to give an indication of gas remaining are almost useless and best avoided.

Regulators are a vital system component, but, to understand factors that affect their function and use, a quick overview of some of the fundamental characteristics of LPG and LPG-burning appliances may be helpful. LPG, for our purposes, takes the form of butane, propane, or a subtle mixture of both. Butane has a higher calorific value so is more efficient per kilo; however, it suffers from the major disadvantage of a relatively high boiling point. Butane will not turn to gas at temperatures below 0°C so will stubbornly sit in your storage tank/cylinder in its unusable liquid form in cold conditions. Propane, though not as calorifically efficient, becomes gaseous at temperatures slightly below −40°C so will be usable in all but the most extreme conditions. The self-fill type LPG available at garage forecourts is essentially a mixture of both butane and propane: optimised by petrochemical companies to suit the climatic conditions in which it's sold.

LPG-burning appliances will have, somewhere on them, a label indicating the gas operating pressure they're designed to work at and, in some cases, there may even be two values quoted depending on whether the gas in use is butane or propane. *Typically*, the gas pressure required by appliances ranges from 28 millibar (mbar) to 50mbar.

Propane, because of its inferior calorific value, ordinarily requires to be delivered to an appliance at a slightly higher pressure than butane in order to burn at the same intensity. However, since 2004, all LPG-burning appliances sold new in Europe have been designed to run at a compromised 'dual-gas' pressure of 30mbar. This pressure was agreed as a standard as it results in the safe functioning of the appliance irrespective of whether the gas in use is butane, propane, or a mixture of both.

LPG in tanks and bottles is stored at a pressure far higher than appliances could cope with and, crucially, the fuel is stored in two states. The lower part of the storage vessel contains LPG in its liquid state whilst the upper part contains 'boiled' LPG in its gaseous state.

Enter the regulator: it is the LPG in its high-pressure gaseous state that the device taps off and 'regulates' to the requisite very low pressure before allowing it to pass into the distribution system for use by appliances. The regulator, then, ideally needs to be optimised to take into account both the type of gas being used and the pressure rating of the appliance(s) being served.

As if this is not complex enough, there is a further twist: not all regulators share the same fundamental design. There are two distinct types: those which affix directly to the LPG storage vessel, otherwise known as 'on-bottle' regulators, and those which fix to a suitable point on the vehicle itself, commonly known as 'bulkhead-mounted' regulators. On-bottle regulators reduce gas pressure *as* it leaves the storage vessel and utilise a short length of purpose-made flexible *low*-pressure pipe to connect the supply into the vehicle's purpose-made gas-distribution system. Bulkhead-mounted regulators, however, do not reduce the pressure of gas as it leaves the storage vessel and therefore require the use of purpose-made *high*-pressure hoses or 'pig tails' to initially link the storage vessel outlet to the regulator before subsequently entering the vehicle's low-pressure distribution system.

Design considerations for LPG systems

The prospect of having a year's supply of gas on board and the luxury of simple (and comparatively cheap) refills may, at first, make large-capacity refillable tanks or cylinders seem like an attractive option. All is not so straightforward, though, as the sheer bulk and weight of mammoth tanks can pose considerable mounting issues and threaten the quest to keep overall weight manageable. Additionally, shipping with LPG on board is often absolutely prohibited and furthermore, forecourts and other outlets dispensing LPG are *not* encountered worldwide. Indeed, in some countries LPG can be extremely difficult or even impossible to obtain. For these reasons, if venturing outside of the developed world (or indeed *within* some parts of it), though a refillable reserve remains desirable, it's highly recommended that you design your system in such a way

that you can also easily incorporate *at least* one locally obtained exchangeable cylinder.

Here though, as alluded to above, arises a problem of compatibility. There is absolutely no standardisation of exchangeable cylinders and even within the same country you might come across vessels with totally different fittings, which demand a completely unique regulator. Fortunately, on-bottle regulators, which are in use domestically, recreationally and commercially throughout the world, offer something of a lifeline. They're cheap, acceptably reliable and, crucially, offer the most easily accessible compatibility solution. Wherever exchangeable cylinders are sold, you'll be able to buy an on-bottle regulator *that is suitable* for use with that cylinder. Furthermore, connecting this to your gas-distribution system is simply a case of attaching the regulator to your length of low-pressure flexible pipe. So far so good … but (maybe unsurprisingly by now) there may be a further problem. The regulator you manage to obtain may well not reduce the pressure of the cylinder contents *to match the requirements* of your on-board appliances. In this eventuality, you should seek advice from your appliance manufacturers

▼ **The simplest version of a remote fill point for refillable fixed tanks and cylinders. This fitting is threaded to accommodate various adapters. Approved high-pressure pipe must be used between this point and the vessel being filled.**

DANGEROUS / ILLEGAL PRACTICES

1. If you find yourself using an exchangeable cylinder, complete with compatible regulator, but this is mismatched to the pressure requirements of your appliances then you should, as stated in the main text, seek advice from the relevant manufacturer before operating any appliance.

2. The flames produced by burners can be indicative of system health:

▪ On hobs, a blue flame with no yellow tips that additionally does not produce sooty deposits on pans and kettles is an indicator of good system health.

▪ In grills and ovens, a *slight* yellow tinge to otherwise healthy blue flames is nothing to worry about.

▪ If flames show long yellow tips, and this is combined with sooting on pans etc., you may well have an overly rich gas mixture.

▪ If the flame lifts away from a burner or does not readily stay alight from all burner apertures there may well be too much air in the mixture. If this also smells 'gassy' and emits smoke from the flame tips *this can be an indicator of carbon monoxide production.*

If your system shows any signs of burning overly rich or overly lean, *do not operate your LPG appliances until you've had the system professionally checked.*

3. In many countries around the world (and in spite of all that has been written) it's actually possible to sidestep nearly all compatibility issues because it *is* (theoretically at least) possible to self-refill exchangeable cylinders irrespective of their country of origin. However, in order to do this, you need to possess the correct hardware, the correct know-how and an understanding that you can quite literally be risking life and limb ... and not just your own. Though theoretically possible then, the practice is *unequivocally* discouraged, not least because it's so easy to overfill cylinders past their 80% safe-fill limit and render them prone to explosive failure. It's not the kind of mistake you get to make twice...

▲ **One of many types of on-bottle regulator. Note the (orange) low-pressure pipe is gas-specific and this must be the case: LPG can quickly degrade non-gas-specific rubber pipe.**

before proceeding. Incorrectly used appliances can – and do – produce lethal emissions and/or go up in flames.

Bulkhead-mounted regulators, though guaranteeing a fixed pressure, do *not* offer the same versatility as on-bottle regulators. This is, essentially, because of the sheer inconsistency of cylinder fittings across the world and because high-pressure pig tails are a comparatively new and not yet generally accepted or supported innovation. Even carrying numerous different styles of pig tail – augmented by even more bottle-fitting-to-pig-tail adapters – is unlikely to provide a foolproof solution. A further reason to sidestep bulkhead-mounted regulators revolves around an issue of reliability. Many owners of these regulators have had problems with the regulator itself becoming blocked with oily deposits and thereby rendering the entire gas system useless. The reasons for this phenomenon are not widely agreed upon, but suffice to say that the prospect of simply being unable to connect to a local exchangeable cylinder, plus the potential for blockages, mean that bulkhead-mounted regulators are not (currently) the best choice for an overland camper.

▼ **A typical bulkhead-mounted regulator reducing gas in the high pressure black pig-tail hose to very low pressure before feeding it into the copper distribution pipework.**

Building the system – general hints and tips

There will, in all probability, be legislation covering the building and commissioning of LPG systems in your country of origin; this is certainly the case in the UK. Naturally you are obliged to adhere to any regulations that apply to you. Notwithstanding *legal* requirements, some purely pragmatic advice follows.

Fixed refillable tanks should be mounted well out of harm's way. There should be no prospect of grounding out the vessel, or its fittings, when traversing trails and poor roads. As tanks are usually mounted with dedicated steel strapping, once fixed, they're at least very secure and not prone to being torn from fittings on rough surfaces.

If you are using cylinders instead of – or as well as – a fixed tank, you'll need to pay close attention to mounting them securely. In a conventional road-bound motor caravan, cylinders can typically sit on rubberised matting and be restrained with the use of a single purpose-made strap. This arrangement is usually sufficient given gentle road use but is far from appropriate in an overland camper. For our purposes, at least two straps per cylinder are recommended, as well as utilising stops to physically prevent the base of the cylinder from 'shuffling' around. A false floor, about 50mm deep created with a circular aperture in which to drop a cylinder's base, is a good way to achieve this. Naturally, the aperture will need to be as big as the largest cylinder you are likely to carry. In the event that smaller cylinders are substituted, the aperture can always be packed out to take up the excess space. An additional mounting issue is one of a cylinder's propensity to rotate *within* its straps to the point where excess stress can be placed on pipework and fittings. Again, depending on the actual nature of the issue, you may have to be creative. However you achieve it, cylinders need to be fixed very securely and ideally within their own sealed (but drop-vented) locker, separate from the habitation area.

The area in which LPG is stored should not be accompanied by anything that could be a source of ignition, so no fuses, light bulbs etc. If the DIY option to safely mount cylinders is proving troublesome, commercially available lockers and cylinder restraints are available to help; however, they can be expensive.

Refillable tanks and cylinders utilise remote-mounted filler tubes complete with their own dedicated fittings. Stick

▲ **Working out the safe positioning of a fixed refillable tank in order that a custom steel mounting rack can be made. The high-pressure pipe to the right is to a remote fill point, the high-pressure pipe to the left is the pig-tail take-off and can be traced to a bulkhead-mounted regulator … forlornly awaiting the construction of an actual bulkhead.**

with standard filling hardware; don't be tempted to try to substitute inferior products. LPG will degrade natural-rubber products and, as it's dispensed from pumps into tanks via the dedicated pipework at very high pressure, it will quickly find any weak spots. The same holds true for the flexible take-off pipework from tanks and cylinders *post* regulator. Use low-pressure pipework designed for the purpose and keep its use to a minimum.

Quality fittings should be used to connect any flexible take-off pipe to a dedicated metal (usually copper) pipe distribution system, which should itself be securely fitted to bulkheads using non-abrasive clips at frequent intervals. At all stages, with all gas pipework, take great care to prevent it coming into contact with any other fixtures and fittings that might cause chafing, and site

▶ **Twin refillable cylinders with on-bottle regulators. The black pipes are filler pipes that connect to the external fill point. Note the home-made aluminium tube/threaded bar bracing between the two bottles. This prevents them turning in their mounts and stressing pipework. Note too the twin straps per bottle and rubber stops at floor level to stop any lateral movement.**

◀ It makes sense to be able to isolate different circuits. The LPG-feed is from the right; individual circuits exit beneath. Note the non-chafing nylon clips used to fix the copper pipe to the wall.

LPG SYSTEM EXAMPLE

Though there are many options to solving the issue of sourcing and storing LPG, for the reasons discussed in the main text, a combination of a user-refillable vessel and a locally obtained cylinder complete with its compatible regulator takes some beating.

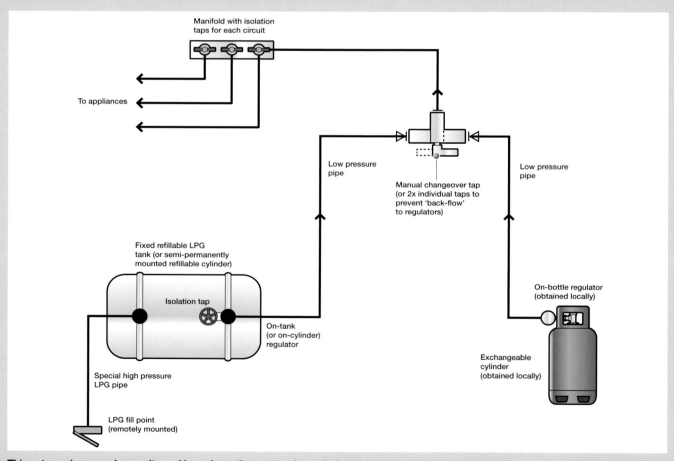

This set-up gives good capacity and is perhaps the most universally (safely) serviceable. The refillable side can comprise either a fixed tank or a semi-permanently mounted cylinder. Though fittings to support bulkhead-mounted regulators are now the norm, alternative fittings are available to allow the use of on-tank/on-bottle regulators. If you have any concern about gumming up a bulkhead regulator, the tank/cylinder supplier should be able to supply the requisite fittings.

it so that it's protected in the event that items rolling around unrestrained in a locker cannot damage it. To distribute gas to separate appliances you should employ a manifold with individual isolating taps. In this way, if a leak develops, or if a particular appliance develops a fault, it's possible to simply cut the supply of gas to the affected circuit whilst leaving all other circuits up and running.

Most gas fittings themselves are straightforward to fit and require no special tools. A pipe cutter and pipe bender are perhaps the only essentials required to create an entire system. Most metal-to-metal pipe joints are of the compression type whilst pre-flared or barbed fittings are generally used to reliably join flexible pipe to the rigid system. Always use a proper pipe cutter to cut metal pipe to length and deburr the cut end before offering it up to a compression fitting. Use of good-quality stainless-

steel hose clips on low-pressure flexible pipe and careful system assembly will ordinarily result in a reliable gas-tight system. Some gas fitters swear by gas-joint sealing compound; others swear by *gas-specific* PTFE tape; yet more say there's no need for any kind of supplementary sealing medium. Whichever option you choose, you should always use purpose-made leak-detection spray to check your work and even if all seems well you *must* get the complete system checked by a suitably qualified fitter before it's taken into use. As highlighted previously in the chapter covering ventilation, gas-drop vents should be installed at suitable intervals around the floorpan that will allow any accumulated leaked LPG to drop out of the vehicle and vent to atmosphere. Finally, fit (at a minimum) a carbon monoxide detector – they are cheap and simple to fit...

▼ **Gas-drop vents are not optional.**

▼ **For when it all goes wrong.**

John Brooks

1 Name

John Brooks.

2 Base vehicle

Mercedes 1124AF – 1995 – ex-police fire engine.

3 Drive

4x4 (switched). Rear diff lock. High/low ratio box. Power take-off. Right-hand drive.

4 Fuel capacity

550 litres in 3 tanks. Racor 1000 fuel filter.

5 Weight when loaded and ready to travel

10 tons loaded (8.6 empty) – and it's too heavy!

6 Reason for base vehicle choice

First one I found/purchased on impulse. I demonstrated a lack of insight/research. I would never buy right-hand drive again.

7 Subframe solution

We originally had a 'professionally' fabricated 3-point torsion-free subframe built in the UK that turned out to be incompetently made: it broke *both* chassis rails. We had a 4-point torsion-free mount fabricated during travels on the Mosquito Coast, Honduras. This was made from the fifth wheel of a truck and still works well. Four truck shock absorbers effectively control subframe movement.

8 Habitation-box construction

Professionally laminated by Coldsaver Panels. These have a GRP surface, ply walls and an insulative core. They are very strong but quite heavy. The whole habitation box was simply bonded together and is finished with aluminium capping to help with weatherproofing.

9 Habitation-box insulation material

Closed-cell 75mm thick walls. Tested to –40 exterior temperatures in Canada. It's over-insulated; I would make thinner walls next time.

10 Habitation-box manufacturer

Assembled by Able Engineering but needed re-bonding within two months, which was exceedingly difficult to do post fabrication.

11 Habitation-box windows

Profiles made by Smart Systems Ltd – these were self-specified and installed; they work very well and are very strong. Glazing produced by Glassolutions and the units feature interior bladders to balance pressure. The interior blinds are by Oceanair. The flyscreens of these blinds do *not* stop mosquitoes and they are very fragile – much like Seitz units.

12 Habitation-box door(s) and locker(s)

Supplied via Able Engineering. Problems have been encountered in very hot temperatures with both entrance door and cargo-hatch door sticking shut.

13 Fit out done by

Entirely self-built.

14 Furniture construction

I used furniture ply, painted with a floor paint selected for its toughness. All furniture panels were bonded together. The furniture has worked well except for a few doors that were not bonded all around their mating surfaces and bowed as a result. It's important to use expensive door/drawer catches as an escaped drawer makes a big mess!

15 Fresh water

500 litres capacity. We use three filters. The first is 30 micron and this is enough for the shower. The second filter is 10 micron and this serves for washing-up water. The third filter is supplied by General Ecology and supplies drinking water. We've drunk everything we've put in the tank and encountered no health problems in three years.

16 Refrigeration

Waeco compressor fridge – 110 litres capacity. This is neither strong nor efficient. We added an extra fan

internally to even out the internal temperature and added a further exterior fan to increase cooling. The duct from this 'extractor' fan supplies warm air, which would otherwise largely be wasted, into the shower room to dry both the shower cubicle itself and clothes.

17 Space heating
Diesel-powered Webasto hydronic furnace with a Kalori water-to-air heat exchanger. This is fast and efficient and kept us warm for a week of −35°C temperatures. I added cleanable air-conditioning unit air filters, which resolved an issue of dust blocking the heat exchanger's fans. The Webasto worked *without* an altitude kit up to 5,000m (but it needs a sea-level blow through every few weeks).

18 Water heating
Hot water is supplied by the above Webasto hydronic furnace through a Surejust calorifier. This also features an electric immersion element backup which we used in Canada when diesel froze.

19 Cooking facilities
Gas cooking from a fixed 85-litre LPG tank (no problems encountered in filling this). We use a Dometic caravan-style 4-burner cooker, which is *very* fragile. This also features an oven, which we use a lot. We also have an electric microwave/oven/grill as a backup.

20 Habitation-box cooling
Caframo Marine Sirocco fans. These have excellent styling, are quiet and have a strong air flow… but they all broke. They were no good for rough roads – I rewired the circuit board to hard-wire to the fan motor. Also, a small extraction fan runs permanently to circulate air, this is silent and helps with condensation etc. We also use two roof vents that flip open, but even when open, they remain entirely invisible from the outside.

21 Leisure-battery charging
Excellent Blue Sky solar panel – 400W. Mains/split charger from Antares TDC (but this is not really appropriate for motorhomes and was very expensive). The truck came with a 2,000W alternator – it's an animal!

22 Things to do differently next time
Have the chassis preparation, torsion-free system and habitation box fabrication all done by a reputable German company. I would even have spare wheel mounts and all fuel-delivery systems etc. built by such a trusted company as this is the stuff that – when it goes wrong – causes a trip to end. I would self-build the interior again, all of it. It's part of the journey and gives great freedom. If you build it, you can fix it.

I would also take better and more recovery gear. Big trucks are very different to pick-up sized vehicles. Getting seriously stuck in a remote area could and has led to the total loss of vehicles. Finally, whereever I have tried to save money, it has caused problems and cost more in the long run. For long-term foreign travel, the best-quality products ultimately save money.

CHAPTER 10

Electrical systems

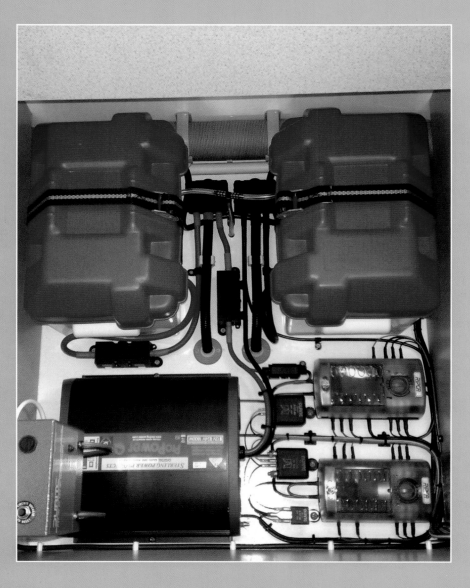

■ The basics

■ Charging systems

■ The question of capacity

■ Inverters

An entire book could easily be written about leisure-vehicle electrical systems. This chapter serves as a mere whistle-stop tour of the topic and its purpose is intended to be twofold: to outline key subjects in order to help with understanding during your own further research, and to highlight some hardware and techniques that have been proven to deliver reliable service in overlanding use.

The basics

A vehicle's starter battery should be utilised for its intended purpose only. Do not be tempted to tap into starter battery reserves to run any domestic equipment. You should never compromise your ability to start your overlander, especially in cold and remote regions.

Instead, a dedicated 'leisure' battery (or battery bank) should be employed to supply power to the habitation area and run *all* domestic equipment. The dedicated battery (bank) can itself be charged from any number of sources, but principally ordinarily utilises the vehicle's alternator.

Conventional leisure batteries (i.e. discounting exotica such as Lithium-ion) are manufactured using different materials and construction methods with the result that three distinct technologies are currently commonly employed: open lead acid, absorbent glass mat (AGM) and gel.

Open lead acid

Open lead acid or wet/flooded cell batteries hold a sulphuric acid electrolyte in liquid form, which will readily slosh around within the internal cells. During charging, if the charging voltage exceeds about 14.6V, this electrolyte can give off potentially explosive hydrogen gas. In order to accommodate this phenomenon, open lead acid batteries are usually vented to atmosphere. Any gas produced is normally carried away in a small vent tube to a point somewhere outside the vehicle where it can dissipate quite harmlessly.

Pros include:
■ Cheap to buy.
■ Easy to replace.
■ Tolerant to most charging regimes.

Cons include:
■ 'Boiled off' electrolyte needs replacing in the form of distilled/de-ionised water.

INTRODUCING LEISURE BATTERIES

■ Leisure batteries generally comprise six internal cells, each producing a nominal 2.12V. These are connected in series internally to produce the familiar finished product with one positive and one negative terminal producing a nominal 12.72V.

■ Internally, leisure batteries have thicker plates and a different design of plate separator to batteries used for starting vehicles and the two different designs should only be used for their intended purpose. Starter batteries are designed to permit a very heavy but very short-term current draw when cranking an engine; leisure batteries are designed to permit a light current draw but over a comparatively long period.

■ In recent years some battery manufacturers have re-badged and marketed starter batteries – usually at inflated prices – as leisure batteries: research the internals of your proposed batteries well before handing over any cash.

■ Leisure batteries perform optimally when they're kept in a high state of charge and gently called upon for power. Rapid and heavy discharge currents – such as those encountered when powering a microwave for instance – are not good for performance or longevity.

■ Equally bad is too deep a 'gentle' discharge, such as might occur when camping in one place for more than a few days. Ideally, as a general rule, leisure batteries should never be discharged below 50% of their capacity.

- Electrolyte can spill if batteries are roughly handled or tipped over.
- Cannot be discharged as deeply or frequently as AGM or gel technologies without significantly shortening the battery's life expectancy.

Absorbent glass mat (AGM)

AGM batteries have a compressed glass-fibre structure pressed against the plates and this absorbs the contained electrolyte. Accordingly, unlike with open lead acid batteries, the electrolyte does not slosh around. With AGM batteries, air is withdrawn from the unit at the time of manufacture and the whole assembly is sealed (apart from the incorporation of a safety valve). Because this type of battery is effectively sealed, and therefore can't readily vent a build-up of hydrogen gas, it's important that the chemistry is not overly stimulated during charging. Maximum charging voltage must be limited to around 14.4V.

Pros include:
- More tolerant to the real-world rigours of partial charge/ deep discharge.
- Maintenance free.
- Can occasionally be pressed into service as starter. batteries because of integral support for plates.
- Better able to withstand short but heavy discharge loads required by items like microwaves.

Cons include:
- Expensive.
- Require limited-voltage charging regimes.
- Potentially difficult to obtain like-for-like replacement in the event of failure on the road.

Gel

These batteries hold their electrolyte in gel form and are completely sealed. Because of the medium employed, they will not spill their corrosive electrolyte under any (normal) circumstances and so can, if required, be mounted on their side or even upside down. Again, because they're fully sealed, and because of the peculiarities of the gel medium, care needs to be taken with charging regimes: general consensus dictates that maximum charging voltage should not exceed 14.2V. Pros are similar to AGM batteries, but gel can also be inverted and roughly handled without fear of spilling electrolyte. Cons are also similar to AGM batteries, but gels are even more expensive and charging regimes even more restricted.

In summary, each technology has its advantages and disadvantages, but unless your needs are specialised, e.g. you'll *regularly* require the capability to deeply discharge, or you need to mount the units otherwise than upright, then because wet lead-acid batteries are universally available and

ALTERNATIVE BATTERY CONFIGURATIONS

Though most batteries are effectively six inter-connected cells built into one self-contained 12V unit, it's possible to buy specialist deep-cycle batteries that comprise altogether different numbers of cells. Accordingly, it has been known for numerous separate batteries nominally rated at, for example 6V, to be wired in series to make banks outputting 12V or 24V. Though performance can be outstanding, wiring is complex and banks tend to be bulky. Additionally, just one failed cell could render the whole bank useless and like-for-like replacements might prove *very* difficult to source on the road. Depending on configuration, the whole array may need to be abandoned and replaced by conventional 12V six-cell units, which will also mean, in very many parts of the world, buying simple open lead acid starter batteries.

do not require bespoke chargers, they're arguably currently still the most logical compromise for providing habitation-box power in remote parts of the world.

Charging systems

There are numerous ways to charge batteries and supply auxiliary power when on the road and these commonly include: the vehicle alternator, solar power, wind power, fuel-powered generators and mains electricity.

INTELLIGENT CHARGERS

Battery charging is an incredibly complicated subject and even amongst purists there are contrasting views. What is agreed upon is that in order to both swiftly and fully recharge a battery *and* to protect it from being overcharged, fluctuating current and voltage rates are required at different stages of the charging process. Essentially, by monitoring actual battery voltage and, ideally, temperature, 'intelligent' multi-stage chargers fully automate this process and optimise both the charging current and voltage as required. Ordinarily, there are three distinct phases to an intelligent charger's regime. Some highly sophisticated chargers also include an equalisation function (a highly specialised conditioning regime). Some battery aficionados swear by this function; others consider it largely unnecessary.

Alternator charging

If your on-board equipment is not particularly power-hungry and if your style of travel sees you moving on most days then you may not actually *need* anything other than the vehicle's alternator to satisfy all of your power requirements. Charging leisure batteries from an alternator is commonly achieved in three ways by utilising either: a split charger, an alternator-to-battery charger or a battery-to-battery charger.

Split chargers

These come in different forms and basically comprise either a conventional relay energised from the alternator, a (now very aged and largely defunct) diode-type battery isolator, or a more modern, electronically controlled solid-state voltage sensitive relay. In each case, when the engine is running, the chosen device is electrically switched and allows charging current to flow to *all* batteries connected to the device – both starter *and* leisure. Power output from your alternator is, as the name suggests, effectively 'split' between banks. Conversely, when the engine is turned off, split chargers break their internal switch and thereby isolate one bank from the other. This means that after the day's drive it's impossible to tap into your starter battery when operating domestic items and the vehicle's starter motor cannot recruit the leisure battery for engine cranking.

Pros include:
▓ Easy to fit.
▓ Easy to replace.
▓ Reliable.
▓ Prevent power being drawn from the 'wrong' batteries.

Cons include:
▓ Reliance on sophistication of alternator's inbuilt regulator for efficiency of charging regime, i.e. they are not intelligent multi-stage chargers.
▓ Both banks must match in terms of voltage, so if your starter battery bank is 24V then your leisure bank must be the same (unless further hardware is incorporated).
▓ Voltage output is not modified and will generally be optimised for open lead-acid batteries (your alternator may produce too much voltage for AGM/gel batteries – this can be checked by measuring actual output at full running speed).

Alternator-to-battery chargers

These are electronically controlled devices that are wired between the alternator and batteries. They 'manipulate' the vehicle alternator's inbuilt regulator in order to substitute charging regimes designed to optimise speed of charging and battery health.

Pros include:
▓ Simple to fit.

▓ Some can be programmed to suit AGM/gel batteries.
▓ Quick charging times .
▓ Incorporate intelligent charging regimes designed to optimise a battery's charge level, condition and longevity.

Cons include:
▓ Expensive.
▓ Reliance upon electronics.
▓ Some versions cannot cope with high-power-output alternators.
▓ *May* be incompatible with *very* modern base-vehicle electronics.
▓ Not (currently) available with a dual 24V/12V output regime, so starter and leisure banks must be matched in terms of operating voltage.

Battery-to-battery chargers

These are electronically controlled devices that connect to both a master and a slave battery. When voltage in the master battery (most usually the starter battery) is above a pre-programmed threshold, i.e. essentially when the master battery itself is receiving a charge from an external source, the battery-to-battery charger 'taps' power from the master battery in order to charge the slave battery (most usually the leisure battery). When voltage in the master battery falls below a pre-programmed threshold, the charger cuts out to protect the master from constant discharge.

Pros include:
▓ Simple to fit.
▓ Some have regimes suitable for AGM/gel batteries.
▓ Incorporate intelligent charging regimes designed to optimise battery charge level, condition and longevity
▓ Mixed voltage versions available that allow 12V slave. batteries to be charged from a 24V master and vice versa

Cons include:
▓ Expensive
▓ Reliance upon electronics
▓ 24V–12V versions often have limited current output meaning potentially slower charge times

The most appropriate way to have your alternator charge your leisure batteries will depend largely on your equipment and personal preference. *Very* broadly though: if your standard alternator has a relatively high output of 80A or more, then split chargers, especially voltage sensitive ones, are efficient, reliable, easy to fit and cheap enough to carry a spare. If your alternator has a relatively low power output then an alternator-to-battery charger can improve charging efficiency. If you have a mixed-voltage system and wish to 'intelligently' charge a 12V battery from a 24V source or vice versa, then battery-to-battery chargers certainly have their merits.

TWIN ALTERNATORS

If you have the physical room and can obtain the necessary hardware, twin alternators are a good solution. Not only can engine and leisure battery systems be kept completely separate, but you have, in effect, a spare alternator on hand too.

Even if you optimise alternator-based charging, in the event that your on-board equipment is power-hungry, or if your style of travel means that you may be parked for several days and you prefer not to run your engine to replenish battery reserves, you may find yourself having to consider supplementary charging systems. Having at least one way to charge batteries independent of the alternator is – in any event – good practice. If the alternator should fail, or if you have engine trouble, at least you will be able to continue to use domestic appliances until the problems are fixed.

CHARGING RATES

Leisure batteries perform at their best when in a high state of charge. Large-capacity battery banks take a lot of power and/or a lot of time to fully recharge. If your onboard systems are extensive and you absolutely *need* a 500+ amp-hour (Ah) capacity, then your charging systems will need to be both powerful and sophisticated. Large battery banks coupled with inadequate charging systems – in real-world travel situations – often result in a *permanently* partially discharged battery bank. Adding more batteries just results in more half-dead batteries: not more power. Conversely, a high-power charging system and a small battery bank *could* result in batteries only superficially reaching their upper voltage capacity and, as a result, not actually being correctly 'deeply' charged. Though opinions vary, received wisdom suggests that for open lead-acid batteries you could do much worse than have a charging system with an output power of approximately 25% of battery capacity. So, if your entire battery capacity is 400Ah, an alternator with an output of 100A would offer a healthy compromise for charging speed *and* ultimate battery performance. NB: this is a *very* rough and ready rule of thumb and the 'intelligent' electronics found in sophisticated devices like alternator-to-battery chargers are purportedly able to override the general principle and simultaneously deliver quicker *and* adequately deep charging regimes.

Solar panels are a *very* popular addition to overland campers and it's undoubtedly true that powerful arrays can, in ideal circumstances, sustain battery life for almost indefinite periods. That said, they're not favoured by all. Here are some considerations:

Pros:
- Able to provide 'free' and silent power to sustain many days' camping.
- Able to maintain batteries in good condition even when the vehicle is not in use – especially useful if alarms/trackers are left permanently armed.

Cons:
- Large arrays and their associated charge controllers can be expensive.
- Very inefficient in conditions when on-board power requirements are often at their greatest, i.e. when it's overcast, cold, wet, and daylight only lasts a few hours.
- Require significant roof space.
- Prone to damage.

Wind generators are sometimes found in use and again, in appropriate conditions, they can maintain battery life for extended periods.

Pros:
- Can provide 'free' power to sustain many days' camping.
- Can, if conditions permit, maintain batteries in good condition even when the vehicle is not in use.

Cons:
- Bulky to stow when not in use.
- Assembly/disassembly becomes tedious.
- Useless in no, or very light, wind conditions.
- Noisy and spectacularly resonant if attached to the vehicle's superstructure.
- Together with associated charge controllers, can be expensive.

Solar and wind chargers (unless they have a very low power output) need to charge batteries via a charge controller. Simplistically, these are electronic devices that both optimise the charging regime and prevent overcharging.

Tapping into purely natural resources to produce electricity is undoubtedly appealing and can, in many circumstances, provide the ideal solution. If bright days or the wind are in short supply though, and particularly if your power needs are notably heavy, you may need to look to fuel-burning solutions.

Fuel-burning generators

Fuelled generators come in many guises ranging from very neat and almost silent methanol-burning units, through LPG and petrol-powered machines, right up to monolithic earth-shaking diesel-burning powerhouses. Providing you have a fuel source, generators of this genre can be pressed into service for everything from simple battery charging right up to supporting very power-hungry appliances like air-conditioning units. Though the ability to produce enough power to (theoretically) run all your equipment indefinitely seems attractive, generators do have their negative sides. There will be at least some weight and storage penalty (sometimes a very significant one), plus the requirement to source and store the appropriate fuel. Additionally, high altitude may affect normal operation of diesel- and petrol-powered units, and, unless your unit of choice is one of the *almost* silent methanol burners, you must be prepared to sacrifice tranquillity. That may not be an issue if the tranquillity is your own, but do *not* expect to be popular with neighbours…

Power from mains electricity

If your style of travel means that you frequently intend to make use of formal campsites with electric hook-up facilities then not only can a site's mains power be used to charge batteries but also to directly power an AC wiring system within the vehicle. Of course, life is not so simple. Around the world, different standards for mains electricity are adopted meaning that AC appliances that work in one world market may not work in another. For this reason, many overland camper builders do not even try to power onboard AC circuits *directly* from hook-up, but instead run any AC equipment they may have installed via a dedicated inverter, whilst simultaneously utilising a fairly cheap-and-simple over-the-counter AC-powered battery charger (of the kind used to charge a regular car battery) to supply the leisure batteries, which are of course – in turn – supplying the inverter. Adopting this method means that, thanks to the moderating effect of the inverter, onboard AC equipment will always be receiving AC power of a known quality.

Naturally though, there may be a problem in as much as the same AC compatibility issue is equally applicable to simple battery chargers: some are more universally operable than others. If you do anticipate encountering varying mains-power supplies, rather than risking the disappointment of battery-charger incompatibility, it might make sense to forget any hope of fitting a truly universal cheap-and-simple charger at the time of your overlander build and instead accept you may have to purchase a cheap charger 'locally', if and when required.

If you have faith in technology and deep pockets, you can also buy your way out of incompatibility woes. It's possible to purchase very sophisticated chargers, or even

combination charger/inverter units that *are* capable of processing incoming AC voltage of differing standards (and even, in some cases, of incoming DC voltages too) and outputting power in a form compatible with your equipment to 'intelligently' charge your batteries *and*, in the case of units with inbuilt inverters, supply power to the on-board AC appliances. Though a very elegant solution, there's no escaping that you'll be placing heavy reliance on potentially irreplaceable-on-the-road electronics.

Given the various pitfalls, and adding to the mix the very real problem that some hook-ups around the world *do not* meet even the most basic of developed-world safety standards (even sometimes those *within* the developed world!), it may be no surprise to learn that some overland camper builders do not even attempt to utilise external mains power supplies at all. If you do pursue the supply of

AC ALTERNATORS

These are popular in marine applications but rarely make the crossover to overlanders. AC alternators supply reliable AC power of a fixed and known quantity and quality when the engine is running. These systems essentially turn your engine into a generator that can produce upwards of 5kW of power. As a result, they are more than capable of running just about any mains appliance you can physically fit into your build. On the negative side, they are expensive and installation is quite involved. Notwithstanding, for many who live aboard boats, these are considered an altogether more convenient solution to conventional fuel-burning generators.

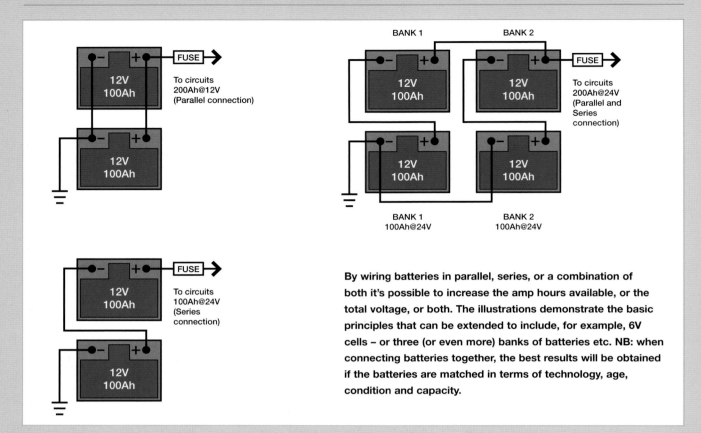

By wiring batteries in parallel, series, or a combination of both it's possible to increase the amp hours available, or the total voltage, or both. The illustrations demonstrate the basic principles that can be extended to include, for example, 6V cells – or three (or even more) banks of batteries etc. NB: when connecting batteries together, the best results will be obtained if the batteries are matched in terms of technology, age, condition and capacity.

By using a pair of busbar-style terminals situated near to the battery bank, the wiring for this example of a 24V 100Ah bank becomes easier to physically manage and is less likely to result in incorrect connections being made.

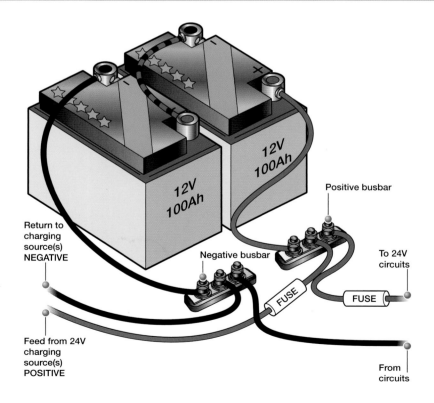

power for onboard AC equipment from an external mains supply, you *must* ensure that the supply is distributed via appropriate consumer units and circuit breakers. Mains voltage can be lethal on contact and is a ready source of electrical fires. If in any doubt, the advice of a qualified electrician should be sought.

The question of capacity

Amp-hours (Ah) is a simple way to quantify battery capacity. If you constantly run a large fan rated at 72 watts powered by a 12-volt supply then it will (simplistically) constantly consume 6 amps (watts divided by volts equals amps). A battery with a capacity rated at 120Ah could then – in theory – run this fan for 20 hours, or an appliance requiring 1 amp for 120 hours, or an appliance requiring 12 amps for 10 hours.

Of course and as ever, things are not so simple. When called upon to provide a very power-hungry appliance, like, for example, a microwave, a 120Ah battery will run out of reserve far more quickly than its 120Ah claim might suggest. This is because high current draw takes a very high toll on battery performance and a battery that can *theoretically* provide 120Ah if slowly discharged over 20 hours might only have a maximum *theoretical* capacity of 90Ah if discharged over just a couple of hours.

For this reason, manufacturers will often quote Ah capacity at a rate that makes their product seem superior. When considering batteries, make sure you compare like with like, preferably focusing on the Ah rating at the *20-hour rate* of discharge – this rate is considered something of a realistic standard and is usually printed on a label somewhere. If it isn't, and the information isn't otherwise readily available, you'll be forgiven for being cynical. Other brands of battery are available…

Furthermore, treat the theoretical Ah capacity with contempt in *all* cases. In highly controlled laboratory conditions with brand-new and fully charged batteries maintained at the optimum temperature, it *might* be the case that a battery can be persuaded – as a one-off – to perform to the claimed standard. In the real world of less-than-optimum charging regimes (batteries rarely reach a genuine fully charged state), fluctuating demands on the circuit, less than optimum temperatures, and the fact that discharging an open lead-acid battery lower than about 50% of its capacity is damaging to its longevity, you will not in reality achieve anything approaching even *half* of the claimed capacity. The 120Ah battery that looked quite promising in the opening paragraph might, in reality, safely yield somewhere loosely around 30–40Ah.

Note well, some travellers cope very well with limited battery capacity, others less so. Your pattern of behaviour and consumption is one aspect of battery capacity

management that is easily overlooked but which is perhaps *the* most important. Consumption (of all resources) on the road can require a huge shift in mentality. It will *always* help to reduce consumption and you could try, in the specific case of battery capacity:

▪ Utilising items like LED lights and small-screen media players.

MONITORING CONDITION

If relying solely on voltage readings, a battery's state of charge can only reliably be monitored when it has been allowed to rest (ideally completely disconnected) for several hours without being subject to *any* charging or discharging loads. When rested, the below readings relate to the *approximate* state of charge of a 12V battery in an ambient temperature of 25°C. Readings are subject to a range because not all batteries perform identically and not all purists agree on definitive readings. Your battery manufacturer should be able to supply you with voltage-specific state of charge (SoC) data specific to the product you are using.

Battery reading (Volts)	*Approximate* state of charge (%)
>12.7	100
12.4–12.6	>74
12.2–12.3	>49
12.0–12.1	>24
<12.0	0

Naturally, under normal travelling conditions, there will be very few *if any* occasions where batteries are not in a state of constant flux. Even if no equipment is actually 'running', batteries will still be subject to quiescent loads from the likes of battery-to-battery chargers and printed circuit boards in fridges and heater controllers.

In the real world then, simple voltmeters and ammeters utilised to spot-test the state of batteries are *not* particularly meaningful. There are more sophisticated monitors available that rely on: a) the installation of shunts to measure current and voltage, or b) a combination of voltage sampling, pre-programmed algorithms and the 'intelligent' incorporation of empirical data (i.e. they 'learn' your battery). Some of these are very popular in marine applications and are reportedly accurate. If you want to make the effort to *reliably* monitor your battery reserves, there isn't a particularly cheap solution.

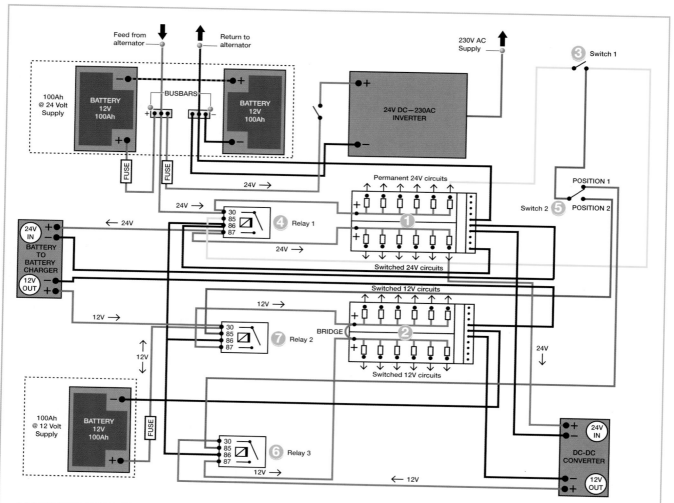

HARDWARE AND CIRCUITS

This example of a field-proven triple voltage (24/12V DC and 230V AC) system fits well with the tenets of simplicity, reliability and reserve systems.

Key:

1 **Distribution block 1.** A 12-way blade-fuse holder consisting of 2 x separate banks of 6 x fuses supplying the habitation box's 24V circuits. One bank of fuses provides a permanent 24V supply; the other bank is switched via relay 1.

2 **Distribution block 2.** A further 12-way blade-fuse holder. The two banks in this instance are intentionally bridged and control distribution to the habitation box's 12V circuits.

3 **Switch 1 (one-way).** When closed, energises relay 3 and also supplies power to switch 2.

4 **Relay 1 (24V/60A).** When energised, supplies 24V DC to the 6 x switched circuits of distribution block 1.

5 **Switch 2 (two-way).** When in position 1, energises relay 3. When in position 2, cuts power to relay 3 and instead energises relay 2.

6 **Relay 3 (24V/40A).** When energised, supplies distribution block 2 with a 12V supply from the DC–DC converter. NB:

even though this relay is rated at 24V, the supply passing across terminals 30 and 87 is 12V – this is not an issue.

7 **Relay 2. (24V/60A).** When energised, supplies distribution block 2 with a 12V supply from the stand-alone 12V battery. NB: this relay too is correctly energised by 24V but manages a 12V supply.

As you work through this system, two things will become apparent:

1 That when switch 1 is left open, all of the relays, the DC–DC converter and the battery-to-battery charger are fully isolated and therefore draw zero current.

2 That no matter whether any single battery, the DC–DC converter or the battery-to-battery charger should fail, the system (with the worst-case scenario of having to move the 12V stand-alone battery into the 24V bank) is always able to supply 24/12V DC and 230V AC.

- Using latching relays where possible. These do not require any power to hold them in (or out).
- Charging laptops etc. whilst actually travelling, then using their built-in batteries when stationary.
- Fully isolating any equipment that's not actually in use (inverters, heater control panels, TVs etc). Leaving them on standby is surprisingly wasteful.
- Cutting internal losses. Each time you subject power to a transformational stage you introduce inefficiencies. An often-encountered example is using batteries to power an inverter, which in turn powers a laptop power-pack – that itself then basically undoes the work of the inverter and re-converts voltage to DC. Chains like this ultimately waste energy (plus they introduce the potential for unreliability).
- Careful management of the compressor fridge (an art in its own right).
- Offsetting heavy discharge. For example, if you're going to run a microwave or hairdryer for a few minutes, run your engine (at fast idle) whilst the appliance is operating.

So how many amp-hours will give true independence?

No one can tell you. How much leisure battery capacity is ultimately required will depend on many factors including (but not restricted to): your onboard equipment, the quality and type of your batteries, your pattern of energy consumption, your alternator's performance and how much you travel each day. In spite of the question of optimum capacity being utterly imponderable, here – anyway – is a tentative attempt at a starting point. Using only an alternator/voltage sensitive split-charge relay combination, and assuming you use a ubiquitous upright compressor fridge, four hours spent driving and a nominal 300Ah of battery capacity at 12V *should* be more than adequate for *two* people to camp for a couple of nights no matter what the season. If you travel alone or with just one other person and discover a four-hour drive and 300Ah *isn't* enough for a couple of nights' camping, then it might help to follow the below steps to power-supply independence. Make one change at a time and only progress to the next step if required.

1 Make sure all your systems are working, your batteries are in good condition and manage your capacity thoughtfully. Unless you run *very high-demand equipment* or are catering for particular needs, an adequately charged and well-managed 300Ah capacity really *should* be sufficient.
2 Optimise alternator performance. Ensure your alternator is adequate and upgrade if it isn't. Alternatively, install a device like an alternator-to-battery charger or aftermarket alternator controller to override the standard alternator's regulator (if compatible).
3 Consider relatively low-output external charging devices (solar panel or small generator).

WORKING OUT CABLE RATING

It's important to use cable with sufficient current-carrying capability to safely and reliably power appliances. Undersized cable can overheat to the point of combustion or, in a less dramatic scenario, inflict a voltage drop that will effectively render it unsuitable for purpose. The information below relates to modern, high-quality single-core cable and is meant only as a rough guide; always take heed of manufacturers' actual specifications.

Cable of cross sectional area (mm²)	Approximate current carrying capacity (Amps)
0.5	11
1	16
2	25
3	33
4	39
6	50
7	57
8.5	63
10	70
16	110
25	170
40	300
50	345
60	415

4 Increase battery capacity by around 100Ah (at 12V).
5 Consider additional or higher-output external charging devices (solar array/large generator).
6 Increase battery capacity by around 100Ah (at 12V)
7 Consider a hotel.

Remember, this model assumes you drive on most days. If you don't, large solar arrays or a fuel-burning generator are likely to prove appropriate additions. In all cases, don't fall into the trap of simply adding batteries *without* addressing consumption and an *appropriate* charging regime. If you do, you are adding little more than expensive ballast.

Inverters

As briefly covered in the previous section on charging batteries from a mains electricity hook-up, mains-fed AC circuits can be of questionable use unless all of your AC appliances are compatible with the specific characteristics of the mains electricity supply in the geographical area(s) in which you happen to be. For many, the solution is to install an inverter to convert battery power into AC and run mains-voltage appliances from that.

Inverters are basically of two types: quasi (or modified) sine wave and pure sine wave. The difference lies within the sophistication of the electronic circuitry and the inverter's resultant ability to perfectly mimic the alternating current oscillations of a true mains supply. Pure-sine-wave inverters will run any equipment without issue but are slightly more inefficient in terms of internal power loss; they also tend to be more expensive. Quasi-sine-wave inverters will run almost everything except for some sensitive electronic equipment but with some equipment, especially if the equipment contains its own power supply unit, can cause irritating clicking or buzzing. Unfortunately, apart from seeking opinion from those who have trodden the path before you, there is no simple way to establish whether your particular quasi-sine-wave inverter will irritate, or run your particular piece of sensitive electronic equipment at all.

Inverter output power is generally quoted in watts and when it comes to selecting a large enough unit, you'll need to determine the *total* power required to run your on-board AC appliance(s), and then add 25%. For example, if you just wish to run a hairdryer requiring 1,200W, your inverter should be rated at a minimum of 1,500W *continuous* (not surge) output power. It isn't always terribly obvious how much power is required to run appliances and bear in mind that for items like microwaves, the headline 'cooking' power might initially mislead. A microwave's cooking power might be advertised at 800W but it will take a great deal more power, perhaps in the region of 1,500W, to actually produce that quoted 800W output. In order to establish the relevant requirements of all appliances, a visit to the small print of manufacturers' specification sheets will be time well spent.

Fitting an inverter is straightforward and essentially only requires a fused connection to the leisure battery. In use, one useful tip is to make sure the inverter is fully powered up and allowed a few seconds under idle before turning on any AC appliances. Activating an inverter with a load already connected, especially if it's a large load like a kettle that's already switched on, can hasten the demise of the unit.

MIXING 24V AND 12V

As many overland campers are built on mid-sized commercial vehicles it's very common to encounter 24V base-vehicle electrical systems. Unhelpfully, the vast majority of habitation box fixtures and fittings are aimed at leisure vehicles, which utilise a 12V supply. 24V versions of most appliances *can* be purchased but they frequently command a premium price. There are several ways round this mixed-voltage issue, the most common of which are:

■ Stick with 24V as far as possible. Accept you may have to pay a little more and use as many 24V appliances as are available. This *can* be done but starts to prove tricky when it comes to some smaller items like TVs and chargers for mobile devices. A small locally mounted DC–DC converter will almost certainly be needed to power *some* smaller items.

■ Run a mixed-voltage system utilising a large 24V–12V DC–DC converter. Run some appliances on 24V and use the converter to power selected 12V circuits too. Some DC–DC converters have substantial current-producing capacity and can easily run appliances as large as heaters and fridges. They're acceptably efficient in terms of internal losses and because output is effectively isolated from any fluctuations in supply voltage, they have the added advantage of delivering a very stable voltage to sensitive electronic equipment such as, for example, televisions. On the downside, if the DC–DC converter should fail, you'll need a contingency to run your 12V circuits.

■ Run a mixed-voltage system utilising a 24V leisure battery bank *plus* an additional 12V leisure battery and use a battery-to-battery charger (or some other suitable 12V charging source) to charge the 12V battery. If this system is adopted – and especially if backed up with an 'emergency' 24V–12V DC–DC converter – you will have a great deal of flexibility should any of the charging components, or even a battery itself fail. (A system such as this is featured in the previous 'Hardware and circuits' illustration.)

■ Use a 24V–12V battery-to-battery charger to connect the starter batteries to the leisure batteries and run *everything* in the habitation box on 12V. This might seem like a tempting solution, but the charging current to the 12V side may be restricted, meaning that only low-power systems can realistically be supported. Also, if the unit should fail in the field then you've lost the ability to recharge from the alternator.

Though each of the above methods is well tested, reasonably efficient and field proven, there are *numerous* other creative solutions to this conundrum. If you choose to go your own way, as always, simplicity and a back-up system will be useful attributes to bear in mind.

Design

1 Choosing energy-efficient equipment like the smallest-screen 12V-specific TV that you are comfortable with and directly powering as many items as possible from DC circuits will help with consumption and reliability.

2 Consider exactly which equipment and appliances you'll be installing and where all hardware will be situated – working out your wiring runs at a very early stage will save an enormous amount of frustration in the long term.

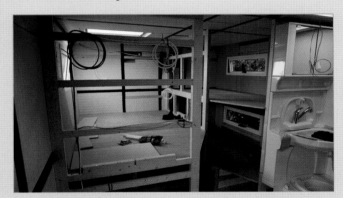

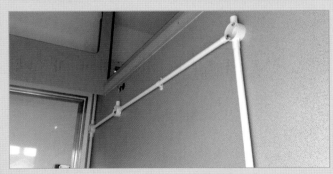

3 Ensure that, post-build, you'll always be able to access all connections and equipment, and also as much of the actual wiring loom as possible. The ability to easily access looms via demountable conduit etc. allows for the possibility of maintenance/alterations without the need to dismantle the full interior.

4 Design in contingency systems. If one critical component like, for example, a battery-to-battery charger should fail, you should have a backup solution.

5 As always, keep it simple – a surprising number of micro-processors and printed circuit boards will insidiously creep into your overlander as you add appliances like fridges and heaters. Faults arising in simple mechanical controls (like these from the versatile and modular CBE range) and electro-mechanical relays are easy to diagnose and cheap to fix.

6 Even seemingly innocuous electronically controlled equipment like this touch-sensitive light can be prone to malfunction. This particular light developed an irritating trait of turning itself on when a different light on the same circuit was operated. Moving its supply to a dedicated circuit cured the issue.

7 Keep the system 'balanced' – remember, charging too quickly can mean batteries are only superficially charged and too large a battery capacity coupled with an ineffective charging regime can result in batteries being permanently undercharged. Either scenario will mean a spiralling decline in battery performance. These batteries are destined for a system with a total capacity of well over 500Ah at 12V but they employ gel technology so are tolerant to partial charge/deep discharge and – crucially – they are carefully managed using a range of quality chargers, including a charge-controlled 720W solar array.

8 If mounting electrical equipment to the floor, consider lifting it slightly to prevent inundation if water should reach it. Humble tap washers are incredibly useful for this purpose and in this image lift a relay by a few potentially critical millimetres. Additionally, tap washers help in reducing the potentially damaging effects of vibration and can be used throughout a build to help isolate all manner of hardware from the worst of such stress.

Batteries

1 These are properly engineered 'leisure' batteries: beware of impostors that are simply rebadged starter batteries.

4 To minimise the possibility of catastrophic short circuits, fuse each battery bank as close to the final output positive battery terminal as possible.

2 For the rigours of overlanding, restrain your batteries well – they are very heavy and full of acid…

5 Mount batteries inside the habitation area or, if this is impossible, try to provide a heat source – cold batteries do not perform well. Note the blown-air heater ducting behind these battery cases, which provides enough residual heat to improve battery performance in very cold conditions.

3 Vent wet lead-acid batteries to atmosphere – hydrogen gas readily explodes and spilled electrolyte causes irreversible corrosion. This tube eventually vents through a hole in the camper's floor.

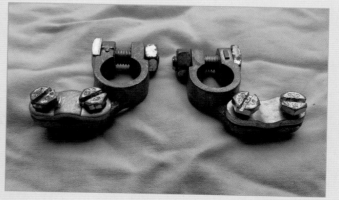

6 Take care if soldering battery terminals: fully support the cable close to any soldered joints. Soldering reduces the flexibility of copper strands and vibration can cause them to break. Furthermore, there are even reports of overheating circuitry causing solder to melt. High quality crimps or terminals with purely mechanical connections are favoured by some.

Wiring

1 For protection and neatness, run wiring through conduit or a commercially available braided sleeving. For a very professional finish, seal conduit/sleeving ends with short sections of heat-shrink material.

2 Always err on the side of caution with cable size – check equipment manufacturers' documentation for advice on the current-carrying capacity required. Use larger cross-sectional area (less resistant) cable if in doubt. Additionally, keep cable runs as short as possible – longer runs mean more voltage drop.

3 Try to avoid poor quality pre-insulated terminals or connectors. Connections made with poor quality versions can be found wanting and can – over time and for a variety of reasons – increase circuit resistance. As a result, though appearing superficially sound, they can be the source of hard-to-diagnose intermittent faults.

4 Multi-way connectors make for very reliable joins and a neat installation. They're available in any number of configurations and are an especially useful way of making neat junctions involving multiple circuits.

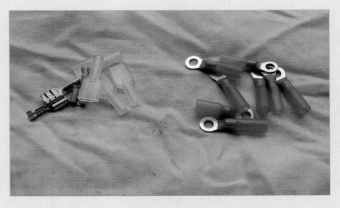

5 High-quality terminals with separate insulation and pre-insulated heat-shrink terminals provide a solid and reliable connection as (if correctly sized) they offer good support for the insulated sleeve of the wire itself, plus they keep out moisture.

6 Don't skimp on the crimp. Invest in a good quality crimping tool – connections will be infinitely more reliable.

7 Ensure you leave enough slack in your battery cables to be able to replace a defective battery on the road – the position and style of positive and negative terminal posts are not standardised. Here, a temporary battery is pressed into service but enough spare cable has been left to allow connections to be made successfully.

CHAPTER 11

Heating and cooling

- Space heating
- Domestic water heating
- Combination heaters
- Integrating the base vehicle's cooling system
- Heating snippets
- Heating summary
- Cooling (and a bit more about heating)

A fairly unusual but clean and good-looking tended stove. The owner reports good performance from this charcoal burner.

As with water and gas systems, because of the bulk and complexity involved, it's best to plan the installation of the hardware and plumbing associated with heating and cooling systems before building furniture.

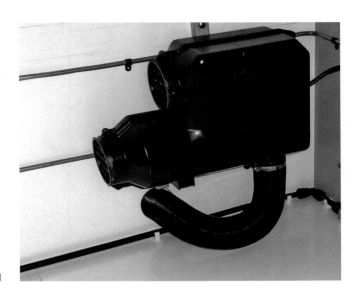

▲ A typical LPG-burning furnace at the early stages of installation prior to ducting being added. This kind of heater can be mounted almost anywhere and in any plane.

Space heating

Heating a habitation box can be achieved in many ways. At the simple end are 'dry' systems like log burners and convector heaters, at the complex end are pumped-hot-water (hydronic) systems that are characterised by fuel-burning furnaces (ordinarily powered by LPG or the same fuel as the base vehicle uses) that heat and then pump hot water through a combination of radiators, underfloor heating pipework and water-to-air heat exchangers. Just getting to grips with the various heating options can initially be bewildering. Buckle down!

Dry systems

Dry systems are so called because they heat air directly without any reliance on firstly heating and circulating hot water. Dry space heaters take innumerable forms but generally, in the overland camper context, the different types can be shoehorned into just a few broad genres: tended stoves, blown-air furnaces and untended convection heaters.

Tended stoves

These are essentially 'contained' open fires that have to be manually set and tended by the user. The fuel used is ordinarily wood, but some stoves burn other fuel such as drip-fed diesel or charcoal.

Pros include:
- Easy to install
- Cheap on fuel
- Heat output can be huge

Cons include:
- Suitable fuel can be hard to source
- Maintenance can become a chore

- Some versions are dirty and smelly
- Heat output difficult to regulate
- Safety issues
- Installation eats into living space

Blown-air furnaces

These are most often vehicle-fuel or LPG powered. They're room sealed and rely on inbuilt fans to circulate heat produced in the furnace, usually via ducting, to selected parts of the vehicle.

Pros include:
- Clean and (if working correctly) odour free
- Can be mounted out of sight or even fully outside of the habitation box
- Highly controllable
- Effective heat distribution
- Fuel (theoretically) in constant supply

Cons include:
- Reliance on battery power
- Can be noisy
- Electronically controlled

Untended convection heaters

These produce heat by burning (most frequently) LPG piped in from the vehicle's gas system. Warmed air emanates from the heater itself, usually by convection only, though some versions can also be equipped with a fan to additionally distribute heat via ducts feeding remote outlets.

PRINCIPLES OF COMMON DRY-SPACE HEATING OPTIONS

▶ A typical LPG-powered convector heater with built-in fan. Warm air can be delivered from the heater itself without the need to use battery power, or, with the built-in fan switched on, can distribute warm air around the vehicle via ducting.

▼ A diesel-powered blown-air furnace distributing warm air via ducting around the vehicle.

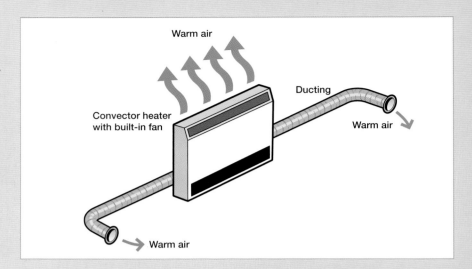

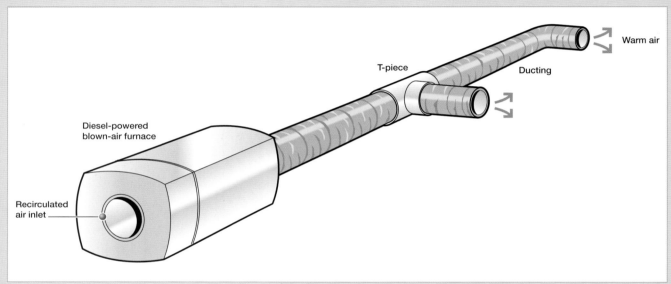

Tended stove

◀ A simple wood-burning tended stove. Heat is always more intense close to the stove and chimney.

▼ A twin blown-air solution utilising both a diesel and LPG-powered furnace. This gives flexibility over fuel source, a reserve system, and the possibility of quick heat-up times if both systems are used together.

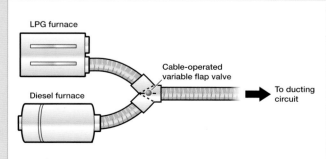

◀ **A typical LPG-burning convection heater. A quiet and non-battery-dependent way to heat an interior.** *(image courtesy of Truma Gerätetechnik)*

Pros include:
- Clean.
- Controllable heat output.
- No reliance upon battery power (unless a fan model is used).
- Quiet.

Cons include:
- Mostly reliant upon LPG.
- Installation eats into living space.
- Heat can be localised or inefficiently distributed (unless a fan model is used).

Each genre of dry-space heater has its supporters and it's not uncommon to see combinations of different types of heating solution in one vehicle. The idea, in keeping with overland-camper good practice, is that back-up systems

▼ **A water-to-air heat exchanger. Hot water pumped through this unit heats air as it's blown over the internal matrix.**

can be brought into play in the event of system failure or the shortage of a particular fuel type. On the subject of back-ups, stand-alone electric heaters of the convection or fan-assisted type are another solution occasionally encountered, but their dependence on an AC hook-up or generator *tends* to mean they're impractical as a primary heating source.

Though acknowledging choice and individual circumstances are very personal things, tended stoves are often reported as becoming a chore to manage whilst all LPG-powered heaters, though arguably the most refined solution, can burn through gas quite quickly and suffer from the single major issue of requiring a constant but potentially unobtainable supply of LPG fuel. For primary space-heating duty, the most conventional solution is a blown-air furnace running from the same fuel as the base vehicle itself, usually diesel. This is not necessarily the right choice for you but it *is* the most usual dry-space heating choice encountered.

Hydronic systems

Remember that, for the time being, even though heaters in the following section are all about heating water, we are only currently considering how the water they heat is utilised for *space* heating. Solutions for heating domestic water, i.e. water used for washing and showering etc., will be covered shortly.

With hydronic systems, a furnace (ordinarily vehicle-fuel powered) heats water and pumps it through a dedicated plumbing system to conveniently placed radiators, underfloor heating circuits, and/or to water-to-air heat exchangers. Such heat exchangers, much like a regular car heater, house a matrix complete with a built-in fan. The fan blows warmed air to any desired places, sometimes through ducting, around the vehicle.

Because of the multiplicity of ways in which pumped hot water can be put to use, hydronic furnaces offer a huge degree of versatility. On the negative side, they're expensive and complex machines, which can be fearsomely difficult to install and, especially if used in installations involving extra circulation pumps and blown water-to-air heat exchangers,

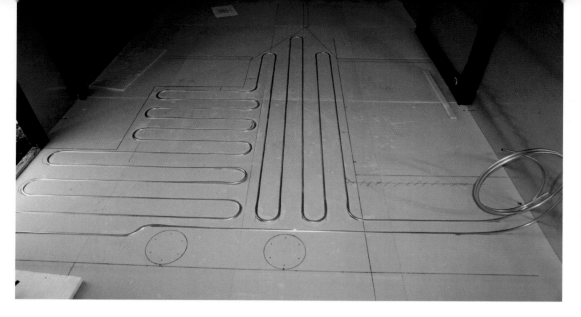

◀ Preparing for underfloor heating courtesy of a hydronic diesel furnace.

can be very demanding on battery power. There is also a *perception* that they suffer from inferior initial heat-up times compared to a dry blown-air system.

Domestic water heating

As with space heating, heating water for washing and showering can be achieved in many ways. In its simplest form, a kettle on a log-burning stove will do the trick. Of course, we can also elect to make life much more complicated.

Instant water heaters

Instant water heaters are not commonly used but are available. Some models are specifically designed to

burn LPG and work with the low water pressure found in leisure vehicles; modern versions also feature room-sealed burners. With this kind of system, there is no hot water storage boiler; water is simply heated as it's pumped through the boiler en route to the showerhead or tap. Though appealing, gas consumption is high and once again the major issue is one of sourcing reliable supplies of LPG. An additional but less obvious issue revolves around water conservation. 'Unlimited' hot water supplies tend to encourage longer showers…

Hot water storage boilers

In the vast majority of cases, domestic hot water is *not* instantly heated as above but is instead pre-heated and

PRINCIPLES OF COMMON HYDRONIC SPACE HEATING OPTIONS

▼ This is a simple hydronic furnace feeding a radiator circuit. Most of the system is plumbed in series but also features an isolatable extension plumbed in parallel.

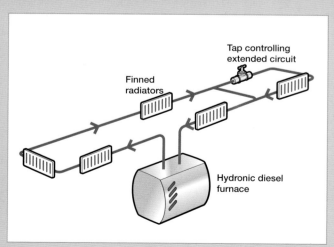

▼ This hydronic furnace feeds an isolatable radiator circuit, an underfloor heating loop and a fan-assisted water-to-air heat exchanger. The water-to-air heat exchanger could also blow through ducting if required.

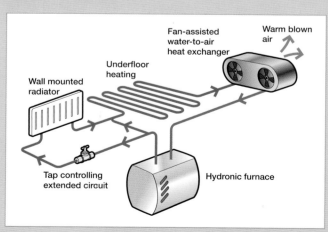

retained in some kind of hot-water storage boiler. As is the case with most matters to do with heating, storage boilers take many forms but all essentially comprise an insulated tank capable of holding anything between 5 and 50 (or occasionally even more) litres. The four most popular ways to heat the water that is stored within are:

■ By pumping hot water through a coil housed within the storage boiler itself – aka a water-to-water heat exchanger/calorifier.
■ By routing blown-air ducting through the storage boiler – aka an air-to-water heat exchanger.
■ Via an immersion heater element. *Most* hot water storage boilers house such an element and indeed boilers are available that can *only* be heated electrically. However, such is the energy requirement of immersion elements that heating water by this method is only really practicable with a mains hook-up, a generator or whilst driving. Elements are usually mains-voltage AC powered but occasionally 12/24V DC versions are encountered.
■ By direct application of heat utilising an inbuilt LPG or vehicle-fuel powered furnace. This kind of boiler houses the hot-water storage tank *and* furnace within one fully integrated unit. They tend to be of a fairly limited capacity (5–15 litres) but have the advantage of being very unobtrusive.

Of all of the ways to heat the water stored in a boiler, pumping hot water through a coil in the boiler itself is a very popular choice. The 'pumped' hot water is itself initially

heated in one of two ways: by a hydronic furnace or the vehicle's engine.

In the case of furnaces, these *can* be the very same units as those used to pump hot water to radiators etc. as described in the hydronic space-heating section, and this exemplifies the earlier-mentioned versatility of these machines. If you imagine one high-output furnace constantly circulating hot water through radiators, under-floor heating circuits, fan-assisted water-to-air heat exchangers *and additionally* a calorifier too, you'll understand how just one diesel-powered furnace can supply *all* space and domestic water heating requirements in one fell swoop.

In the case of the 'pumped' hot water initially being heated by the vehicle's engine, this is most usually achieved by tapping into – either in series or in parallel – the vehicle's own heater matrix plumbing. By routing the vehicle's engine coolant through a calorifier in this way the heat otherwise totally wasted by cooling the engine is effectively utilised. If you travel most days, it makes a great deal of sense to utilise the 'free' heat produced from this source. Making the best of both worlds, it's even possible to purchase twin coil calorifiers that enable use of both a furnace *and* the vehicle's coolant supply to heat the stored contents.

▼ A single-coil 15-litre calorifier. This particular storage boiler is heated by tapping into the base-vehicle's cab-heater circuit (via the black pipes). Note the thermostatic mixer valve to the left of the image. Note too the three securing straps mounted on 'tap washer' bobbins. On rough roads, calorifiers will do their best to break free – the larger they are, the more restraint they need.

CALORIFIERS

Calorifiers are essentially no more than a simple insulated storage tank with one or two lengths of coiled pipe running through them. Water supplied from the camper's fresh-water system sits within the storage vessel and is gradually heated by hot water pumped through the coil(s); some calorifiers also contain an electrically powered immersion-heater element. When a hot-water tap is opened, cold water is pumped into the calorifier which displaces hot water in the storage vessel to the tap you just opened. Though essentially simple devices, here are some general points of interest:

- Thermostatic mixers/anti-scald valves. At the point where hot water leaves the calorifier, you'll often find a thermostatic mixer; this can usually be user-set to ensure water is delivered at a specific temperature. The mixer draws in a little cold water from the cold water side of the plumbing system and mixes it with the hot water drawn from the calorifier before distribution to the opened tap.
- More hot water than you bargained for. Because the thermostatic mixer draws in cold water, every litre of *hot* water you draw from the calorifier will result in more than a litre of *mixed* water at the tap. This only works whilst water temperature in the calorifier is *greater* than the temperature set on the thermostatic mixer but, essentially, means that a fully heated calorifier will deliver slightly more heated water than its nominal capacity.
- Cooling effect relating to size. As hot water is drawn off, cold water is introduced into the calorifier so the smaller the overall capacity, and the longer the water is allowed to stand, the greater the cooling effect of the incoming water will be. A 15-litre capacity is ordinarily enough for two *consecutive* showers and some washing-up water. Longer or *non*-consecutive showers might be better served by a unit of 20–25 litres' capacity.
- Over-sizing. Larger calorifiers (over 25 litres) start to introduce unhelpful issues relating to weight, bulk and security of mounting; plus, they take more energy and time to heat and can discourage good water conservation habits. Bigger is not always better.
- Heating time. Given direct and efficient plumbing, an engine running *under load* will heat water stored in a 20-litre calorifier to a shower-ready temperature in *approximately* 15 to 20 minutes, depending on ambient temperature and the initial temperature of its contents.
- Insulation. If well insulated *and previously untapped*, agreeably warm (but *not* hot) water will still be available the morning after the previous day's drive.

- Hydronic furnace input. If heated from a hydronic furnace instead of, or in addition to, the vehicle's engine, you can have, to all intents and purposes, hot water at any time.
- Electric immersion elements. The same applies, if you are on hook-up, or have some other way of generating sufficient power, immersion elements can also mean hot water at any time.
- Safety valves. A feature usually found on calorifiers is a safety valve. This will open as the heated water expands to relieve internal pressure. It will 'spit' a little hot water every so often so careful positioning of the valve's associated drain pipe is required. An accumulator or expansion tank in the hot-water system will minimise operation of the safety valve. Valves can also often be manually opened to facilitate a full draindown for frost protection.
- Mounting location. Ideally, to avoid any airlock issues, the calorifier should be mounted *below* the height of the header tank of the system that feeds it; be that the vehicle engine or a hydronic furnace. Mounting the calorifier as close to the taps it feeds as possible will provide the most consistent temperatures.
- Reinforced take-off pipe. Because the water exiting the calorifier can be *very* hot, it can overwhelm and burst some fresh-water plumbing fittings. For this reason, it's wise to install a short steel-reinforced take-off pipe to take the initial thermal 'hit'.

▶ **A consequence of too-hot water in a pipe not designed to take high temperatures. This pipe wasn't even particularly close to a heat source.**

▶ A simple single-coil calorifier is the easiest way to utilise engine coolant to both heat and store domestic hot water.

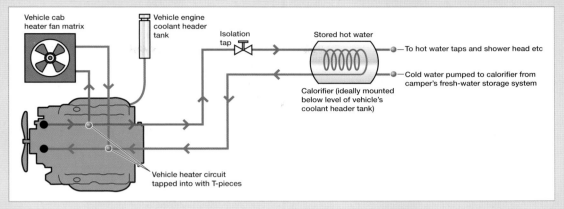

Vehicle cab heater fan matrix

Vehicle engine coolant header tank

Isolation tap

Stored hot water

To hot water taps and shower head etc

Cold water pumped to calorifier from camper's fresh-water storage system

Calorifier (ideally mounted below level of vehicle's coolant header tank)

Vehicle heater circuit tapped into with T-pieces

▶ A simple LPG-powered furnace with a built-in hot water storage boiler.

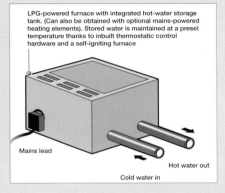

LPG-powered furnace with integrated hot-water storage tank. (Can also be obtained with optional mains-powered heating elements). Stored water is maintained at a preset temperature thanks to inbuilt thermostatic control hardware and a self-igniting furnace

Mains lead

Hot water out

Cold water in

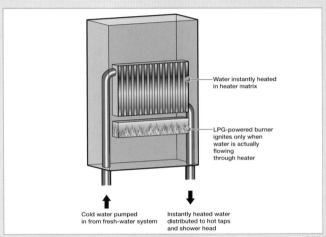

Water instantly heated in heater matrix

LPG-powered burner ignites only when water is actually flowing through heater

Cold water pumped in from fresh-water system

Instantly heated water distributed to hot taps and shower head

▲ An instant hot water heater.

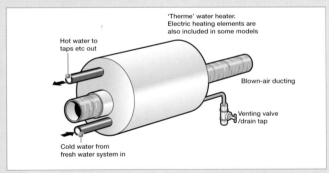

Hot water to taps etc out

'Therme' water heater. Electric heating elements are also included in some models

Blown-air ducting

Venting valve /drain tap

Cold water from fresh water system in

◀ An interesting and surprisingly rarely used water heater. This simple and ingenious air-to-water heat exchanger simply feeds a blown-air duct through a storage container, which slowly but surely heats the stored water contents. Though of limited capacity, this would make for an excellent auxiliary or back-up hot-water supply.

▶ A typical twin-coil calorifier supplemented with an electric heating element. This set-up allows either the vehicle's engine, an onboard hydronic furnace, or electricity to heat domestic hot water.

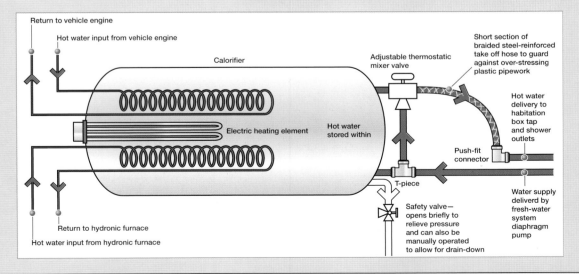

Return to vehicle engine

Hot water input from vehicle engine

Calorifier

Adjustable thermostatic mixer valve

Short section of braided steel-reinforced take off hose to guard against over-stressing plastic pipework

Electric heating element

Hot water stored within

Hot water delivery to habitation box tap and shower outlets

Push-fit connector

T-piece

Water supply deliverd by fresh-water system diaphragm pump

Safety valve— opens briefly to relieve pressure and can also be manually operated to allow for drain-down

Return to hydronic furnace

Hot water input from hydronic furnace

Combination heaters

Combination heaters are primarily diesel or LPG fuelled and take care of both space and domestic water heating in one neat, self-contained unit. Though they all ultimately perform the same functions, heaters in this genre do not all utilise the same methodology. Some heat space by employing a blown-air system, others heat space by employing a hydronic-based system. In some cases, they also incorporate an AC electric element that can be used to heat space in the event that you're on AC hook-up or have a generator running.

As far as the domestic-water-heating side of their functionality is concerned, the solution in all cases is to integrate a (usually quite small) hot-water storage boiler within the self-contained unit adjacent to the furnace, which, more often than not, will also incorporate an AC-powered immersion heater element. Again, if you *are* on hook-up, have a suitable generator, or can power the element whilst driving via an inverter etc., this addition may be a useful one.

In each case the space- and water-heating functions can be operated independently of one another so if it's too warm to fire up the space heater but you need a hot shower then domestic water can be heated without having to fire-up the space heating side of the system. A useful aside with this kind of heater is that when operating the furnace for space heating, domestic water contained within the boiler will usually be heated to a reasonable temperature just from the residual heat generated by the space-heating operation. In

other words, when heating space, you'll usually gain some 'free' warm water.

In the event that you do *not* wish to utilise your vehicle's engine coolant as a source of heat for domestic hot water, then a combination heater – particularly if utilising blown-air rather than hydronics for its space-heating function – is probably amongst the neatest, simplest to install and altogether most efficient solution to *all* of your heating needs. Indeed, the benefits are recognised by professional manufacturers: LPG-powered combination heaters particularly are often the default heating solution in conventional motorhomes.

Integrating the base vehicle's cooling system

As may now be apparent, what initially sounds like a fairly straightforward notion, i.e. heating space and water, can involve a genuinely mind-bending range of solutions. If you're not already utterly baffled, there are two additional layers of complexity that you may wish to mentally wrestle with.

The first of these layers involves using the vehicle's own coolant system to heat space in the habitation box. Essentially, the vehicle's heater matrix circuit – in addition to being extended to provide domestic hot water by pumping coolant through a calorifier as described in previous sections – is commonly *further* extended to incorporate a radiator or two, or a water-to-blown-air heat exchanger. By incorporating these space-heating components, the

PRINCIPLES OF COMMON COMBINATION HEATER OPTIONS

▼ **A hydronic combination boiler. This kind of system is popular on some boats and on very high-end conventional motor caravans.**

▼ **This is a combination boiler that utilises blown air instead of circulated hot water for space heating. This kind of set-up is the most common system fitted to conventional motor caravans. Though an LPG version is illustrated, diesel-powered versions are readily available.**

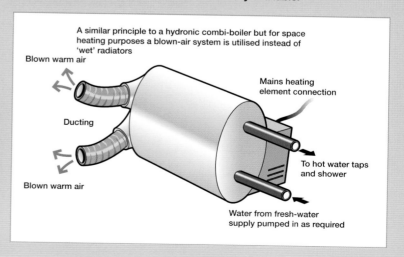

LPG-powered hydronic combination boiler.
This unit heats and stores domestic hot water at a preset temperature. The operation is fully automatic. Additionally, the unit circulates hot water to radiators etc via a different 'loop'. The domestic hot water and hydronic functions can be operated independently.

To hot water taps and shower head

Mains heating element connection

From radiators etc
To radiators etc

Water from fresh water system pumped in as required

A similar principle to a hydronic combi-boiler but for space heating purposes a blown-air system is utilised instead of 'wet' radiators

Blown warm air

Mains heating element connection

Ducting

To hot water taps and shower

Blown warm air

Water from fresh-water supply pumped in as required

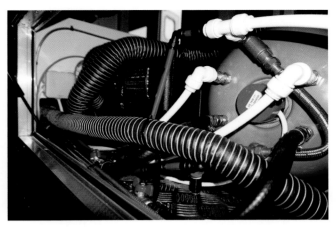

▲ **Heating systems can rapidly become incredibly complicated.**

habitation area can be heated during the day's drive simply by recruiting energy that would otherwise just be wasted as a by-product of engine cooling. However, though the notion is attractive, care should be taken not to over-extend such additions otherwise – especially in very cold conditions – the engine may fail to reach its optimum operating temperature.

The second layer of complexity involves using a furnace – usually vehicle-fuel powered – to (directly or indirectly) heat the vehicle's engine coolant. The idea behind this arrangement is that the base vehicle's own inbuilt heater fan and ducting system can then be utilised to heat the cab space without the engine running and furthermore – what is for many exponents of this idea the most useful benefit – the engine itself can be pre-heated to maximise the chance of an efficient start even in the most extreme of sub-zero conditions. Of course, as well as maximising chances of the engine actually starting, because the coolant is fully pre-heated the vehicle's inbuilt heater can instantly supply hot air, something that is of massive benefit in defrosting frozen windscreens, plus intrepid travellers.

The hardware, plumbing and electrical systems involved

▼ **A water-to-water heat exchanger. This allows transfer of heat both ways between the engine coolant and domestic hydronic circuits. Both circuits, however, remain sealed from one another.**

in incorporating the base vehicle's cooling system into bespoke space-heating solutions ranges from *reasonably* straightforward to very involved. The illustrations overleaf will hopefully add some clarity to the basic options.

Heating snippets

Here are some further snippets that may assist in your contemplation of the design and installation of heating solution(s):

Diesel furnaces

■ Glow plugs. Diesel furnaces demand a heavy current draw at startup as an inbuilt glow-plug needs to pre-heat incoming diesel in order that it will initially combust. In some cases, this is the case at shut-down as well where the glow plug can be called upon to help in a 'self-clean' routine. The glow-plug time is usually minimal but your wiring and batteries *must* be able to cope with the short-but-heavy current draw otherwise the furnace may refuse to start.

■ Hysteresis. To avoid too many start-up/shut-down cycles and thereby minimise reliance on battery-draining glow plugs, many diesel furnaces are programmed to allow a relatively large temperature differential between cycling down and re-firing. As a result, they can be *poor* at maintaining a constant room temperature. They will initially burn fiercely but reduce their output as they approach your chosen thermostatically preset room temperature. When the preset temperature is reached *some* heaters will stop burning fuel, cycle down, and not re-ignite until room temperature has dropped *sometimes uncomfortably*. As a battery-saving alternative, *some* heaters do not cycle down at all. Instead, they continue to burn fuel and produce heat but at a very low rate. In these cases, it falls to users to simply switch off manually if the habitation area becomes too warm. These regimes are designed to conserve battery power *not* to optimise end-user comfort.

■ Zero idle. *Some* blown-air diesel furnaces, having reached the required room temperature and cycled down, will stop supplying heat but will *not* turn off all their functions completely and are specifically programmed to continue recirculating ever-cooler air. This is purportedly so that the recirculated air temperature can be monitored within the heater casing and when it's sensed to be sufficiently cool, it indicates to the heater that it's time to re-ignite. Unfortunately, this has real-world negative effects. It results in the unwelcome *cooling* of a warm habitation area, unnecessary noise, and an unhelpful draw on battery reserves. If you are going to purchase a blown-air diesel heater, you'd be well advised to ensure it has a 'zero idle' capability, i.e. that it will shut down *all* of its mechanical functions completely between cycles and *not* continue to blow cooler air around.

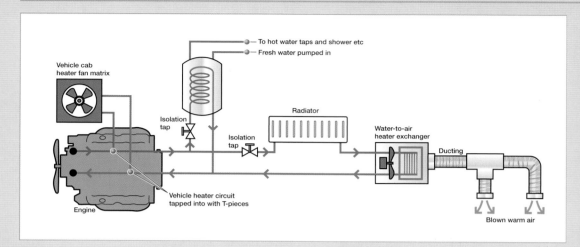

◄ This set-up allows the engine coolant to not only heat a calorifier for domestic hot water but also to heat a small radiator and a water-to-air heat exchanger to enable the habitation box to be warmed up whilst driving.

▶ This system uses a hydronic furnace to pre-heat engine coolant and circulate it to the vehicle's own cab heater matrix plus a calorifier. NB: This set-up is highly simplified for illustration purposes and can be modified to include thermostats and one-way valves to favour heating the engine block or the heater matrix initially and then heating the 'secondary choice' once a set temperature is reached.

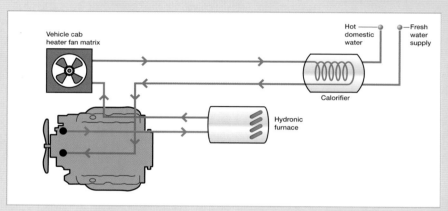

▼ Using a water-to-water heat exchanger the engine coolant can be pre-heated courtesy of the hydronic furnace primarily used for habitation box heating. Because the engine coolant is warmed, it can also provide a heat source for the vehicle's own cab heater matrix etc. Conversely, when driving, the engine coolant heats up the water-to-water heat exchanger enabling heated water to be pumped around the habitation box circuits, heating the box as you drive. NB Auxiliary pumps are needed to circulate hot water in the 'secondary' circuit – whichever that happens to be at any given time.

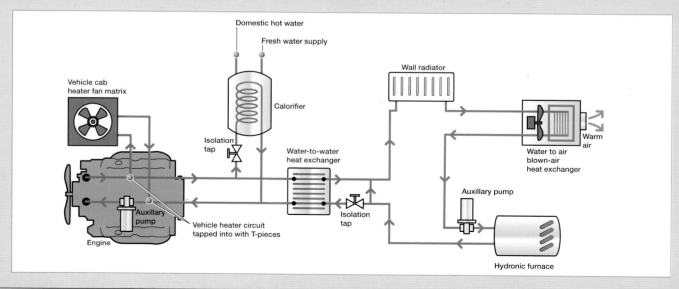

- Metering pump tick. Diesel heaters require a metering (aka dosing) pump to deliver fuel to the furnace. These pumps 'tick' audibly and, notoriously, drive some people to distraction. Careful siting of the pump and the use of purpose-made pliable rubber mounts can help enormously in reducing this infamous noise.

- Altitude issues. Diesel-powered furnaces do not operate well at altitude. Anything over a *sustained* 1,500m *might* start to cause trouble. At altitude, notwithstanding the thinner air found there, the heater's dosing pump (unless modified) will continue to deliver fuel at its pre-programmed rate. This results, effectively, in an over-fuelling scenario that will eventually manifest as 'sooty' deposits and, ultimately, a clogged furnace. Different manufacturers have different solutions and some of these are specific to the particular furnace in question. The only answer for reliable operation at altitude is to seek manufacturer's advice (usually, extra altitude-compensating hardware is required), or to utilise an alternative heating system.

- Waxing. Though petrochemical companies appropriately prepare fuel for different climates, in very low temperatures diesel can turn 'waxy' and will not flow. Diesel heaters may fail to work in very low temperatures unless the fuel supply is insulated or otherwise protected.

- Exhaust noise. Exhaust noise from diesel heaters, even through a silencer, can be substantial. When combined with metering pump tick, your popularity amongst neighbours may border on 'generator' levels.

- Over-cycling hydronic system. In some hydronic systems, a sensor in the diesel furnace monitors returning water temperature and if this is close to the temperature of the water leaving, the heater may compute room temperature has been reached and cycle down. Unfortunately, it might well be the case that hydronic circuit is 'short' or otherwise has insufficient opportunity to 'lose' heat so the habitation area may well not actually ever reach an agreeable temperature before the heater cycles down. In these cases, builders need to find ways to reduce the temperature of hot water returning to the heater. This might mean incorporating a valve to reduce the volume of flow to one part of the circuit if components are plumbed in parallel (dedicated calorifier circuits are often a culprit), or, if all components are plumbed in series, extending the overall circuit and running it through extra heat exchangers. Of course, *over*-extending the circuit can also lead to poor performance or failures. Balance is the key.

- Bad fuel. Poor-grade fuel can quickly prevent diesel heaters from working and on-the-road maintenance may be required if diesel quality is very poor. To improve the chances of avoiding foreign objects and water entering the metering pump, it's best practice to draw fuel via a stand pipe that doesn't reach all the way to the bottom of the fuel-supply tank.

- Comfortable room temperatures. Because LPG is highly flammable and very easily ignited without the need for a glow plug, LPG heaters can be designed to cycle on and off constantly without fear of draining batteries. As a result, high-quality LPG heaters *tend* to be the best solution for fully automatically maintaining a comfortable room temperature.

- Other plus points. LPG furnaces tend to be easier to install than their direct diesel rivals and are often quieter in use. Additionally, they're not as prone to failure at modest altitude, will not suffer fuel delivery problems until at least −40°C (if used on propane), and are less arduous on leisure batteries.

- Of course, if you can't source LPG, these positive attributes are utterly useless.

- Dump valves. Many proprietary hot-water storage boilers have built-in valves that open automatically in low temperatures to protect the storage boiler from frost damage. These *can* be irritating as they will often open at temperatures well above freezing and unceremoniously decant your hard-won hot water. They can also operate in low-voltage situations. Many people work out a way to override them…

- Specialist hydronic coolant. Hydronic system components, particularly pumps, can be damaged if used with plain water only. Manufacturers' instructions regarding correct coolant mix must be followed to the letter.

- Mismatching metals. In a similar vein, hydronic component internals can be corroded if dissimilar metal plumbing fittings are used in the same coolant circuit. Again, heed manufacturers' advice.

- Induction roar from blown-air heater recirculation inlets. The induction roar from recirculation inlets can be substantial. For a quieter experience, recruit air from a (well-ventilated) storage locker etc. rather than from the habitation area directly.

- Blown-air ducting size. Ducting comes in many diameters and manufacturers confusingly disagree on a standard for quoting sizes of duct and fittings. Some refer to *internal* dimensions, some to *external* dimensions. Essentially, the most frequently used ducting (referred to as *either* 60mm *or* 65mm) is the same size *no matter* the manufacturer. It has a 60mm internal diameter and 65mm external diameter. This ducting slides perfectly *into* '65mm' fittings made by one proprietary manufacturer but *over* '60mm' fittings made by others.

- Blown-air ducting systems. There are countless types of ducting fittings, adapters and outlets available that

This section is not intended as a 'how-to' guide, but instead to highlight how much there is to think about when fitting a heating system. This is just a *very* straightforward blown-air diesel heater installation.

1 The underside of a diesel-powered blown-air heater. The convoluted black pipe is the combustion air inlet, the metal pipe is the furnace's exhaust, the wiring is the feed for the dosing pump and the thin black pipe the diesel-fuel feed. The collar surrounding all the pipework locates the whole assembly and if the heater is conventionally mounted inside the vehicle, requires a very large hole to be cut through the floor.

2 One very large hole in the floor later... the view from underneath. Placement is vital to make sure all the pipes and tubes etc. can be accommodated in accordance with operating parameters (outlined in the installation manual) and kept out of harm's way. Note the exhaust silencer – this is not really optional as these heaters can be noisy in operation.

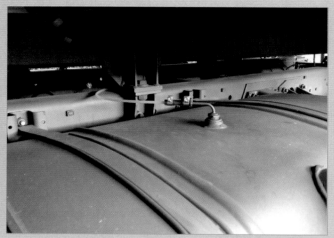

3 A supply of diesel fuel needs to be established. Feeding heaters from standpipes is good practice. Keeping the standpipe well short of the bottom of the tank means you'll never use all of the fuel you require to actually drive and there's less likelihood of debris clogging the heater's pump.

4 The dosing pump in situ. The 'tick' from these can be torturous so mounting them in a totally flexible rubber 'P' clip as per this installation is highly recommended. This prevents the 'tick' from resonating through the entire vehicle.

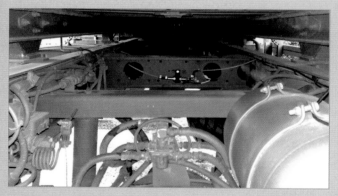

5 Though small, physically siting the heater can be surprisingly awkward. Follow manufacturers' instructions regarding placement and ensure you won't be compromising the subsequent siting of furniture or other hardware.

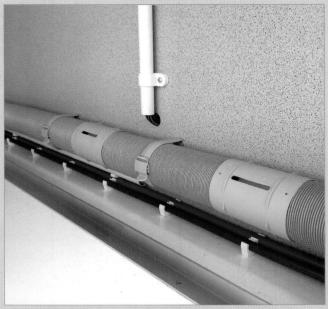

6 An internal wiring loom will need to be accommodated for the heater's controls and room temperature sensor (if fitted). The loom can be shortened or lengthened, but hacking into it could lead to warranty issues so it's arguably better to accommodate extra length by running a 'surplus loop' somewhere out of sight.

7 Ducting distributes heat to all parts of the vehicle but it can take some trial and error to perfect even heat distribution. The small pipes in this installation feed an underfloor section and protect the water tank and its fittings from freezing.

9 An example of fine tuning. All manner of ducting is available. These subtle outlets are basically to ward off the build-up of condensation in the garage area of this installation.

10 One of the many reasons why ostensibly small heaters can be tricky to locate: the associated ducting, pipes, wiring, etc. soon make them very space hungry – remember this is an example of one of the very simplest of installations!

8 Underfloor section covered.

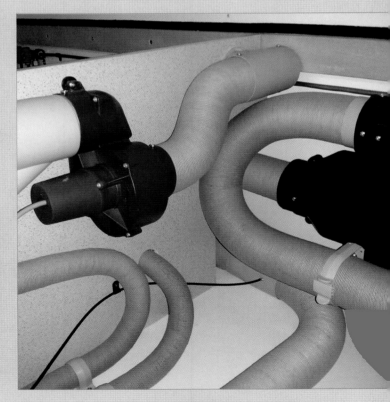

allow the construction of the most incredibly elaborate and infinitely tweakable of systems. It may take a few attempts to get warm air distribution just right so start in the knowledge that you may have to add further outlets and simultaneously restrict the flow from those nearest the heater. Also, beware the common trap of too-long an overall system. Outlets at the end of such systems can actually blow cold air! Build systems in stages and tweak as you go.

■ Battery and water system benefits. Running ducting or hydronic plumbing through battery compartments or through water tank lockers etc. can be of benefit. When kept warm, batteries will perform better and vulnerable water installations will be protected from frost.

■ Total reliance on AC-powered heating elements. For anyone thinking of sidestepping the issue of diesel furnace unreliability at altitude by employing electric heating elements powered from a generator, bear in mind that the generator's internal combustion engines may struggle to work at altitude too.

Heating summary

In summary, first an important point to note: all of the various principles illustrated in this chapter are just that, illustrations. In many cases they are simplified just to give you an idea of the options. None are prescriptive and each and any could be mixed and matched to suit personal requirements. That said, remember well the tenets. Full-blown hydronic systems that interface with the vehicle's own coolant system – though in reliable use in many real-world overlanders – can be fiendishly complicated to install and maintain. Such systems sometimes require the addition of numerous check valves, thermostats, header tanks, solenoid valves, supplementary wiring and switches, drain valves and so on. There is no doubt that going this route is a big commitment and, in more cases than not, will require at least *some* expert advice. Problems associated with complex hydronic installations often require professional problem solving on an installation-by-installation basis.

When it comes to decision time, as with just about every other aspect of an overland-camper build, there's no definitive right and wrong, just more or less appropriate solutions given your own circumstances and intentions. However, after everything is taken into account, the most popular choices amongst others that have already trodden this path tend to be:

■ For space heating: either a ducted blown-air or relatively simple hydronic system, in both cases powered by a furnace that burns the same fuel as the base vehicle (usually diesel).

■ For domestic water heating: a calorifier heated by the

base vehicle's coolant and/or a hydronic furnace, which again uses the same fuel as the base vehicle.

These popular solutions may or may not be the right choice in your own case but they *are* a proven choice for (most) worldwide travel. That said, in cases where consistently high altitudes will be encountered, or when you're absolutely sure that you'll have a reliable supply of LPG, then gas-based systems are arguably an altogether more refined and, on balance, reliable solution.

Ultimately, it bears repeating that rather than swear allegiance to just one fuel type, it may well be better to use a combination of heater types and be secure in the knowledge that, in the event of failure or lack of fuel, you have a contingency. With heating, a secondary system is a very worthwhile consideration and arguably even indispensable if your travels will take you to very cold climates.

Cooling (and a bit more about heating)

Vehicle cab cooling was covered in Chapter 4 and, when it comes to cooling the habitation box, options are broadly similar. In summary, the main choices are: to fit a self-contained, electrically powered air-conditioning unit, to utilise an engine-driven compressor system, or to adopt the simple solutions of evaporative cooling by making use of good ventilation and decent-quality fans.

Electrically powered air-con units

Self-contained air-conditioning units that are large and powerful enough to cool an entire habitation area are almost exclusively designed to work on mains voltage, usually supplied courtesy of a hook-up or a generator. In order to run such air-con units whilst the vehicle is being driven, dedicated DC kits can also be purchased. These bespoke (and expensive) DC kits are essentially sophisticated inverter/controller packages designed to automatically sense and manage the unit's power-delivery source, whether the power is supplied from a mains-voltage hook-up or the vehicle's batteries.

Some self-contained air-con units are designed to be mounted out of sight in a convenient cupboard whilst others are designed to be roof-mounted. Whichever type is preferred, there's no escaping that air-conditioning systems are power-hungry entities and even units at the smaller end of the scale can have requirements of 50+ amps at 12 volts. Accordingly, it's simply just not practicable to use this kind of cooler for extended periods from battery power alone. Regarding effectiveness, in high ambient temperatures (30°C plus, for example) it takes a *very* large and powerful unit to make a significant difference to habitation box temperature, smaller units may improve conditions *slightly* but are never going to be powerful enough to create a truly cool interior. Effectively then, to *substantially* cool down an entire habitation box, unless you have a large and powerful air-con unit and a reliable AC supply, self-contained electrically powered systems are only ever likely to provide a partial solution.

Rather than be drawn into a spiral of acquiring ever larger electrically powered air-con units and generators, one strategy that may be worthy of pursuit is to restrict cooling efforts to a relatively small self-contained compartment set aside as a dedicated 'cool' space and to utilise a relatively compact air-con unit to cool this area alone. In these circumstances it may be possible to use a unit designed to cool a truck cab (of the type discussed in Chapter 4) and to power this directly by DC. Were this strategy applied to a sleeping area, it might then *just* be possible, using battery power alone, to ensure a *reasonably* quiet and cool night's sleep whilst off-grid. If your battery capacity is insufficient, a methanol-powered generator wouldn't add to the air-con's noise levels too much but would, naturally, require a healthy supply of fuel cartridges if used nightly over the course of a long trip.

Coolers as heaters

Electrically powered air-conditioning units generally include a function that, given the availability of sufficient power, can be used to *heat* habitation box interiors as well as cool them. This, however, may not be as useful an attribute as first appears. If utilising the heating function for sustained periods in low temperatures, depending on design, ice *can* form on the condenser/evaporator, causing internal malfunction. In other words, when used for extended periods in very cold conditions, the heater may effectively freeze up. Research this issue well if you intend to rely on the heating function of an air-conditioning unit as anything other than a supplementary and very occasional heat source.

Engine-driven compressor air-con systems

Cab air-conditioning systems powered by an engine-driven compressor can be extended by the use of a dedicated evaporator serving the habitation box to *significantly* cool living quarters when the vehicle engine is running. As outlined in Chapter 4 though, this kind of installation is not for the faint-hearted and will require bespoke plumbing and control systems. Of course, such systems don't work at all once the vehicle's engine is stopped and, furthermore, one hairline fracture in a pipe or a barely leaking 'O' ring can mean the whole installation is reduced to little more than a weighty and expensive source of frustration. In spite of the technical complexity and potential for unreliability though, an engine-compressor-based system has the potential to deliver genuinely worthwhile cooling power and if much of your travel will be in very hot areas then this approach may well prove worthwhile.

Low-tech solutions

Given the incomplete, often less than reliable and sometimes eye-wateringly expensive solutions that dedicated air-conditioning apparatus offers, *many* builders decide that practicable habitation-box air conditioning is a project too far and simply rely on good ventilation and good-quality fans. It's worth bearing in mind, if going the fan route, that many roof vents can helpfully be obtained with fans inbuilt and some of these are even two-way meaning air can be drawn in as well as extracted. If you adopt the low-tech approach, a much-vaunted bush technique/ elementary science project (that really works) is to hang wet towels and pass air over them. This can remove a useful amount of heat energy in what is, essentially, an evaporative cooling process. With low-tech solutions, you *may* not stay quite as cool, but you *will* save installation and maintenance headaches, plus a good deal of cash.

▼ **An ice formation caused intermittent failure of this electrically powered air-con unit when working as a heater in very cold temperatures.**

▼ **A huge evaporator being incorporated into a habitation box for use with a full engine-driven air-conditioning system.**

Thomas Hübner

1 Name
Thomas Hübner (magictom).

2 Base vehicle
DAF Leyland T244 – 1990.

3 Drive
AWD 4x4.

4 Fuel capacity
580 litres is possible. 300 litres from 1 x permanent tank plus 280 litres from an ex-bulkhead tank, which is not always fitted but can be bolted to the left side of the shelter when needed.

5 Weight when loaded and ready to travel
8.5 tonnes.

6 Reason for base vehicle choice
I love the looks... Strong basic truck without electronics, single wheels, good engine, permanent all-wheel drive, roomy cab (2+2 sized). Cheap to buy at €5200.

7 Subframe solution
Self-designed 3-point torsion-free subframe, fixed at front, pivoting at rear.

8 Habitation-box construction
Ex-army radio box, length extended by me by 1 metre. Aluminium frame and aluminium skin.

9 Habitation-box insulation material
Closed-cell foam of 82mm.

10 Habitation-box manufacturer
Dornier – but heavily modified by me.

11 Habitation-box windows
Seitz S7 and S4.

12 Habitation-box door(s) and locker(s)
Original Dornier shelter door relocated by me from the rear to the side.

13 Fit out done by
Self.

14 Furniture construction
Birch plywood.

15 Fresh water
200 litres.

16   Refrigeration
Engel Kompressor-Kühlbox MD-60-F, EEK: A

17   Space heating
I have an oil stove: a HAAS & Sohn Ziller 422.40 (5kW) plus a Webasto diesel-powered blown-air heater (6kW).

18   Water heating
Instant propane-powered hot-water boiler – Junkers Therme (17kW).

19   Cooking facilities
2-burner gas stove inside, 3-burner gas stove outside.

20   Habitation-box cooling
By opening windows, doors and roof-mounted 'pop-top'.

21   Leisure-battery charging
Solar panels, battery charger, split-charge relay from the alternator.

22   Things to do differently next time
Nothing.

CHAPTER 12

Interior space and furniture

- General layout considerations
- A place for everything
- Build techniques
- Specialist structures
- Hardware
- Upholstery

This chapter is designed to be helpful whether you're still at the early stages of a project and are seeking inspiration for the use of interior space, or are well advanced with your build and are beginning to think about furniture, materials and construction techniques.

General layout considerations

First, an underpinning principle. Weight distribution is something that should be considered no matter what the details of your layout preference might be. It may seem obvious, but when you're engrossed in trying to maximise the use of every last millimetre it's something that can easily be overlooked. Ensure that, where possible, any *heavy* fixtures and fittings are carried at a low level and evenly distributed left to right. Fore-aft location is usually less of an issue, but, as covered before, placing very heavy items like large water tanks *behind* the line of the rear axle is bad practice. Overhead lockers and full-height cupboards are popular fixtures, but be mindful that with overland campers especially, the lower the centre of gravity the better. On very uneven terrain, when the habitation box is leaning precariously, the fact you made your tinned-food storage locker at floor level just might save the day!

After taking into account weight distribution, layout choice is a *very* individual thing and what will be perfect for a lone traveller might be totally untenable for a family with young children. Whatever the overall constitution of the crew, here are some general considerations, some of which may initially seem counter-intuitive:

■ Me space. Living on the road in a *very* confined space for months on end can be wearing. Even the strongest of relationships can be tested at times and it's wise to have at least one segregated space where individual pursuits like reading, writing, or simply sitting in a bewildered silence can be done without disturbance. It's not particularly necessary to have a totally closed-off space; the creative use of cupboard placement or partitioning will serve just as well.
■ Separate beds. A very personal choice but one which many seasoned travellers eventually gravitate towards. Not only is this notion an extension of the 'me space' principle but, depending on layout, can have practical advantages too. One of the most frequently cited is that if using just one bed, such is the relatively confined space within a camper that nocturnal visits to the toilet will often mean one partner having to physically clamber over the

other. After several hundred elbows-in-the-face (or worse), the humour starts to run thin…
■ Seats. You'll inevitably spend a great deal of time seated in the habitation box. This may sound incredibly obvious, but it's important that your seats are comfortable. Beware of building *all* your seating to support a formal upright posture. When working on a laptop or dining, upright seating against a table is undoubtedly the best choice. However, when such seating is used for general lounging, it can, unless very well designed, lead to incessant fidgeting in an attempt to get comfortable. Building seating that allows occupants to sprawl/relax with feet up is rarely something that is regretted.

A place for everything

It helps to be organised on the road. Having to move your partner, then a cushion, then lift a locker lid – all to retrieve a pan – does not sound onerous, but it can, after months, become such a hassle that you're almost guaranteed to make a sandwich instead. It's hugely advisable to plan your storage solutions before you start to build furniture.

Specialised storage

Some items and circumstances are worthy of special consideration. Specialised storage areas may need to be created for:

■ Awkwardly shaped items. It will prove worthwhile, before starting construction, to make an inventory of the awkwardly shaped things you intend to take with you on the road and then to ensure that you build in solutions to accommodate these. Things like laptops, cameras, fishing gear, umbrellas (the list goes on) that pose few storage problems at home can prove awkward to accommodate in the confined space of an overlander.
■ Crockery. On rough roads, pots, pans and crockery have a particularly tough time. Solutions to avoid breakages are many and varied, and some builders even go so far as to create bespoke receptacles or foam moulds for each individual piece. Melamine crockery and plastic mugs/glasses may lack a certain sophistication, but they can take a lot of abuse and are both a lightweight and practical solution.

INTERIOR STORAGE SOLUTIONS

Here's a pictorial guide to some effective storage solutions. Some of these appear ridiculously obvious with the benefit of hindsight, but it *can* require several trips with possessions in utter disarray before the chaos is tamed.

▲ Under this built-in seat footrest the compartment has been partitioned to securely accommodate a laptop and optical equipment. Dimensions are such that the items are prevented from moving around when driving on rough roads. Note the magazine/map pocket on the underside of the lid too.

▼ This overhead locker is above the cooking area and is a storage area for food. Partitions help to organise contents, stop movement in transit, and maximise space.

▶ These shelves were built around the dimensions of the polypropylene storage boxes pictured. This is a simple way to keep things organised and doesn't require elaborate furniture-making techniques. Note the brushed-nickel retaining rails. These are simply cupboard door handles from a high street DIY store. The moulding in the front of the boxes has been shaped with a small sanding wheel to lock them into position behind the rails.

▼ By keeping smaller items in resealable polybags, fiddly items can be readily found and all available space can be utilised.

A further use of Really Useful Boxes. This 50-litre version is fastened to the floor beneath a seat base and is used to retain heavy food items (mainly tinned). Note how tap washers above and below the box's base are used to spread the load of the 12-gauge fixing screws. A further 33-litre box stacks on top of this one and is held in situ by the underside of the hinged seat base. Many weeks' worth of emergency food can be stored in this single box.

Hanging space for jackets etc. is useful. This alcove drops into a 'garage' area and is placed directly over a calorifier and a blown-air heater duct outlet – this keeps damp at bay.

Plenty of hanging space in heated shower rooms comes in handy for managing drenched outdoor gear.

- Hanging things. Topcoats and fleeces that are frequently used are a hassle to constantly fold away and retrieve, and, if you travel with some formal-wear, some items will not take kindly to folding at all. At least *some* hanging space will prove useful.

- Shoes. Smelly, bulky, dirty, awkward and sometimes damp: these are not good habitation box companions. Solutions range from boxes to shoe-trees. One good solution is to move the problem and store all occasional footwear (like walking boots) in an outside locker and to rely mainly on just one easy-to-slip-on pair for just about everything you do. Just one 'multi-use' pair per person kept inside the habitation box presents a much easier and far more pleasant storage proposition. When the occasion dictates, use your multi-use pair to retrieve the appropriate occasional footwear you require and reverse the process when you're done.

- Drying things. When it's raining outside, dealing with wet clothing can be awkward so consider a 'staged' system for dealing with the aftermath of wet/muddy pursuits. A waterproof holding area is a useful first stage where items can be unceremoniously dumped while you get into dry gear. Thereafter it will be of use to have some hanging space in the washroom where water can freely drain into a shower tray or similar. As a final stage, and to accommodate more general 'airing' duties, some dedicated hangers or laundry lines in spaces that benefit from residual heat from heaters or the engine will absolutely earn their keep. For skiers, or if your outdoor pursuits regularly result in lots of wet and dirty gear, a full height, waterproof, heated exterior locker is well worth incorporating.

- Valuables. Build in some hidden areas. Some even build in a fairly obvious decoy safe with a few token items therein that can be removed with only a little sacrificial damage.

This is by no means an exhaustive list of considerations when it comes to a functional and efficient use of interior space. The points raised simply illustrate the kinds of ideas that should ideally be wrestled with before committing to furniture construction. Once again, a thorough appraisal of your *actual* individual needs will pay dividends.

Keeping it simple

Strong polypropylene boxes, particularly if supplied with secure lids, can be incredibly useful and versatile. Items can be grouped in boxes according to function and boxes can be stored close together and even stacked to maximise the 3D storage potential of even the smallest of spaces. If furniture is designed around the dimensions of boxes, it's even possible to do away with the need to worry about creating too many bespoke doors and compartments; a shelf of suitably restrained good quality boxes is a very simple, reliable and cost-effective solution to many storage issues.

Build techniques

When it comes to building furniture and dividing up interior space, there are many possible solutions. If you are a bespoke cabinet maker, or have some other specialist relevant craft, then this section is not going to be of much use to you. For those without time-served skills, there are broadly two accessible routes to the creation of interior structures: skinned frames and structural board.

Skinned frames

With the skinned-frame method, just as the name suggests, a framework is constructed to form the basic structures required and this is then skinned in a thin and lightweight material of choice. In many instances, the framework is skinned on both sides to effectively create a hollow box-section structure.

▲▲◥ **Frames and skins both pre- and post-varnish. This structure will eventually form a locker. Note the solid timber edge to the left of the leftmost panel…**

▼▶ **… it has been bonded to eventually form an attractive and functional 'edge' to the panel at the butt joint.**

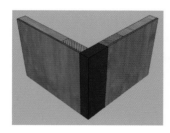

Pros include:
■ Frames are relatively quick to build and can cheaply and easily be mocked up to check if layout ideas will work.
■ The overall structure can be usefully lightweight.
■ Thin skinning material can be comparatively easy to work.
■ If skins are damaged in use, replacement is usually possible.
■ If closed-cell foam or a similar material is incorporated into

the hollow-box structure, this can provide very effective insulation against noise and heat and is a good choice for furniture bases that house diesel furnaces etc.

Cons include:
■ Thinner/inferior-quality skinning material may readily warp with changes in temperature and humidity if not comprehensively affixed to the underlying framework.
■ Skins can be time-consuming to cut to size.
■ Can be comparatively labour intensive and time-consuming overall.
■ Making exposed edges of the hollow box-section structures look neatly finished can require time-consuming bespoke solutions.
■ Can be too flimsy to form seat bases unless extra frame members are employed.
■ Thin skinning material will not reliably hold screws so fixing things like heater controls and switch panels can prove more awkward.

Framework is usually made from softwood and the skinning material – though very often purpose-made 3mm laminated decorative ply – *can* be any material that suits individual taste. Ordinarily, a nominal 3mm is the most usually encountered skinning material thickness, but thicker sheet can be used and, if it is, some of the disadvantages of this build method can be overcome. The trade-off is that the major advantage of a light overall construction weight, i.e. one of the major reasons for favouring this build method in the first place, is then completely lost.

For skinning materials around the 3mm-thick mark, given the inherent risk of warping, it's important to use high-quality board that will resist the effects of temperature and moisture. Materials that readily absorb moisture, like untreated MDF for example, should be avoided. Appropriately authenticated marine, or hardwood plywood are popular choices and if these are screwed, bonded or otherwise securely fastened to underlying framework with supporting struts with centres of no more than 300mm apart, the result can be stable and attractive.

▼ **Made with skins of cherry-veneered ply, these locker doors make for a superb finished example of the skinned-frame method.**

PURPOSE-MADE DECORATIVELY LAMINATED PLY

Made specifically for the construction of aesthetically pleasing and hard-wearing fixtures and fittings, purpose-made decoratively veneered ply is a very popular choice amongst professional and DIY builders alike. The material is available in many different thicknesses but 3mm and 15mm are perhaps the most popular choices. The former is traditionally used for the frame-skinning method, the latter for structural boarding. In the manufacturers' construction process, a very thin layer of decorative melamine (or comparable material) is bonded to one or both sides of a suitable plywood. The finished product provides an attractive and easy-to-work solution for the self-builder. Veneer finishes can range from a simple pure black or white, through many attractive colours and sheens, to convincing replicas of exotica like carbon-fibre sheet.

Many companies make such products and standards are variable. At the lower end of the market poor-grade ply and paper veneers may feature; these will not be up to the rigours of long-term overland camper use and are best avoided. At the upper end of the scale, high-quality, very lightweight ply is used together with quality coatings that it's claimed are very resistant to delamination. NB: Even in top-end products imperfections in the ply and laminates *can* still be found and care should be taken to inspect sheets carefully and work around any minor flaws once construction begins.

If, amongst the many products available you still can't find one to suit, you *can* get your own laminates made. If going this route, you could even specify materials of choice and have, for example, a 0.5mm GRP, 3mm ply, 0.5mm GRP construction to provide an especially hard-wearing and water-resistant, strong and light material. Naturally, quality and price will vary dramatically.

Structural board

With the structural-board construction method, again as the name suggests, sheets of structural material of anything between approximately 12 and 18mm thick are used to form most, if not all of the internal cabinetwork.

Pros include:
- Reasonably easy and relatively quick to work.
- Neat and attractive finish.
- Inherently robust, strong and stable.
- Easily able to hold screws for fittings like coat hooks and switch panels etc.

Cons include:
- Overall weight can be high unless specialist lightweight boards are chosen.
- Can be comparatively expensive if using high-end materials.
- Ideally requires the use of table saws/circular saws and a decent-sized workshop to ensure clean cuts and straight edges on larger panels.

As long as it's able to deal with changes in temperature and humidity, the type and finish of structural board is entirely a matter of personal choice. Once again though, purpose-made decoratively veneered ply is highly favoured. If decoratively veneered ply does not appeal, birch ply is a very popular alternative. This material is fine-grained and has few natural blemishes. Additionally, because it's fabricated using many comparatively thin elements, it features proportionally more glue than would be found in a ply composed of fewer elements and this helps with strength and stability. Once suitably stained and varnished (or otherwise finished), birch ply is noted for its aesthetic appeal and all-round suitability as a structural board. One other material that is worthy of mention is bamboo. When formed into laminate panels, this is a relatively lightweight and attractive solution with an end grain that, unlike some plywood, is itself visually appealing.

▲▼ Five-ply bamboo board has been used on this build to make – amongst other things – very attractive overhead locker doors. The edges have been routed to soften the profile but the end grain has not been 'edged'. This is the natural (tung-oiled) appearance of the product.

1 It's a good idea to mark out where furniture will go before starting to cut panels. Modifications are relatively easy at this stage, less so later on.

2 The starting point for a good proportion of furniture making is often the humble batten. Here, this 22x22mm beech section is bonded with Sikaflex 221 and also screwed to the retaining wall. On this particular build, for battens supporting heavier items like bed bases, 22x50mm beech sections were used.

3 In appropriate (hidden) locations, simple butt joints are perfectly adequate. For strength, this joint is bonded as well as being back-screwed in the two countersunk positions visible.

4 In cases where panels may need to be removed (this panel hides some electrical items) it may be necessary to retain easy access to screws. If this is the case, heads can always be covered by purpose-made caps. A good tip is to use the kind of cap that sits in a counter-bored hole. These are much neater and far more secure than the kind of cap that is held in situ by a screw head.

5 Counter-bored screw caps.

6 For joints where it's impossible or undesirable to use battens or brackets, dowels make for a very strong and visually unobtrusive junction. The interior wall towards the right of shot has been prepared to accept three dowels.

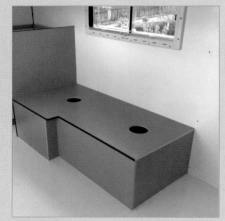

7 A dowel in situ ready to accept a facia board.

8 Simple dowel centre-sets make exact dowel placement relatively straightforward. When drilling dowel holes, especially if this is into thin edge sections of material (as per the previous image), it's good practice to run the drill bit through a sturdy and known-square piece of wood. This acts as a rudimentary jig to keep the drill bit perpendicular to the material being prepared for a dowel.

9 Impromptu but reasonably effective drill jig.

10 Very few panel joins in this build have any visible means of fastening, even from within the lockers. In addition to dowels, biscuit joints occasionally feature. Additionally, all joints are bonded with Sikaflex 221.

11 Biscuit joints require a special cutter but are especially well suited to making neat and strong butt joints in structural board.

12 In cases where a panel is already fairly solidly located, it's possible just to rely on good-quality adhesive sealer for some butt joints. This panel is secured with battens and dowels at various points, but the top edge is simply bonded with Sikaflex 221. Note how the joint is not butted fully up to the roof. 2mm spacers have been set into the upright to ensure sufficient adhesive sealer remains in the joint to make a secure bond.

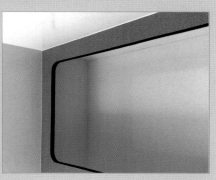

▲ **This stunning interior is simply painted structural board and is almost exclusively just bonded together.**

Construction with structural board usually begins with establishing fixing points on the habitation box interior, generally in the form of wooden battens screwed and/ or bonded into place. These provide a solid foundation to which structural board can readily be fixed. Thereafter, depending on the strength of joint and quality of aesthetic finish required, boards can be physically joined in many ways ranging from simple brackets or modesty blocks, through more time-intensive but less visually intrusive methods like bonding, dowelling or biscuit joints, right up to (for those who possess the skill and devotion) dovetail joints etc. There are no hard and fast rules, as long as the joints are strong enough and you're satisfied with the finished look; that's all that really matters.

Edging

In the case of decoratively veneered structural board particularly, where exposed plywood edges are an inevitable and unsightly part of the build process, some kind of edging not only makes the job look properly finished but also protects the vulnerable laminate from peeling. Edging choices are many and varied and are by no means limited to commercially available solutions. Of the more commonly used purpose-made materials are:

- Iron-on edging. This is available on the roll and is simply laid out on the edge of the board to be covered before quite literally being ironed into position. The heat from the iron melts pre-impregnated glue and bonds the edge to the surface. After application, some trimming with a craft knife or chamfering with fine sandpaper may be required to remove excess material.
- Knock-in edging. This kind of edging requires a slot to be routed into the end grain to be covered, into which a barbed extrusion sits to hold the edging firmly in place. Different styles are available but none look particularly refined if led round sharp angles. Any corners that require edging ideally need to be radiused if they're to neatly accommodate this style of moulding.

EDGING CHOICES

Here are a few images to give a few ideas when it comes to finishing the exposed edge of structural board:

▶ **Iron-on edging** is quick and fairly easy to apply. It's reasonably robust but can be damaged if caught with a sharp edge etc.

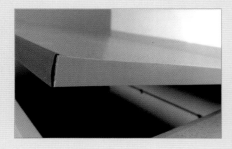

◀ **More robust** than iron-on edging, this knock-in edging is a very popular choice. Like iron-on, it can be purchased in many colours and can also be obtained in different profiles to suit different applications.

▶ **Cutting the** slot for knock-in edging is simple with a router and the appropriate cutter.

▶ **Purpose-made** over-the-counter extrusions are very neat.

▶ **For edges that** are likely to be caught with heavy items, sections of angle can also be used. This can be obtained in any number of materials and if lightly bonded into place can readily be replaced if damaged. Here, 25mm aluminium angle is used to protect a vulnerable corner.

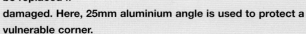

▼ **For focal points,** with a little bit of extra effort, pleasing results are possible. Here, suitably mitred sections of beech are glued to the edge of structural board and finished with a beeswax application.

▶ **These wooden** corner-mouldings were laboriously finished with teak varnish before being deployed…

◀ **Knock-in edging** looks awkward and is ill-fitting if led round too sharp a corner. Radius the edges of furniture board to obtain a much neater finish.

▼ …the results are, quite simply, stunning.

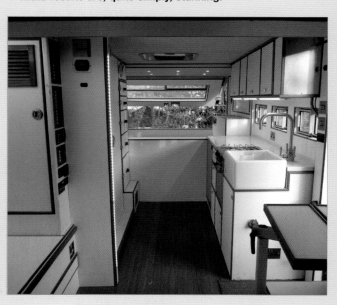

Extruded corner mouldings. Where boards meet at right angles, for example at the corner of a cupboard, pre-moulded radiused corner profiles can be purchased into which the ends of both boards simply slide and can then be screwed/bonded in place

Though these and other purpose-made materials are readily available, it's possible to use any number of alternative approaches to custom-make edging to suit taste and function. Many different solutions have been utilised from plastic strips, through hardwood fillets, to aluminium right-angle section. Effectively, there are no bounds to edging choices and many very attractive and functional finishes can be created. Your own solution is as valid as anyone's.

Specialist structures

Though the title may sound rather grand, the structures covered in this section are anything but; it's just that the frame and skinning/structural board methods are perhaps not the best choice for their fabrication.

Counter tops

Kitchen and shower-room worktops need to be hard-wearing and to be able to stand up to water inundation. The simplest solution for reliable service is to borrow from domestic builds and use purpose-made kitchen counter tops. These usually comprise some form of reconstituted wood bound with resin and laminated with a waterproof and hard-wearing exterior. Such counter tops are reasonably lightweight, easy to cut to shape and, especially if they're properly sealed with a simple silicone sealant where exposed edges are left after creating holes for basins and hobs etc., just get the job done. Naturally, any material can be pressed into service for worktop duty and if weight and budget aren't an issue, Corian, marble, granite and similar tops are at your disposal, although these will almost certainly require a specialist supplier to cut materials to your specification.

Beds

In a nutshell, bed bases need to be exposed to circulating air. If they're not, they will trap moisture and become the breeding ground for all sorts of interesting cultures, amongst which moulds and mildews are usually the first to make their presence known. Laying a mattress directly onto a solid surface will, sooner or later (depending on climatic conditions), create problems. Several methods are commonly employed to overcome this issue and these include:

Purpose-made sprung-plastic bases. It's possible to purchase highly engineered supports that basically comprise a multitude of moulded plastic components which, depending on how you choose to assemble them,

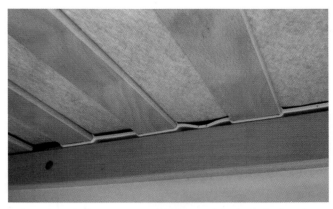

▲ **8mm beech slats support this 90cm wide single bed and allow good levels of ventilation. Note the purpose-made guides that space out the slats evenly and the use of 50mm deep battens to support the bed structure.**

can be customised to provide more or less resistance under various parts of the mattress. These, as well as allowing a customised springing solution, also allow the requisite circulation of air.

Simple lattices. Air circulation is achieved by simply building up thin lattice layers underneath a mattress. These can be of any appropriate material and when constructed resemble a trellis of the kind used to support climbing plants.

Purpose-made bed slats. By using slats, ideally in combination with made-for-the-job guides that hold them at the correct distance from one another, it's possible to leave the underside of the mattress almost completely exposed for maximum circulation. With slats it's also possible, by specifying different thicknesses, to customise the amount of support provided.

Naturally, custom-made solutions are also possible; all that's required to head off problems is to create some or other structure to ensure a ready flow of air and to occasionally lift/turn the mattress.

▼ **Froli springs allow 'tweakable' support as well as the free circulation of air.**

Hardware

When it comes to hardware like hinges, handles and catches, many of the most suitable solutions can be found on the shelves of local DIY stores or from suppliers to the furniture-makers' trade. Many leisure-vehicle traders supply lightweight fittings of the kind found in conventional motor caravans and, though some of these are perfectly trustworthy, it's true to say that many are very flimsy. Plastic hinges and catches designed for use a couple of weeks a year in a caravan may not be up to extended trips over tough terrain. If you do purchase hardware items from a leisure-vehicle outlet, look for heavy-duty options. In particular, very large doors and drawers may need strong, burst-proof catches able to deal with restraining the mass and forces at play. Again, these are easy to obtain, just avoid anything that's obviously flimsy.

Overhead, aircraft-style lockers are a particularly testing environment for hardware. These are very popular and useful structures but can present long-term issues when it comes to getting the conventionally top-hinged doors to stay put in their open position. In most cases, doors are held open either by sprung hinges or gas struts. Repeated use fairly commonly leads to eventual hinge

▽ Burst proof catches are a wise fit, especially on heavy doors.

▲ These push-button catches are marketed for leisure vehicles but are a heavy-duty option and are sufficient to restrain moderately heavy drawers.

failure, drooping struts, or a loosening of the screws that hold the hinges or struts in situ. Repeated loosening and retightening of the fixing screws can then lead to eventual failure of the fixing substrate (i.e. your cupboard wall) itself. Remedies include: using high quality parts, placing sprung hinges at no more than 150mm centres to help spread load, using the longest screws possible, or sidestepping the potentially troublesome issues entirely by using an alternative solution like a sideways-sliding panel or tambour doors.

◣ After hundreds of repetitions overcoming their inbuilt resistance, sprung hinges/gas rams can place a lot of strain on retaining screws.

▽ Tambour doors are simple, lightweight and reliable (but expensive).

▶ **These slats hold this seat's back cushion about 10mm from the wall and allow enough air circulation to stop condensation creating damp patches.**

Upholstery

Unless you have the skills and a capable sewing machine, soft furnishings are probably best left to professionals. Specialist companies can make foam-based upholstery in just about any shape and configuration imaginable, so if you fancy some deeply wedged backrests, knee rolls, a particular stitching pattern, custom piping, custom densities and thicknesses of foam, matching scatter cushions etc. then all you need to do is design your bespoke requirements and give the company specific instructions – along with your payment…

For those who fancy their DIY chances, seating cushions commonly comprise five elements:

■ A foam base, usually of a high-density foam of about 100–150mm thickness.
■ A 'topper' comprising a low density foam of about 25mm thickness.
■ The covering material of choice.
■ A breathable backing for the unseen side/cushion underside.
■ Zips to allow cover removal for repair.

Very simplistically, the foam base is cut to shape and a topper is cut to fit exactly on the upper/facing side of the base. The covering material of choice is then stitched to the topper before both are laid on to the base and the covering material trimmed to fit. The breathable backing is also trimmed to fit and then – the really skilled part – the covering and backing material are all sewn neatly together and a zip added in the process. If all has gone well, the completed cover is then stuffed with the foam base and the result is an extremely neat and highly bespoke item. To keep cushions in place, it's customary to sew a short section of hook and loop tape on to the backing material. Hook and loop strips can then later be stuck/stapled to

the appropriate furniture surface (if actually required) to prevent any unwanted slippage.

Foam mattresses are constructed along similar lines but tend to use more of a medium-density foam as occupant weight is spread more than when seated. That said, it's down to preference and any foam is possible. Furthermore, composites can be made that comprise, for example, a mid/high density or latex-foam base with a memory-foam topper.

If you do take on a soft-furnishing project of your own, or entrust the job to a third party with the relevant upholstery skills, it's vitally important to ensure your materials all meet the applicable fire-retardant standard. The confined spaces within leisure vehicles make this absolutely non-negotiable. Sub-standard materials just aren't worth the risk.

The problems of damp caused by of a lack of air circulation around mattresses *can* also raise its head with other soft furnishings like seat cushions. This is not as common as with mattresses and much will depend on your own vehicle's propensity for building condensation. In certain climatic conditions, the points at which upholstery butts up to exterior walls, especially if the inner skins of exterior walls are something like smooth GRP, can see damp forming. This is because the cushions act as an insulator, effectively stopping the warm air inside the habitation box from reaching exterior walls and thereby allowing localised cold spots to form. Moisture held in the air will readily settle out on any localised cold spots and create moist areas right at the point where upholstery meets wall. Areas furthest from heat sources are the most vulnerable. To reduce the level of the problem, it's wise to slightly space upholstery from the walls and allow air to freely circulate. This can be achieved by the addition of simple lattices; they do not have to hold cushions very far from walls and indeed, once upholstery is in situ, it's not easy to tell that they even exist.

CHAPTER 13

Kitchens and washrooms

PART 1 – KITCHENS

■ Refrigeration

■ Cookers

■ Kitchen hardware

PART 2 – WASHROOMS

■ Showers

■ Toilets

Kitchens and washrooms are worth time and effort to get right. An indication that they are working well is that you simply use them without a second thought; when they don't work well, their use can become something of a chore.

Refrigeration

There are a few options when it comes to keeping food, drink and any other desired commodities cool. At the simple end are cool boxes and these come in two fundamental forms, passive and powered. Passive boxes usually come in the form of a hard plastic insulated shell, into which are placed ice packs and your commodities. Cooling effects are minimal and temporary. Powered cool boxes are generally similar in construction but instead of ice packs they utilise a thermoelectric process known as the Peltier effect to keep contents cool. Ordinarily powered by 12V DC, simplistically, the thermoelectric process promotes the transfer of heat from within the box to atmosphere – hence the internal cooling effect. Powered cool boxes are limited in cooling ability and not terribly effective as a substitute for a true refrigerator. That said, a small cool box in the vehicle cab is a good way to keep a refreshing drink or cool flannels to hand.

Given the limitations of cool boxes, a fully plumbed-in refrigerator (with or without a freezer facility) is the norm for overland campers and these too come in two basic forms:

- Absorption fridges. These essentially use a heat source to circulate refrigerant that, thanks to an evaporation/re-absorption process, removes heat energy from within the fridge and dissipates it to atmosphere. The heat energy that circulates the refrigerant can originate from electric heating elements or by burning LPG. Because they can use AC, DC and LPG energy sources, this type of unit is often referred to as a three-way fridge.
- Compressor fridges. These fridges do not rely on a heat source to circulate refrigerant but instead rely upon an electrically powered pump.

Absorption fridges

Though three-way absorption fridges are physically able to use AC voltage, DC voltage and LPG to power the refrigerant-circulation process, the energy required to operate them is comparatively high. As a result, the AC function is effectively only viable when mains electricity is available and the DC function is effectively only viable when the vehicle's engine is running. Ensuring DC power is only available when the engine is running can be achieved in several ways; the traditional method is to wire in a simple relay energised from the vehicle's alternator. It is, of course, *physically* possible to wire in an absorption fridge in such a way that it can recruit battery power without the engine running but to do so would flatten the supplying batteries in very short order.

Modern absorption fridges are very sophisticated and many have built-in electronic management units that enable an automatic energy selection function. These systems will prioritise for an AC or DC voltage supply if either is available and only fall back on the use of LPG where necessary. The selection process is totally automatic; no user input is required.

Pros:
- Able to recruit various energy sources.
- No significant impact on battery reserves.
- Very quiet in operation.

Cons:
- Will not work if tilted more than a few degrees – not easy to avoid in the terrain encountered in an overland camper.
- Requires exterior venting so large holes (usually two) need to be created in the habitation box wall adjacent to the fridge mounting location.
- Comparatively complex to wire, plumb in and vent.

Compressor fridges

Compressor fridges can utilise AC or DC voltage to run the compressor and a cooling fan. They offer a comparatively simple installation and are the default choice in most overland campers. However, in spite of their relative simplicity and popularity, they are not without reliability and installation issues. Compressor fridges can be very sensitive to input voltage and may refuse to function if they 'sense' voltage is low. It's particularly important to keep cable runs from the batteries as short as possible and to use cable with a sufficient cross-sectional area to avoid voltage-drop scenarios. Manufacturers usually provide guidance on the cable required for the length of run adopted. One well-known supplier, for example, advocates the use of 8mm² cable for a run of 4m, and 12mm² cable in the event that the run is 8m (in both cases using a 12V supply). Follow manufacturers' guidance closely and if in doubt use slightly thicker cable than may seem logical.

Pros:

- No requirement to cut sizeable vent holes in the habitation box.
- Comparatively simple to fit requiring only minimal wiring.
- Will work whilst tilted (within reason).

Cons:

- Unlike absorption fridges with an LPG option, compressor fridges rely solely on electrical energy so place very high demands on battery reserves.
- Comparatively noisy in operation – site them *well* away from sleeping areas!

Ventilation

Whether you eventually choose the absorption or compressor option, when it comes to mounting your unit of choice it's very important to take into account the requirement for adequate air circulation. The heat produced by the cooling process needs to be effectively dissipated and a ready supply of cooler air is required to help in the ventilation regime. Because of the LPG-burning function of absorption fridges, a *significant* amount of heat is produced and there is no practical choice but to cut large holes in the habitation-box wall to both allow adequate air flow and to exhaust combustion gases. NB: These vents can let in insects etc. and, because of the volume of air throughput, can also be the source of unwelcome draughts.

With compressor fridges particularly, it's easy to fall into the trap of imagining that because they are entirely self-contained and only require the attachment of two wires to burst into life, they can be shoe-horned into spaces just a few millimetres larger than themselves. If you do this, the fridge simply won't work properly. It's wise to establish the manufacturer's guidelines for the ventilation requirements of your unit of choice *before* committing to a purchase; do not rely on the physical dimensions of the unit; significant additional space above, below and behind, will almost certainly be required.

With both kinds of fridge, some owners add additional out-of-sight fans to aid in the heat-dissipation process and this is undoubtedly a wise move if you plan on spending extended time in hot climates.

▲ **Even though a compressor fridge is utilised on this overlander, the owner took no chances with ventilation and installed this attractive external vent to dissipate heat.**

Uprights versus chest units

Simplistically, hot air rises and cold air falls. In the case of upright fridges particularly, every time the door is opened, hard-won cooled air spills out: you can easily feel this effect if you happen to be barefoot. If you're camped off-grid, this is bad news in terms of a toll on resources. In the case of compressor fridges, you'll be making heavy use of your batteries and in the case of absorption fridges LPG reserves will be avoidably depleted. Good practice dictates that the door should be opened as infrequently and for as short a time as possible. More useful good practice can readily be found via a quick internet search and it makes good sense to adopt an energy-conscious regime. To put energy consumption into perspective, even with *careful* use of a medium-sized compressor fridge in a modest ambient temperature of 25°C, it's easily possible to consume *more* than 20 amps at 24V (40 amps at 12V) in a 24-hour period.

▼ **In Australia in particular, chest units on sliders are very popular and are even used to facilitate outdoor dining.**

▲ **Boxes in a conventional upright unit help with organisation, fridge and contents protection, and can also help prevent 'cold-spill'.**

Fridge/freezers with a chest design, i.e. those that have a lid rather than an upright door, do not lose the cooled interior air nearly as readily as upright units and, to avoid taking up valuable worktop space, can be mounted on purpose-made

CLIMATE CLASS

The effective operation of fridges (and particularly their inbuilt freezer compartments) is affected by ambient temperature. Fridges may not work correctly if operated outside of their design parameters. The operable ambient-temperature range of units results in a 'Climate Class' designation. Classifications are:

SN (sub-normal) –
    designed to work within the range 10–32°C
N (normal) –
    designed to work within the range 16–32°C
ST (sub-tropical) –
    designed to work within the range 18–38°C
T (tropical) –
    designed to work within the range 18–43°C

Be sure to ascertain the range of temperatures at which your fridge/freezer will effectively operate before committing to a purchase. One anomaly to watch is that if you are in cooler climates and allow temperature in the habitation box to drop, you could, paradoxically, run into refrigeration problems. Unexpected defrosting of the freezer compartment in single-thermostat fridge/freezer combination units is one of the first signs that ambient temperatures are too low for the unit to cope.

sliders. Chest designs are popular as they tend to be more energy efficient and have fewer voids when packed; contents are also less likely to be thrown around on poor road surfaces. On the downside contents tend to be slightly less accessible: the item you want is *always* right at the bottom.

With upright units, it's possible to borrow a couple of the positive attributes conferred by a chest design with the simple use of a few fridge-friendly boxes. Contents can be effectively compartmentalised thereby making the most of available space. Keeping items in boxes also prevents too much unwanted movement and, depending on the nature of the contents, potential damage to internal walls. By using relatively deep boxes in the lower part of the fridge, some of the cool air that would otherwise just spill out can – to a degree at least – be retained.

Reliability

Modern versions of both absorption and compressor fridges can suffer reliability issues and these (assuming adequate ventilation) are often traceable to their reliance upon electronic controls. Additionally, the gas burners in absorption fridges can suffer from a build-up of deposits, rendering them unreliable. It's worthwhile seeking advice from a technician who specialises in repairs of the kind of fridge that you ultimately fit and to equip yourself with a useful supply of recommended spares, especially for extended or remote trips.

Some builders use two small fridges instead of one large one to ensure that they retain at least some cooling capacity in the event of failure. If both units are constantly powered up, this is a less power-efficient path to tread than a single unit of comparable overall capacity, but it does give the reassurance of a back-up system. Extending this idea, using one unit only to cool and the other as a simple insulated storage space (maybe with the addition of an ice pack) until it's actually required as a functioning back-up, is arguably the ultimate set-up in terms of energy efficiency and reserve systems, if funds and logistics allow.

Cookers

Some combination of hob, grill and oven is to be found in most overland campers. It's not unusual to find that ovens and grills are sometimes omitted, but for extended time on the road, a wide range of cooking options is highly desirable.

Cooking by diesel and LPG

By far the most popular cooking fuel with fixed appliances is LPG. Diesel hobs and ovens have a small and dedicated following, but, no matter how intuitively logical they may seem, in the real world they simply lack convenience. All of the negative sides of running a diesel furnace (covered in Chapter 11) apply to diesel cookers. These 'negatives'

COOKER SNIPPETS

■ Glass lids are prevalent on leisure-vehicle hobs (and sinks) and look very neat when installed. They can seem, on the face of it, like a very good idea. The main selling point is that the glass lids, when down, provide additional worktop space. In reality, the lids *can* be more of a nuisance and often lead to a constant Tetris-like shuffling of equipment and tasks. Some love them; some find them *permanently* in the way. You'd be wise to give the matter some careful thought before purchase.

■ Sparking ignitions. Electronic ignitions sometimes fail. Piezo igniters are generally more reliable, but these too can be problematic as the sparking nodes and burners build up deposits, cleaning is often only a temporary solution and can sometimes make matters even worse. If you are in a position to specify, keep auto-ignitions as simple as possible. No matter which auto-sparking system you get, you'll very probably end up manually igniting burners at some point. Don't forget to pack matches or a lighter.

■ Rattles and squeaks. If you don't close the habitation area off when driving, hobs, grills and ovens are nearly always a source of *really* irritating noises. Fixes range from judicious bending of wire racks etc. to wrapping components in tea towels.

■ Occasionally, alternative fuel sources are utilised for cooking duty and if LPG, diesel and electric heating sources do not quite fit with your own plans, looking to solutions employed by those who spend months at sea can prove worthwhile.

▼ **The live-aboard occupant of this overlander has strong maritime connections and chose an alcohol-burning hob. This version also has electric elements, which are used if a suitable shore supply is available.**

▲ **A very simple two-burner hob. This unit has no auto-ignition, so there's very little to go wrong.**

most significantly include a heavy reliance on battery power for ignition and potential problems at altitude. Additionally, it takes some considerable time for appliances to reach operating temperature: it can literally mean 20+ amps and 10 minutes to bring about a simple cup of tea. Thereafter, if you turn the cooker off, there is a cycle-down time of a few minutes, during which time it's generally not possible to re-start it – so too bad if you didn't put enough water in the kettle. And then there are the issues of often-reported fault warning lights and coked-up burners... On the plus side, installing diesel cooking opens up the possibility of running a completely LPG-free vehicle and for some owners this makes the inconveniences well worth living with.

LPG-powered hobs, grills and ovens are comparatively convenient and reliable, and place no burden on battery reserves. There is a staggering range of units available, from the very simplest no-inbuilt-ignition single hob up to very clean-looking auto-igniting ceramic hobs. Though choice is a very personal thing, as with all aspects of an overland camper build, simplicity is a good guiding principle.

Cooking by electricity

Cooking by electricity requires a great deal of energy and in order not to foreshorten the life of your batteries (or even destroy them) the energy requirement dictates that when an electric heating element/microwave is operating you ideally need to either:

■ Be on a hook-up. This is usually a good solution but there can still be problems: remember that different standards for mains electricity are adopted around the world, plus, on very many campsites the actual amperage available at individual outlets will not be sufficient to cope with high-power consumers like electric hobs – campsite blackouts are a frequent result of over-optimistic appliance usage.

- Use a generator. Again this is usually a viable option as long as the generator is working reliably and you (and your neighbours) don't mind the noise.
- Run the vehicle's alternator. This will help offset the worst of negative impacts on batteries but is not really very convenient, environmentally friendly or efficient if used at every mealtime.

In most real-world terms then – unless you have *massive* battery reserves and a very sophisticated, powerful and super-reliable charge-management system – relying *primarily* on electricity for cooking is not wholly practicable. If you are not persuaded and *do* wish to pursue the electrical option (even if just when the occasion lends itself) it would make sense to select usefully low-power devices like Ramoska-style cookers. These meet with consistently positive reviews and smaller versions particularly are unlikely to trip even the shakiest of campsite hook-ups. Similarly, small electric travel kettles rated at about 1,000W can – if used appropriately – prove an ally and contribute usefully to the long-term preservation of gas reserves. 12/24V DC-powered microwaves are available but are no less problematic in terms of power consumption than their AC-powered counterparts, plus they require the installation of very large-section power-supply cable in order to operate reliably and safely.

Kitchen hardware

Some sinks are specifically designed for, or marketed towards, the leisure-vehicle and marine markets. Many styles and finishes are available and range from the very ordinary

FITTING KITCHEN ITEMS

With refrigerators, cookers and sinks etc., physical installation is relatively easy and mainly a matter of following manufacturers' instructions. Be sure to use as many good-quality (ideally stainless-steel) screws of sufficient gauge and length as possible to fully restrain heavy items like fridges and ovens, and make sure they're well braced using additional framework and supports if necessary – rough terrain will quickly find any weakness. A fairly popular option with fridges is to mount extra blocks of closed-cell foam against the unit's exterior to improve insulation and therefore efficiency. As long as the integrity of the mounting and the adequacy of ventilation are not compromised, this is a useful way to reduce the LPG or electrical consumption of the unit.

to units that incorporate, for example, fully integrated LPG-burning hobs. Available space and taste will inform choice, but just two things to consider might include whether you want a specific draining-board-type function – and on which side of the hinged-glass-lid fence you stand.

Miscellaneous items of hardware such as kitchen roll and tea-towel holders should be on the sturdy side. As with other hardware components, flimsy plastic items that are designed to shave off a few grams in a caravan may not be up to the rigours of overland travel. Robust items primarily intended for domestic use are far more reliable.

PART 2 – WASHROOMS

Showers

Shower curtains are clingy! Though they are reasonably efficient at stopping unwanted shower water from reaching every last corner of the shower room and ruining toilet rolls etc., in the confined space of an overland camper they *can* make showering a relentless fight against fabric and an altogether less-than-pleasant experience. Unless you have a particularly generously sized washroom and can place a curtain at some considerable distance from shower users, a solid partition or a full 'wet room' are better options.

Fitting a solid partition is not difficult. Material like polycarbonate sheet can be purchased pre-cut to your exact dimensions and the availability of various high-quality fixings and hinges specifically designed to support washroom glazing means it should be possible to rig up a suitable screen in even the most awkward of spaces.

Whether you go with a curtain, a screen or a wet room, washroom walls need to be entirely waterproof – water escaping into the fabric of the build is definitely a scenario to avoid. There are several ways to ensure a water-tight build but nearly all are based – in one way or another – on the use of a fairly thin sheet of waterproof material bonded to an underlying structural support and then sealed at all junctions with a suitable adhesive sealer. Thin sheets of GRP are a good choice but specialist companies and high-street DIY stores alike sell all manner of sheeting material that has been successfully pressed into overland-camper-washroom service. Some materials are even specifically sold as washroom linings and sport a pseudo-tiling effect or other finishes designed to improve aesthetics.

In your final choice, there are two issues that need close

◀◣ **This stable-door-style shower partition is made of polycarbonate and is held by stainless-steel hinges that have a 'click-stop' function to hold them in the open position. Making the door two-piece makes for easy access to the storage areas behind and also makes for a suitably stiff shield. A full-height one-piece shield of 6mm polycarbonate would be far too flexible.**

attention. First, the lining-sheet material must not be prone to excessive expansion and contraction as this will, over the course of time, work away at any bonding or fixings that have been used to attach it to the underlying structure, as well as the sealer used at all panel junctions. Second, the bonding agent used must be suited to the lining material *and* to the material used as the underlying substrate. Contact adhesives are typically used, but care must be taken to ensure compatibility with *both* of the materials to be laminated. Long-term failure of self-bonded laminated board is by no means a certainty but *is* fairly common (not just in washrooms) and once a showering area is built, it's extremely difficult to disassemble without significant disruption. If you have any doubts, there's a good argument for having washroom wall panels professionally laminated.

If you do have washroom wall panels professionally laminated, two or three full-sized sheets of a three-element composite comprising a thin skin of GRP, a stable ply of about 12–15mm, and a further thin skin of GRP mean that you'll have some excellent material from which to build storage cupboards, shelves, and any other washroom structure desired. With such a building material, providing care is taken in construction and sealer is effectively applied where all panels meet, the entire washroom is likely to give years of reliable service. Whilst on the subject of careful construction, one worthwhile tip (repeated in other parts of the book) is to completely seal the end grain of all panels used in a washroom build with your adhesive/ silicone sealer of choice *before* they are assembled so that if water *should* find its way past the finishing bead of sealer, it won't be absorbed by vulnerable material and cause structural damage.

Washroom doors

A full-height door is generally desirable to separate the shower/ablutions area from the rest of the interior. Such doors and their requisite frames *can* be fabricated from scratch, but arguably the easiest solution is to employ one of the professionally made integrated frame-and-door solutions as discussed in Chapter 8. Beware though: the door is unlikely to be designed to be watertight and for this reason, by far the best strategy for avoiding a deluge in the habitation area when showering is to try to avoid a scenario where the door itself forms part of the showering area. If this is not possible, the use of hinged solid shields or even

1 This washroom was constructed from Vöhringer furniture board, which had first been home-laminated (on the room's internal walls only) with 3mm polypropylene sheet. High-quality contact adhesive was used in the lamination process and the composite panel left for several weeks in different temperatures to check all was well before it was used in construction. The panel remained stable and the room was built. However, months later, a particularly hot day saw the polypropylene expand at a rate too great for the adhesive to cope with and the whole room delaminated spectacularly. ▶

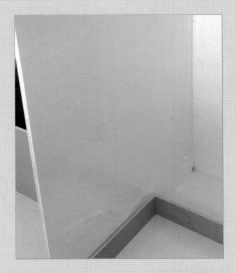

2 The room, by this stage, could not be disassembled so a 'fix' was required. Over a hundred 5mm holes were drilled through the polypropylene layer only and then 3.5mm countersunk self-tapping screws were used – concealed in chrome-effect plastic caps – to mechanically fasten the polypropylene back into place. The 'oversize' holes (concealed under the caps) now allow the polypropylene some room to expand and the walls have remained watertight and intact since. Sikaflex 512 was used in each hole to keep water from working into the Vöhringer, and the screws, being countersunk, helpfully centre the chrome caps. ◣ ▼

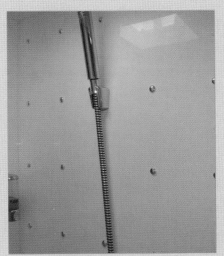

3 How to do it properly. Professionally laminated GRP-skinned panels being used to make a washroom. Do it once – do it right!

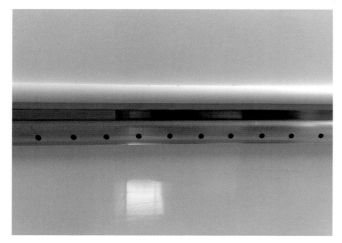

▲ **Modifications in progress to ensure this ready-made door and frame prevents water from finding its way into the habitation area. The door's interior panel skin is 3mm polypropylene so is, itself, waterproof. The door frame has been drilled to allow appropriate drainage and a section of purpose-made self-adhesive 'drip-strip' has been added to direct water running down the inside of the door panel directly into the shower tray. At least three further 'fixes' were required on this particular door.**

a well-restrained shower curtain are good ways to cover the interior face of the door and sidestep any potential issues.

In the event that none of these strategies are practicable or desirable, it may be necessary to come up with some creative solutions to ensure that the door will dutifully keep water within the washroom. This can be tricky, though, and problems will need to be solved on a case-by-case basis. If you are faced with the dilemma, a good strategy is to spray a small quantity of water on to just one small and discreet

section of the door/frame; watch where it runs, then divert it as required. Patience is a virtue and it will almost certainly be necessary to repeat the whole spray-watch-fix operation several times before all issues are finally sorted.

Shower trays

Pre-moulded shower trays are easily obtained from leisure-vehicle parts suppliers and, in spite of differences in style, size and quality, often share common features. They are generally moulded in a thin, ABS-type material and, as a result, are fairly flimsy as supplied. In order to collect and direct water into the tray, they're generally moulded with a fairly generous apron and there will usually be, within the tray's moulding, provision to locate one or two drain points. Twin drainage points are useful as they maximise the chance of being able to drain successfully, even if parked on a slope.

When it comes to fitting, pre-moulded trays usually require locating in a simple (usually wooden) box-type structure. The purpose of such a structure is simply to locate the tray and support the aprons; it should never be called upon to bear *any* of the weight of a showering occupant. Instead, it is crucial that the entire base of the tray is fully supported and this is best achieved by ensuring it sits firmly and directly on to a perfectly flat floor. Or *almost* anyway… a good tip is to cushion the tray's base by laying it on a thin piece of *very dense* but slightly shock-absorbent material, like a section of foam camping mat for example. This not only makes for a superior underfoot experience but helps to spread occupants' weight and to take up any slight irregularities in the moulding/floor surface. Under no circumstances should you leave any *unsupported* gap between the base of the tray and the floor; deformation of the moulding under footfall *will* (eventually) lead to failure.

Even if correctly mounted, pre-moulded-tray failure is not

▼ **For pre-moulded shower trays, a box structure similar to this is required to both locate it and support the tray's apron. Note the vent – this allows circulation of air and provides a handy inspection facility.**

▼ **The underside of a pre-moulded tray during construction of the supporting-structure framework. Note the tray's mouldings for twin drain points and good pre-planning to accommodate runs of semi-rigid plumbing pipework.**

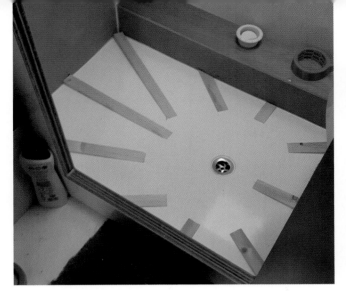

▲ An example of an unusual home-made shower tray build. The drain plug is not – as first appears – in a pre-moulded tray. It is instead mounted directly in the habitation box floor and 'wedges' of gently tapered wood have been bonded in situ to face it.

▲ A flexible base of marine ply is Gorilla-glued/Sikaflexed/ screwed to both the 'wedges' and floor. This creates just enough of a curve to ensure that water is instantly directed to the drain hole.

◀ To seal the whole base of the wet room, the builder in this particular case built up numerous layers of a special waterproof anti-slip polyurethane coating.

▼ The finished job looks very smart and any ongoing maintenance should be far more straightforward than would be the case with pre-moulded ABS trays.

uncommon so some builders accept the weight penalty of a sturdier, domestic-quality tray and yet others create their own trays from scratch. All sorts of home-made solutions have proved reliable and range from custom-fabricated stainless-steel units, through hand-laid fibreglass mat and resin constructions, to fully custom-moulded GRP units (ironically often made using a broken pre-moulded tray as a buck).

If you have reservations about creating a shower area from scratch, it's possible to purchase self-contained modular shower cubicles specifically designed for leisure vehicles and though these are lightweight and a good way of retaining water they can be quite expensive and are, like most trays, often moulded in fairly flimsy ABS. It's not unusual to find these large mouldings cracking in unsupported areas or around areas of stress such as shower head mounts. If you do source a self-contained shower cubicle that will physically fit in the space you have available, be sure to bond supporting battens behind the moulding to reinforce stressed areas and crucially, as outlined above, don't forget to support the shower tray base.

Given that, even with very diligent builds, it's possible for water to get behind panels and beneath the shower-tray structure, it will prove a very worthwhile exercise to liberally coat everything that will ultimately be out of sight with silicone sealer (or similar). In the event that water does creep through gaps in panels, or if your shower tray does develop hairline cracks, you will hopefully buy yourself enough time to effect repairs before structural damage is done.

Toilets

Though there may be some initial attraction to an American RV or marine-style ceramic bowl toilet complete with its own remote 'black water' holding tank, the reality is that waste from such dedicated holding tanks can – unless you are touring the campgrounds of North America – be *very* difficult to legitimately dispose of. Suffice to say that the cost, work and complications associated with rigging up the hardware required by such a system are significant and, in the context of remote and unsupported overland travel, the *practical* advantages are arguably zero. In summary, it's far more practicable to stick with the tried and tested solutions of a permanently mounted or free-standing cassette toilet.

Whether permanently mounted or free standing, cassette toilets are basically of a two-piece construction comprising the upper seating area and a lower holding tank. When assembled, the unit is made usable by the action of a simple sliding blade. When opened, this blade allows the toilet to be 'used', but when closed, it effectively seals off the holding tank contents and any associated odour. When convenient, the upper and lower components can be separated and the sealed contents of the holding tank disposed of.

Permanently-mounted cassette toilets

With permanently-mounted cassette toilets, the seating area is fixed to the internal structure of the vehicle and is also, ordinarily, plumbed into the domestic fresh water system in order to supply water for the flushing function. The holding tank, meanwhile, sits within an integrated moulding below the seating area and when de-coupled slides out in a completely sealed state from a convenient hatch. Though not compulsory, this hatch is ordinarily sited in an exterior wall

in order that the contents don't have to be carried through the vehicle's habitation area. A door frame that enables construction of the access hatch is usually supplied with the toilet kit.

Relevant to overland use, it's worth bearing in mind that it's possible to purchase versions of permanently-mounted cassette toilets that have *separate* flush tanks, i.e. they are not plumbed into the vehicle's fresh water supply. Those who prefer this arrangement cite as advantages the relative simplicity of installation and the fact that 'clean' grey water can be recycled and used for flushing duties. Furthermore, if you are so inclined, perfumed additives can be added to the flush tank to give the perception at least of a splendid-if-slightly-sullied floral bouquet. Flushing is generally achieved by a small built-in electric pump that requires a DC connection to the vehicle's electrical system.

Pros:
- Almost domestic appearance.
- Can be purchased in a 'bench' style or with a swivelling bowl that helps to maximise space.
- Cassette disposal is slightly more sanitised and refined than with free-standing units.
- Allow addition of an extraction unit to draw any potential odours from the holding tank whilst the toilet is in use.

Cons:
- Relatively involved to fit.
- Units plumbed into the vehicle's water supply for flushing. draw on (potentially) precious fresh-water reserves.
- Occupy a relatively large floor and wall space.
- Air displaced from the holding tank when the toilet is in use may cause smells (unless an extraction unit is fitted).

◀ ▼ **A 'bench' style permanently-mounted cassette toilet being mocked into position. The white ABS moulding will eventually be fully integrated into the washroom whilst the dark-coloured holding tank seen below can be separated and extracted from the (supplied) exterior locker door.**

Free-standing cassette toilets

With free-standing cassette toilets, the upper-section seating area incorporates a tank that holds flush water and, as the name suggests, the whole unit is completely portable so can be used and stored anywhere. Flush water has to be added to the upper section and is then pressurised, usually by a built-in hand pump, so that when a button is pressed a flushing action (of sorts) is achieved.

Pros:
- Extremely easy to fit.
- Least demands on space.
- Cheap.
- Easy to replace.
- Can be slid into a cupboard when not in use.
- Fixing kits available to semi-permanently mount.
- Grey water can be recycled and used in the separate flush tank to preserve fresh-water reserves.

Cons:
- Can look rather unsophisticated.
- Flush water tank has to be manually filled.
- Flushing action is not *usually* as effective as that of a permanently mounted unit.
- Air displaced from the holding tank when the toilet is in use may cause some odours.

When it comes to fitting permanently-mounted cassette toilets, templates supplied with the kit make marking out the toilet's physical location and, crucially, its relationship with the required cassette-removal door aperture a fairly straightforward matter. Plumbing and wiring are no more complicated than any other appliance and a few screws will see the major components in situ. Free-standing cassette toilets, naturally, require no fixing at all but if you do elect to semi-permanently mount them, then a separately obtainable mounting kit can be screwed to a suitable floor surface. As an alternative, a slightly raised floor section with a suitably sized aperture cut into it will allow the lower portion of the holding tank to be dropped snugly in to prevent any unwanted sliding around. And don't forget to strap it down!

Use on the road

Great and lengthy debates rage about the most efficient and least offensive ways to both actually 'use' cassette toilets and, thereafter, how long to 'store' and finally dispose of the contents. Here are just three hard-won 'living-with-an-elaborate-bucket' observations:

- If you make use of alternative facilities where practicable then living with a cassette toilet becomes less of a chore. The less you use it, the less you are obliged to reap what you sow.

- Changes in pressure caused by fluctuations in temperature, and particularly with altitude, can lead to some 'interesting' dynamics when the sliding blade is opened. If you are changing altitude, either leave the blade slightly cracked open or keep the lid firmly down when you first operate the blade and allow pressures to equalise. You may need some disinfectant wipes.

- The use of *genuine* biological additives (or no additives) means that waste, in emergencies, can at least be buried or disposed of into septic tanks or public toilets etc. with minimal environmental impact. Chemical additives *do* slightly mask unpleasant odours but mean (ethical) disposal is so much more of an issue.

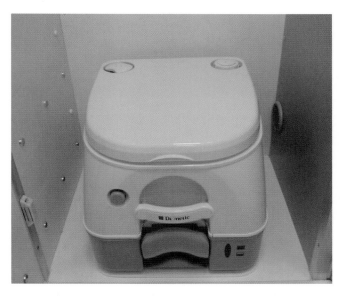

▲ ▼ **A simple free-standing cassette toilet. This particular unit is kept in situ with an optional-extra semi-permanent fixing kit.**

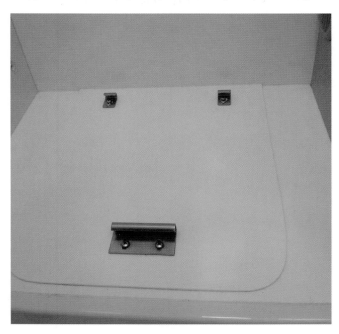

Patrick O'Neal

1 Name
Patrick O'Neal.

2 Base vehicle
1988 Mercedes 1017A.

3 Drive
Selectable – 4x2 (RWD) or 4x4 (AWD).

4 Fuel capacity
500 litres in 2 tanks: 1 x 350 litre, plus 1 x 150 litre (reserve).

5 Weight when loaded and ready to travel
Approximately 80% of manufacturer's design weight.

6 Reason for base vehicle choice
Robust. Worldwide availability of parts.

7 Subframe solution
Galvanised custom-made subframe rigidly fixed to the truck's chassis at the rear. The subframe rests directly on an intermediary frame which itself is connected to the truck's chassis rails (the intermediary frame was an original fitting from the truck's military days). The subframe is allowed to separate from the intermediary frame towards the front of the box and the degree of separation is controlled by opposing springs.

8 Habitation-box construction
three-element GRP-skinned composite panels comprising GRP-insulation-GRP. The floor also contains a fourth plywood element.

9 Habitation-box insulation material
PU foam.

10 Habitation-box manufacturer
ORMOCAR.

11 Habitation-box windows
Dometic Seitz S4 plus 1 x (very expensive) KCT porthole in the habitation door.

12 Habitation-box door(s) and locker(s)
ORMOCAR.

13 Fit out done by
Self.

14 Furniture construction
All self-built using poplar ply sheets, professionally laminated on both sides (by ELS Panels of Spalding). The panel edging is ABS strip bonded into place and then trimmed to the exact panel width – this was a very time-consuming job. The Corian worktops were professionally cut to size, but I think that job could also have been a DIY project with the right tools.

15 Fresh water

500 litres in two tanks. I have installed 3 x prefilters comprising 1) a coarse grit filter, 2) a finer particulate filter and then 3) a charcoal filter. These pre-filters then deliver 'clean' water to 2 x Seagull filters – one delivering fully purified water to the bathroom sink and one to the kitchen sink.

16 Refrigeration

Dometic Waeco 140-litre compressor.

17 Space heating

A 10kW Eberspächer diesel-powered furnace circulates hot water to finned radiators and also to 2 x water-to-air heat exchangers. These utilise built-in fans to supply warm blown air if and when required.

18 Water heating

The above Eberspächer also feeds a 15-litre calorifier plus a further water-to-water 'plate' heat exchanger that acts as an interface with the coolant of the base vehicle's engine. Using this plate, plus two auxiliary inline pumps, means that no matter whether the Eberspächer or the engine coolant is producing hot water, the hot water produced can be utilised (via the plate) as a heating source for the 'other' system. In other words, hot water produced by the Eberspächer furnace can be used as a heating source to (indirectly) pre-heat the engine block, and hot engine coolant can be used as the heating source (again acting through the plate) for space and water heating in the habitation box.

19 Cooking facilities

Four-burner LPG-powered hob plus an LPG oven and grill.

20 Habitation-box cooling

Two built-in 12V extractor fans.

21 Leisure-battery charging

1) An alternator-fed 24V to 24V battery-to-battery charger. 2) A 720W (at 24V) solar array. 3) A Xantrex multi-volt AC to DC charger.

22 Things to do differently next time

Fit a larger (25-litre) calorifier to provide more of a capacity buffer for cold water drawn into the cylinder.

Conclusion

Well, that's just about all there is to it. Simply put, self-building an overland camper is hard work but is eminently achievable and it bears repeating that the rewards associated with fully independent overland travel in a vehicle of your own creation are genuinely difficult to overstate.

If you do commit, an honest appraisal of actual needs, good research and planning, and subscription to the underpinning principles of simplicity, reliability, durability, reserve systems and multifunctionality *will* pay dividends. This is not to discount innovation though; creativity, flair and personalisation need not necessarily be mutually exclusive of the underpinning principles. Indeed, you may already have thought of new and more effective ways to evolve the well-established tenets.

When your project gets underway, be prepared for extraordinary highs and all-consuming lows. Some days you can do no wrong, others you'll make a hash of everything you touch. Some days you'll have everything to hand; others you will grind to a halt for the sake of a solitary missing nut. Sometimes suppliers will defeat you with faulty or incorrect goods; sometimes they'll go the extra mile to help you out. On days when things aren't going so well, it's most definitely best to *stop*; part of the skill set is knowing when to take a break.

Balance is the key to maintaining enthusiasm and productivity. You'll need to be dogged in your approach, but you'll also do well to recognise that you're probably in too deep if the project is *all* you can think about. Strive to keep the momentum going but don't allow yourself to become consumed; this way you'll maximise your chances of building to the best of your ability *and* enjoying the journey.

Good luck…

▼ **You know you're in deep when you start to blend in with your project.**

Useful contacts

Given that almost all research is now internet-based, this appendix is geared towards helping you to shortcut your way online to the various products, suppliers, materials, services, resources and contacts that nearly all UK-based overland camper builders eventually chance upon anyway. The list is not necessarily a recommendation or endorsement of the companies, products or services that feature and you would be well advised to extend your research to gauge levels of end-user satisfaction before committing any of your budget.

In some cases the search strings will return results for a specific website; in other cases you'll be presented with a range of results that might include, for example, retailers, reviews, links to forum threads etc. In all cases, you're encouraged to delve further and read widely! Although the list is primarily UK-based, many of the entities have a global reach and the chances are that searches based on the suggested strings will at least open up lines of enquiry in domestic markets worldwide.

Company / Product / Service etc	Suggested search string
Accordion boot crawl-through seals	cr laurence accordion
	mediatunes accordion OR accordionboot.com
Adhesives and / or sealers	gorilla glue
	sika group OR sikaflex adhesive sealer
	soudal adhesive sealer OR soudal.com
	uksealants.co.uk
Base vehicle fuel/air-system fittings	centre tank services OR centretank.com
	lancashirehose.co.uk
	mendahose.co.uk
Batteries (genuine 'leisure' open lead-acid)	banner leisure battery
	exide leisure battery
	varta leisure battery
Bed supports	bedslats.co.uk
	froli bed systems
CAD package (free)	sketchup-make
Calorifiers	alde calorifier
	quick nautic calorifier
	surecal OR surejust.co.uk
Cookers	alcohol hob OR spirit hob
	dometic cramer
	gn-espace.com
	ramoska
	scan-terieur can
	smev
	thetford spinflo

Company / Product / Service etc	Suggested search string
Electrical systems	antares.co.uk
	batteryuniversity.com*
	bepmarine.com
	cbe switches
	conrad anderson
	durite.co.uk
	masterplex.co.uk
	morningstarcorp
	nasa marine bm1
	roadpro.co.uk
	smartgauge electronics
	sterling-power.com
	vehicle-wiring-products.eu
	victron energy
	xantrex
Fans	caframo fan
	fantastic vent
	hella marine fan
Fasteners and fixings	rawlplug
	westfieldfasteners.co.uk
Flyscreens and blinds	dometic seitz blinds
	fiamma blinds
	horrex flyscreen
	nrf blinds
	oceanair.co.uk
	reimo blinds
	remis blinds
Forums	expeditionportal.com*
	sbmcc.co.uk*
	silkroute.org.uk*
	the hubb OR horizonsunlimited.com/hubb*
	theoverlander.org*
Fridges	engel refrigerator
	vitrifrigo refrigerator
	waeco refrigerator
Furniture	elspanels.co.uk
	modernlaminates.co.uk
	morland-uk.com OR morland furniture board
	vöhringer ply OR voehringer.com
	wisa multiwall OR wisaplywood.com
	woodveneeruk.co.uk
Generator (methanol powered)	efoy fuel cell
Habitation box – doors and lockers	magnummotorhomes.co.uk
	olearymotorhomes.co.uk
	transportwindows.co.uk
	vehiclewindows.co.uk

Company / Product / Service etc	Suggested search string
Habitation box – external hardware	albert-jagger.co.uk
	cbf.uk.com
	metals4u.co.uk
	seascrew.com
	whb horsebox supplies
Habitation box – hatches and vents	dometic heki OR seitz heki
	fiamma vent
	lewmar hatch
	marinemegastore.com
	mpk vent
	omnivent
Habitation box – insulation	celotex insulation
	styrofoam rtm
Habitation box – panel capping	captrad.com
	ormocar.de
	service metals group
Habitation box – panel manufacturers	coldsaver panels
	commercial vehicle roofs OR cvr-uk.com
	omnia panels
	service metals group
	the coretex group
Habitation box – windows	dometic seitz window
	duration windows OR duration.co.uk
	glassolutions
	kct windows
	kellettwindows.co.uk
	smartsystems.co.uk
	vanglas.de
Habitation box builders (for self-fitting)	bocklet.eu
	exploryx.de
	fuess-mobile.de
	langerundbock.com
	ormocar.de
	procab.net
	qualiticonversions.com
	woelcke.de
	zeppelin-mobile.de
Heaters	ca4u OR caravanaccessories4u.co.uk
	eberspächer
	morco heater
	propex heatsource
	truma heater
	webasto heater
Hinges, catches, stays etc.	häfele
	wixroyd.com
Interior trim / soft furnishings	as pickering
	automobiletrim.com
	megavanmats
	noisekiller nk group
	regalfurnishings.co.uk
	woolies-trim.co.uk

Company / Product / Service etc	Suggested search string
Ladders	fiamma ladders
	whb horsebox supplies
Leisure vehicle fit-out suppliers	caravan accessories kenilworth OR cak tanks
	grasshopperleisure.co.uk
	leisureshopdirect.com
	magnum motorhomes
	marcle leisure
	obrienscamping.co.uk
	olearymotorhomes.co.uk
	rainbow-conversions.co.uk
LPG tanks and cylinders	autogas 2000
	gasit
Plastic, acrylic, polycarbonate etc. sheet	theplasticpeople.co.uk
Specialist paint / coatings	new venture products OR protectakote
Specialist services (insurance)	adrian flux
Specialist services (chassis / downrating)	svtech.co.uk
Specialist vehicle disposal and suppliers	adventure-trucks.com
	atkinson vos
	hopdeals.com
	jsharples.co.uk
	ljacksonandco.com OR jackson rocket site
	mantra military vehicle OR achleitner.com
	mascus.co.uk
	mobile.de english
	ovik cameleon
	witham specialist vehicles OR mod-sales.com
Storage solutions	beenybox.co.uk
	really useful boxes
Subframes	qtwo aufbaulagerung
Suspension modifications	grayston engineering OR springassisters.co.uk
	marcle leisure
	midland road springs OR leafsprings.co.uk
	springcoil.co.uk
	vb air suspension
Suspension seats	jennings-seats.co.uk
	kdr seating
Tambour doors	waivis tambour
Toilet taming	Biomagic
	SOG toilet kit
Vehicle preparation and recovery equipment	mattsavage.co.uk
Water tanks	barratt tanks OR tank.me
	ft-design.de
	tanks-direct.co.uk
	tek-tanks
Water treatment	aquatabs
	accepta water treatment
	general ecology water OR seagull filters
	katadyn filter
	sanogene chlorine dioxide
* Research resources	